# A Call to Duty

*The Life and Times of Leslie E. Gehres*

## William J. Stewart

## THE MAN IN THE ARENA

*It is not the critic who counts; not the man who points out how the strong man stumbles, or where the doer of deeds could have done them better.*

*The credit belongs to the man who is actually in the arena, whose face is marred by dust and sweat and blood; who strives valiantly; who errs, who comes short again and again, because there is no effort without error and shortcoming; but who does actually strive to do the deeds; who knows great enthusiasms, the great devotions; who spends himself in a worthy cause; who at the best knows in the end the triumph of high achievement, and who at the worst, if he fails, at least fails while daring greatly, so that his place shall never be with those cold and timid souls who neither know victory nor defeat.*

**Theodore Roosevelt**

# Dedication

In honor of Captain Leslie E. Gehres and
his gallant crew who,
on March 19, 1945,
through outstanding leadership,
skill and bravery saved the
USS *Franklin* CV-13

# Contents

# William Stewart

William Stewart grew up in the footsteps of Rear Admiral Leslie E. Gehres, the hero of Dr. Stewart's hometown of Newark, New York.

As a boy, he watched as the dashing naval aviator flew into town and landed his state-of-the-art pursuit plane in a field behind Dr. Stewart's home.

As a young man, he and millions of Americans throughout the country watched in horror, then with growing pride, as Admiral Gehres sailed home the USS *Franklin* after the ship had endured a crippling attack from a Japanese warplane.

And, near the end of his long and eventful life, Dr. Stewart decided to write a biography of Gehres, a book that would show the man, warts and all, at the bar of history.

Admiral Gehres, whose rise from seaman to commander of a mighty aircraft carrier is the stuff of American dreams, deserves such a biography. Professor Stewart, using material about Gehres' life that has been overlooked or unavailable to previous historians and authors, has constructed a life's journey that places the swashbuckling, old school Gehres in context. The photographs, personal recollections, and analysis Dr. Stewart brings to the story of Rear Admiral Gehres and the USS *Franklin* could and should lead to a reexamination of the man who captained "The Ship That Would Not Die."

Dr. Stewart's life is as much a memorial to Gehres as is this book. The admiral's virtues of courage, leadership, and dynamism undoubtedly were absorbed by Dr. Stewart.

Professor Stewart graduated from Newark High School in 1938. Perhaps to emulate his aviator hero, Dr. Stewart joined the Army Air Corps in 1943 and served through its transformation into the United States Air Force.

During his military career, Dr. Stewart served in increasingly more responsible support assignments. In North Africa, he was awarded the Certificate of Commendation for his work as base sergeant major for the Air Transport Command. He earned letters of commendation for his service in the Canal Zone with the Caribbean Air Command and for his role as a chief clerk with the 3650th Support Squadron in New York. He was awarded a Certificate of Appreciation from the Army Air Forces honoring his service in WWII. Dr. Steward, who was also stationed in North Africa, Italy, the China-Burma-India Theater, Bahrain, England, and various bases in the United States, continued his studies during his 20 years in the Air Force.

Upon his retirement in 1963 as a master sergeant, he attended the University of Cincinnati. He earned a Ph.D. from the College of Education in 1968, and continued there as a professor until retirement in 1983.

Dr. Stewart had an enormous impact on his students and stayed in regular contact with many of them for the rest of his life. His students remember him with fondness. At a moving memorial for Dr. Stewart, Steve McMillen, one of his PhD. awardees spoke of him in words one would associate with a loving son or protege.

Another of his students, Steve Martin, mentioned Dr. Stewart in the preface of a book he published on management. "Bill ran our program in the School of Education and was famous for his stories," he wrote. "He was a character with a diverse set of life experiences—career military veteran, entrepreneur, and educator. He continually amazed us with his ability to repurpose stories to fit the idea he was illustrating. I appreciated his creativity and positive outlook on life."

In a personal message to Dr. Stewart, he wrote: "My career since UC has been very fulfilling and l owe you a debt of gratitude for that. You helped me create a solid foundation on which I've been able to build. You played a key role in my development and I'm forever grateful to you. I am following your example working hard to help those coming up behind me."

Like Admiral Gehres, Professor Stewart did not believe in leaving anyone behind. He was a coach, counselor, mentor, and teacher to generations of younger men and women enrolled in the University of Cincinnati's Adult/Technical Doctoral Program.

Dr. Stewart was also something of a swashbuckler. He took a courageous stand in his academic career during the Cold War, when he published an academic paper that was one of the first to analyze the experiences of American POWs during the Korean War.

In the 1970s Dr. Stewart and his wife, Eleanor, built an ocean-going trawler they named *Pamaleng*. Their sailing led them to Central America, where they invested in beachfront property. Along with a partner, Willis Peterson, the Stewarts built and ran a small resort on the island of Guanaja off the northern coast of Honduras. Named Club Guanaja Este, the resort included a lodge, three acres, and one mile of beachfront.

Upon his retirement to Englewood, Florida, Professor Stewart embarked on the adventure that would consume the rest of his life, the biography of Rear Admiral Leslie Gehres.

He became a well-known figure in printers' shops, post offices, and libraries in Southwest Florida as he developed sources and gathered material. He set up a network of correspondents throughout the United States as he painstakingly gathered oral histories and documented Admiral Gehres' life. He met with veterans of the *Franklin*, several of whom had relocated to southwest Florida within driving distance.

He also was active in his community as a member of Community Presbyterian Church and the American Legion Post 113.

His wife, Eleanor, emerged as a major facilitator of Professor Stewart's work, helping to organize and catalog the reams of documents and primary sources such as monographs, personal letters, and recordings. As Dr. Stewart's health flagged, Mrs. Stewart became the spirit of the book, incorporating her husband's vision as she worked with me to complete it.

In August of 2016, she was gratified to see Dr. Stewart's hometown high school district rededicate a memorial display to Gehres which had been founded by Dr. Stewart.

Her fidelity to Professor Stewart's vision helped make this second edition of *A Call to Duty* a reality.

*James Abraham*
*Editor and publisher*

# Introduction

This book is a story about a boy's ambition to join the U.S. Navy and succeed. Through hard work and perseverance, Leslie E. Gehres rose from the lowest enlisted rank to rear admiral. He was a by-the-book, no-nonsense officer who achieved many significant accomplishments during his thirty-two-year U.S. Navy career.

He was the first enlisted sailor to rise to command a super-aircraft carrier, the USS *Franklin* CV-13. During a fierce naval battle off the coast of Japan on March 19, 1945, through his outstanding leadership and the work of his skilled crew, he saved his ship and the lives of many sailors. The men of the *Franklin* became the most decorated crew in the history of the U.S. Navy.

Rear Admiral Leslie E. Gehres was recommended for the Medal of Honor for his heroic service while in command of the USS *Franklin*. However, in his appearance before the Board of Decorations in Washington D.C., he declined the honor.

"It is the commanding officer's primary duty to save his ship and its crew to the best of his ability, and I have done nothing beyond and above the call to duty," he said. On May 21, 1945, aboard the battle-scarred flight deck of the USS *Franklin* in the Brooklyn Navy Yard, Rear Admiral Gehres was awarded the Navy Cross.

Rear Admiral Gehres, as the commander of Fleet Air Wing 4, helped take war to the Japanese from the Aleutian Islands through continuous bombing of enemy installations. His planes performed the first continuous bombing raids of the islands of northern Japan.

For his services in the Aleutian and Kurile Islands, Rear Admiral Leslie E. Gehres received the Distinguished Flying Cross from the U.S. Army. The U.S. Navy also awarded him the Legion of Merit and Gold Star.

Earlier in his career, Gehres organized and led the Nine High Hats aerobatic stunt team. This team was the forerunner of today's Blue Angels and was nationally recognized, winning many top awards.

In 1930, Gehres flew as lead pilot in a U.S. Navy expedition that produced the first clear motion pictures of a full eclipse.

In 1938, he helped catch a renegade ex-Navy officer who was working undercover for the Japanese.

After retirement in May 1949, Rear Admiral Gehres distinguished himself in many worthwhile community, state, and national activities. He held leadership positions in several businesses, as well as in political and social organizations. One of his more important contributions was his work with the Valley Forge Freedoms Foundation, speaking about American patriotism and citizenship. He was especially proud of helping young people understand, respect, and support these values.

With Bob Wilson as his campaign manager, Rear Admiral Gehres ran for the U.S. Congress from San Diego in 1950. He lost the election. Two years later, they switched roles and Wilson won. Rear Admiral Gehres was chairman of the San Diego County Republican General Committee for twelve years. In this position, he organized support for the successful elections of Presidents Dwight Eisenhower and Richard Nixon, Governor Ronald Reagan, and Senators William Knowland and George Murphy. Gehres was a strong supporter and mentor of Pete Wilson (no relation to Bob Wilson), who became mayor of San Diego, a U.S. Senator and later governor of California

The story of Rear Admiral Leslie E. Gehres represents a life of dedication, leadership, and achievement that should be an inspiration for generations to come.

*Caspar W. Weinberger,*
*Former Secretary of Defense and*
*Chairman of the Board, Forbes, LLC*
*Washington, D.C.*

# Preface

It is a privilege to be able to write the life's journey of such an outstanding American as Rear Admiral Leslie Edward Gehres. My aim is to provide a full, honest, and balanced portrayal of his life as he lived it. There is a scarcity of written material about Rear Admiral Gehres. Nevertheless, through diligent research efforts, I was able to compile the biography of this remarkable American.

Leslie E. Gehres was born in Newark, a small rural town in upstate New York. Newark provided a diverse environment that helped to nurture his inquisitive and adventurous spirit. Such a setting provided him with the ability, motivation and character to realize his early ambition to join the United States Navy. Gehres achieved the rank of rear admiral and had a successful civilian career after he retired from the Navy.

Rear Admiral Gehres was Newark's hometown hero, who had earned worldwide status. I also grew up in Newark. I had some of the same school teachers that Gehres and my parents had when they were schoolmates in the old Washington School in Newark. These teachers never hesitated to incorporate Gehres' accomplishments in their classroom sessions. I remember a plaque that hung on the wall of my eighth-grade math classroom, where Gehres and my parents studied in earlier times. The plaque read:

*"A winner never quits and a quitter never wins!"*

I am certain that this simple quote helped to inspire Gehres and many other students to pursue and succeed in the service of their country and the society in which they lived and worked.

From an early age, I was made aware of the impressive legacy of Rear Admiral Gehres, from his youthful antics to his outstanding U.S. Navy career and civilian pursuits.

I remember many times when I witnessed Gehres flying his biplane into town and landing on the makeshift old Newark Airport. This landing strip was called Bailey's Lot, owned by the local Bailey family. It was a large, flat pasture where the slow-moving aircraft of that era could safely land and take off.

As the Bailey family did not use this land for any agricultural purposes, they did not object to its use as an airport. This field was behind my parents' home on

South Main Street. From there, it was real handy for some of my buddies and me to see Lt. Gehres safely maneuver his plane and jockey it into a secure landing position. He generally flew in from the south. He would park his plane at the northern end of the landing strip, abutting pasture land owned by my uncle, William Merson. At times, Gehres would hire us boys to guard his plane while he was visiting. The task did not pay much, but it did not require any real effort on our part. Frankly, I am not sure what we were supposed to do if someone approached the plane with over-zealous intentions. Usually we boys found a soft cool spot under one of the plane's wings and took a nap.

There was generally a small group of local townspeople at Bailey's Lot for Gehres' arrival. Such a group might include his uncles, Elliot and Erwin Thomas; other relatives, and some of his old-time friends including Newark's Mayor Harry Parker, Boh Bloomer, Eugene Morgan, Karl Herman, Joe Stewart (my father), Harold Stiles and possibly others. After the formalities of greeting his onlookers, Gehres was ready to proceed on his local round of visits.

The shortest exit from Bailey's Lot was west across my uncle's lot and past my parent's house. At that point, Gehres would usually stop and visit with my mother and grandmother, who was a good friend of Phebe Thomas, Gehres' mother. At times my father and uncle would also be present.

If we were lucky, my brother and I could listen to the conversation. Our role was strictly that of listeners, not contributors. Nevertheless, it always provided a unique learning experience for us.

After a short visit, Gehres would proceed to one of his uncles' homes and have lunch. After lunch, he would visit with his other uncle, and hopefully some other relatives and friends. If he had time, he would also be able to make a short trip to some of his local haunts or Sodus Point, to revisit hangouts of boyhood days. By late afternoon, Gehres would head back to Bailey's Lot and take-off.

Karl Herman, or one of his mechanics, was usually available to help Gehres start his engine. Gehres would give his engine a good warm-up surge, then take off and head toward downtown Newark. Gehres would perform several aerobatic stunts. After completing his downtown demonstration, he would buzz the local Washington School. Gehres would then turn his plane south for his home base, the U.S. Naval Air Station, Anacostia, Maryland.

After Rear Admiral Gehres retired from the U.S. Navy on May 1, 1949, he entered civilian life with the same energy and dedication he had brought to his naval career. He became the vice president of a large West Coast business consortium. He also held leadership positions in political, government and social organizations, including the Freedoms Foundation of Valley Forge, Pennsylvania.

My special interest in writing a biography of Rear Admiral Gehres stems from a conversation that I had with his nephew, Leslie Van Huben. Based on my knowledge of Gehres' life and my interest in his career, he suggested the possibility of my writing his biography.

My immediate challenge was the scarcity of documentation of the life of Rear Admiral Leslie E. Gehres. However, Van Huben put me in touch with Gehres' daughter, Leslie Girard, and her family. They provided me with an abundance of personal information and material relating to Admiral Gehres and provided ongoing support. I received invaluable input from my parents, who were schoolmates of Gehres, and other members of my family and Admiral Gehres'. His uncles, Elliot and Erwin Thomas, were very good sources.

Former Secretary of Defense Caspar Weinberger was gracious enough to write an introduction to this work, and former California Governor Pete Wilson has contributed an oral history included in the appendix. Both men became acquainted with Gehres after his retirement from the U.S. Navy, when Gehres pursued a successful political career.

The life of Rear Admiral Leslie E. Gehres is an engrossing tale that should spark the adventurous spirit of both young and old. He was able to fulfill his earliest boyhood ambition to join the U.S. Navy and succeed.

The librarian at the National Museum of Naval Aviation, Pensacola, Florida, said it simply and best after reviewing Gehres' career records: "Gehres was quite a man." Newark is fortunate to have had such a distinguished hometown hero pass its way.

*William J. Stewart*
*Englewood, Florida*

# Leslie Girard

Life with my father was an experience like that of many children of military families. Changes of duty gave him the opportunity to choose a different travel route each time to show his family a new part of the country, always visiting historic points of interests.

Patriotism was alive and well in our home, full stop at Colors, full explanation of each and every national holiday, discussion of current events at the dinner table, and of course, full attention to the Army-Navy football game.

We were never strangers in a strange land. There were always service families we knew from previous stations who could show us the ropes around town and school. There were always other military friends to visit where conversations centered around the newest aircraft, ships, or military tactics. Family visits to aircraft carriers were always exciting and a view into the life of a naval aviator.

The Japanese attack in December '41 was not a complete surprise. When we were at Pearl on Ford Island war was expected, we just didn't know when. There were frequent air raid drills and we were directed to our assigned bomb shelters.

Wartime was the same experience for everybody; eyes and ears glued to newspapers and radio. Peacetime was a blessed relief and a new life in civilian territory. Patriotism and America First ruled the Gehres household until the day he died. My father loved his country, his country's history, the Navy, his family and his friends. He left a life of "small town boy makes good" to inspire his grandchildren and great-grandchildren and perhaps some young person who reads his story.

The Gehres-Girard family is grateful to the author, William Stewart, for his inspiration, research, time, and devotion to this biography and to his wife, Eleanor, for her support and assistance.

*Leslie Gehres Girard*
*Daughter of Rear Admiral Leslie E. Gehres*

*Newark's Union Street in the late 19th century.*

# I
# Newark, N.Y.; The Early Years

*"A boy has the right to make dreams and take adventures down uncharted paths leading to the fulfillment of his most passionate ambitions."*

**Mark Twain**

Toward the end of the 19th century in upstate New York, Newark was a pleasant and thriving community along the banks of the Erie Canal. Nestled comfortably in a beautiful little valley surrounded by a ring of drumlins, Newark was a picture-perfect setting in Wayne County.

With the exception of Rochester, Newark was the most populous and prosperous town between Syracuse and Buffalo. It had a population of slightly more than 5,000. Although officially it was only a village, Newark functioned like a small city. It was a major trading and industrial center with both small and larger manufacturing such as woodworking, canning, tobacco, machine, and automobile factories. An agricultural community surrounded Newark with a prolific countryside abounding in rich orchards, nurseries, and large upland fields of various grains and tobacco. Because of the rich farmland, pioneers officially named the township Arcadia.[1]

Newark was the primary shipping center for most of the commerce produced in this area and it was the hub of five railroads providing direct freight and passenger service to the leading commercial centers within a 500-mile radius and beyond. One railroad, the Rochester and Eastern Railway, was the town's largest employer, with two 250 full-time workers at its Newark terminal.[2]

First-generation Dutch and Germans settled Newark, with English, Scots, Irish, and French immigrants. Italians arrived a few years later. This population provided Newark and its surrounding countryside with an abundance of hard-working and dedicated people with a strong kinship to their community and country. They contributed to the steady growth of local business and the general success of the overall community.[3]

At exactly seven o'clock in the evening of September 23, 1898, Dr. Fhutten delivered a healthy baby boy who was destined to become famous as a World War II U.S. Navy hero. His name was Leslie Edward Gehres. He was born in his grandfather's house on upper Church Street in Newark.[4]

The roots of the Gehres family lie far from the deep blue waters of the oceans where Leslie Gehres would make his name. The surname is prevalent across the near Midwest into upstate New York, where Leslie Gehres' branch of the family settled during the 19th century.

Leslie's father was Charles F. Gehres, who was born in Alloway, New York, in 1859; he died in 1905. He was a carpenter. His mother was Phebe A. Thomas, born in Millport, New York, in 1868. She is listed in the Newark business directory of that era as being a hotel housekeeper. Leslie had four sisters: Winifred, Flora, Margaret, and Bernice. He also had an older brother, Carl, who died in infancy.

Leslie's grandfather, Peter Gehres, was born in Bavaria in 1827, as was his grandmother, Margaret H. Beisher, in 1836. Peter first settled in Lyons, New York, and became a blacksmith. However, he soon moved to Newark, where he purchased a hotel and some land. He owned and operated the European Hotel in Newark for many years.

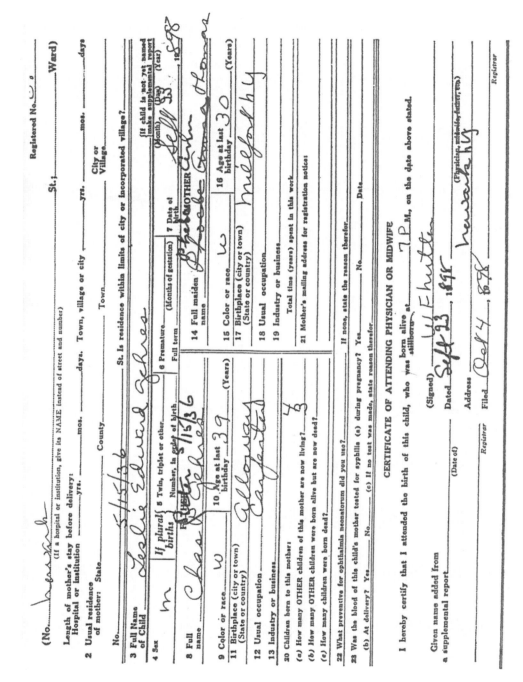

*Gehres' birth certificate*

*Above, the Gehres family home in Newark from 1899 to 1909; below, Gehres' home from 1910 to 1912.*

**Thelma Prutzman**

He announced his purchase in an optimistic manner, with a small listing that ran in an 1869 edition of the Newark Business Journal. It read, in part:

EUROPEAN HOTEL, Corner Canal and Charles St., Newark, N. Y. Having recently purchased and re-fitted the above house, I am prepared to accommodate the traveling public. A bar well stocked with choice liquors, lager beer, &c.
PETER GEHRES, Proprietor

*Winifred Gehres*

Shortly after Leslie's birth, Charles Gehres moved his family to 501 Mason Street in Newark. They remained at that address until 1910, when they moved to the north side of a double house located just south of the Episcopal church on South Main Street. They remained at that address until the fall of 1912, when they moved to Rochester.

Leslie's father died in 1905 in a local construction accident when the boy was only eight years old. The combination of the loss of his father and a growing disinclination toward school made Leslie a growing problem in the household. His mother, Phebe, lacked the time and energy to keep Leslie in line. Phebe allowed the oldest sister, Winifred, also known as "Virgie," to take over the responsibility of reining in her younger brother. She was a strong factor in developing Leslie's positive traits.

Winifred was a no-nonsense person who demanded the same from her sisters and their younger brother. As Leslie grew to manhood, he recognized the value of Winifred's discipline and sense of responsibility. Acquaintances who knew Gehres as both a boy and a man say that the perseverance and tenacity he learned in his early life were among his strongest attributes.[5]

By the time Gehres reached the eighth grade, he had developed a love of the sea. Even at a young age, he had been able to find the time and means to visit the New York State Naval Militia in nearby Rochester. Gehres was convinced that he wanted to join the U.S. Navy. Such an ambition was a respectable goal for a young boy in the early years of the 20th century, as America gained naval ascendancy.

In 1898, the year of Gehres' birth, the U.S. Navy came of age in the Spanish-American war. Gehres probably grew up hearing stories of how Admiral Dewey had destroyed the Spanish fleet in Manila Harbor, or about the dash by the battleship USS *Oregon* as it sped from the west coast to the battle zone in the Caribbean Sea.

Another Spanish-American War hero, Admiral William T. Sampson, was born and raised in the nearby canal town of Palmyra, New York. During World War II, the U.S. Navy Basic Training Center along the eastern shore of Seneca Lake, south of Geneva, New York, was named in his honor and became known as Sampson Air Force Base. Today this land is a state park.

In 1907, when Gehres was nine, President Theodore Roosevelt sent the "Great White Fleet," four squadrons of battleships and escort vessels, on a world tour. From December 1907 to February 1909, the ships called at ports across the globe, a potent symbol of American power.

In his early youth, while living in Newark, Leslie Gehres was known as an intelligent, inquisitive and adventurous boy. He was not above skipping school. In the summer months, his favorite pastimes were swimming and fishing in the Erie Canal along with occasional trips to Sodus Point. In the fall and spring, fishing in the Erie Canal and nearby Ganargua Creek was always at its best. There was also hiking in Bailey's Woods. In the winter, ice skating, ice fishing and sledding held his interest, along with frequent visits to the library where young Gehres could read about the world. Gehres did not feel comfortable in the structured school courses that existed in the overall school curriculum at that time. Instead he sought real-life experiences through personal contact and observation. Reality education added significantly to his common-sense approach to learning and life.[6]

Many facets in Gehres' early life undoubtedly affected his route to success. Newark and its surrounding communities produced an abundance of self-made men, such as William M. Stewart, the promoter of the famous Comstock Lode and later a Nevada senator. Famous artists from the region included Dewitt Parsall, painter of western scenes, and Ann Collins, a talented painter of race horses. Among her clients were Bing Crosby and John Wayne.

Perhaps one of Newark's most successful early residents was Isaac Singer, who worked as a journeyman machinist in the John Daggett Machine Manufacturing plant on South Main Street. Singer was a skilled machinist with a bent towards experimentation and innovation. He is credited with developing the first successful sewing machine while working at the Daggett plant. Henry Wells, who later joined forces with Henry Fargo to form the Wells-Fargo Company, was also from the area.

Gehres often visited the Erie Canal's triple-tiered double locks in Lockville, East Newark. The barge crew members represented a unique cross-section of humanity, from young boys to old men and women with a wide variety of nautical experiences. Many of the crew members had served not only on the canal barges, but also on larger ships that plied the waters of the world. Some had served in the U.S. Navy. For Gehres, these individuals provided him with a wealth of information about life on the high seas and the lands beyond.[7]

## *Sodus Point*

While Newark provided Gehres with many outlets and worthwhile experiences, he was really interested in the ships of the sea—the larger ships. To see these ships of the ocean and the Great Lakes, he had to venture to nearby Sodus Point. Located on the southern shore of Lake Ontario, Sodus Point was a port of entry to the United States, leading shipping center, and summer resort.[8] There Gehres found the ships he wanted to see, and got to talk with the crews, and sometimes the passengers, aboard these ships.

To get to Sodus Point from Newark required a twenty-five-minute train ride on the Northern Central Railroad. During the summer, there were several round trips from Newark to Sodus Point each day. Newark served as a hub for other railroads providing direct service to Sodus Point from Washington, D.C., and other points throughout the northeast.

Sodus Point was a charming little town that gained notoriety during the War of 1812, when two battles took place between the British, their Indian allies, and the local militia. There was little damage, and the scuffles ended in draws, with the British and Indians retreating.[9]

Sodus Point provided good lodging and restaurants, along with many waterside activities and educational and religious opportunities. Gehres often visited Sodus Point with his family and friends. The rail fare for kids was usually about 25 cents round trip. But if money was scarce, then the local box car would do, especially if the kids wanted a little spending money once they arrived. Sodus Point was not without its entertainments. It had a large promenade sporting a grocery store, dance hall, several bars, icehouse, hotdog-and-hamburger stands, soup-and-potato bar, boat service and a movie theater. Also, located nearby in Willow Park was a Ferris wheel, a well-decorated merry-go-round and the railroad station.

***Old Sodus Point Lighthouse***

**A modern view of Sodus Point**

Sodus Point was also a regional port and terminal for water and rail commerce. It supported two large shipping trestles for unloading various commodities produced locally, shipped in by rail, or trans-shipped from other ports in the Great Lakes. Sodus Point had a U.S. Customs House, where people entering or leaving the United States, as well as foreign crew members, had to register and obtain proper documentation.[10] For Leslie Gehres, this location offered many of the answers he sought regarding life at sea and the lands beyond.

Sodus Point at that time was not only a popular resort and busy port of entry and commercial center, but also a haven for retired ship's officers and crew members. They were always ready and willing to tell their shipboard stories to anyone who would listen. The old sailors walked the streets, sat in the parks, and visited the establishments on the promenade. Such situations provided young Gehres with many opportunities to approach and listen to their remarkable nautical tales of bygone days.

One of Gehres' highlights was the opportunity to observe the larger ships as they entered the narrow, two-piered channel to Sodus Bay. He especially marveled at the maneuvering by the crews of the large windjammers in negotiating the channel between the two piers.[11]

These majestic ships, usually fully rigged, were able to accomplish this difficult task in a gingerly manner without the aid of auxiliary power or a tugboat. Once they arrived in Sodus Bay, they would continue under sail to the trestle area unassisted. They used a tugboat only to assist in the docking. Gehres was able to meet the steamship and windjammer crews. Language was seldom a problem as most of the ships came from English-speaking countries such as Canada, England, Ireland, and Scotland.

Those ships that navigated the St. Lawrence River had a dangerous journey because the lower reaches of the river were particularly hazardous with shallow water, unstable rapids and underwater rock formations. While it was not an easy journey for the steamships, it was usually a very difficult and dangerous voyage for the windjammers.

John Masefield, the English poet laureate, best described the longing for the sea when he wrote "Sea Fever."

*I must go down to the seas again, to the lonely sea and the sky,*
*And all I ask is a tall ship and a star to steer her by,*
*[...]*
*And all I ask is a merry yarn from a laughing fellow rover,*
*And quiet sleep and a sweet dream when the long trick's over..[12]*

There were other interests in the area that attracted him. Gehres was undoubtedly familiar with *The Last of the Mohicans*, by James Fenimore Cooper. In the summer of 1823, Cooper rented a cottage on Sodus Bay at Charles Point, where he wrote this Indian tale. Gehres, who traveled around Sodus Bay on the local ferry, was able to locate and visit Cooper's cottage on Charles Point.[13]

A notable visitor to Sodus Point in Gehres' time was John Philip Sousa, the famous bandmaster and composer. With direct train service from Washington, D.C., to Sodus Point, Sousa was able to make weekend sojourns to this popular resort. Sousa liked to fish on his visits, and he also led a small band in Sunday afternoon concerts in Willow Park.[14]

Gehres' love for sailing was strong, whether the boat was large or small. Sometimes he was able to sail on a relative or friend's small craft, such as a lark or star class sailboat. If there were no sailboats available, a rowboat or canoe would do.[15]

While at Sodus Point, Gehres and his friends occasionally visited both the older and newer lighthouses. The older lighthouse was no longer in use and served as the home for the U.S. Coast Guard lighthouse keeper and his family, along with quarters for the lighthouse keeper's assistants. The newer lighthouse was located at the end of the western harbor pier.

Gehres and his friends liked to swim in Lake Ontario where the water was cool and clean. On some days, the bay waters were a better swim as they were warmer. The water was also a lot different from the muddy confines of the Erie Canal in Newark.

They also liked to fish in the bay as its waters usually yielded good frying fish. The boys usually fished in the afternoon to make sure that the fish would keep on the journey back to Newark.

Izaak Walton described fishing in Sodus Bay:

*Green are the waters, green as bottle glass*
*Behold them stretched thar.*
*Big muscalonges and Oswego bass*
*Are chiefly cotched thar.*[16]

When the sun began to set, Gehres and his friends knew it was time to board the last train back to Newark. The train left from Sodus Point's downtown Lake Shore Station. When the boys arrived safely back in Newark, they divided their catch of fish and went their separate ways. After a full meal and expounding on his day's adventures, young Gehres was ready for bed. The next morning he would awaken early, have breakfast, and head out the back door for another day of adventure.

Gehres helped his family by developing a newspaper route and several other enterprises. He was a hard worker. Perhaps his most significant venture into the world of entrepreneurship was when he built a newspaper monopoly. He delivered the morning edition of the Rochester newspapers, including the *Rochester Democrat & Chronicle*, hours before any other newsboy had the papers.

Palmyra, ten miles west of Newark, was a central distribution point for newspapers in the region. The *Democrat & Chronicle*, the major paper, usually did not arrive in Newark until early afternoon, as it came down from Palmyra on a slow New York Central train that made several local stops before arriving in Newark. Gehres would take an early morning trolley to Palmyra. There he would buy at wholesale a generous supply of the *Democrat & Chronicle*. He would then haul his bundle of newspapers on the next eastbound trolley and head for Newark. If he was lucky, Gehres would be able to catch an express trolley both ways.

By the time Gehres arrived back in Newark, it would still be fairly early in the morning. He would set up his location downtown and sell the morning editions of the *Democrat & Chronicle* and other newspapers. Newspapers were the primary source of local, regional, national and international news and advertising. Good early morning newspapers were in demand, and prompt delivery was well rewarded. Ambitious newsboys such as Gehres received handsome tips.

Paying for trolley rides to and from Palmyra was never much of a problem for Gehres. His uncles Erwin and Charles Thomas worked for the trolleys. They knew young Gehres was working to help support his family, so they let him ride free.

*Two of Gehres' sisters, Flora and Bernice, flank their mother, Phebe.*

## *Farewell to Newark—Destination Rochester*

Following her husband's death, Phebe Gehres was employed by her father-in-law as the housekeeper of his small European Hotel. Unfortunately, in early 1912 Peter Gehres lost his hotel (legend says it was gambled away in a poker game), and Phebe was out of a job. Finding work in Newark was not easy, and wages were low. In the fall of 1912, Phebe decided she could no longer afford to live in Newark even though she loved being near her close relatives and many friends. Relatives in Rochester had told her that the job market there was better, with many jobs available. Also, in Rochester there would be a better opportunity for finding employment for her children.[17]

In the early morning of a cool, late autumn day, Phebe gathered her clan together at the corner of West Maple Avenue and South Main Street. They caught an express trolley on the Rochester, Syracuse and Eastern Railway for Rochester. It would be a short, 30-minute ride. Perhaps the Gehres family was saddened by this move, but Phebe thought that Rochester would provide better opportunities for herself and her children. It would prove to be the correct decision.

Over the years, Newark has carried its scars with the grace and dignity befitting the *grande belle* that she is. Looking back at Newark and its surrounding community, there were few locations in Gehres' time that could have offered such a wholesome and abundant environment. Rear Admiral Gehres' hometown provided him with many of the tools and incentives for a successful and rewarding life.

*Gehres' uncles, Elliot and Ervine Thomas, with Gehres'*
*mother, Phebe*

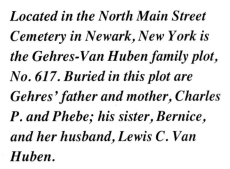

Located in the North Main Street Cemetery in Newark, New York is the Gehres-Van Huben family plot, No. 617. Buried in this plot are Gehres' father and mother, Charles P. and Phebe; his sister, Bernice, and her husband, Lewis C. Van Huben.

*Gehres as a young officer, circa 1920s*

# II
# Rochester and Early Service

*"A chance to go to sea is a wonderful thing, for it allows a seafaring lad to smell the ocean air, and cast his roots in exciting adventures, both at sea and in distant lands."*

**Alan Villiers**

Relatives had already located more affordable living quarters and work opportunities for Phebe Gehres and her family. She felt that with a regular job paying decent wages their lives would improve. Also, with work opportunities for her older children, they could help support the family. Leslie quickly found

**John Towers**

employment at the Yawman and Erbie Manufacturing Co. and enrolled in high school. However, while coasting his sled down a hill in Highland Park, Gehres broke his leg. He quit school, believing he could no longer actively participate in sports. Also, he was not particularly interested in his school's curriculum.[18]

Gehres' mother sensed the futility of trying to force formal education on her son. Gehres' favorite worthwhile interest was the New York State Naval Militia. Phebe could understand her son's interest in the robust, hands-on education the service would provide. However, Gehres was underage; the minimum age for acceptance was eighteen. Evidently, Gehres was able to convince his mother of the advantages of enlisting. Phebe agreed to sign a statement indicating that Leslie was eighteen years of age. In 1914, Gehres enlisted as an ordinary seaman in the New York State Naval Militia, Sixth Division, in Rochester, New York. As Leslie Gehres was a large, robust and healthy lad, he had no problems passing his physical examination.

Information supplied by his family, friends, his birth certificate, and the naval archives dispute several of the alleged ages Gehres listed on official documents. His actual age at the time of enlistment was probably fifteen and possibly fourteen.

*Glenn
Curtiss*

Actually, he is in good company, as a number of high-ranking U.S. Naval and other military branch officers also enlisted underage.

Rochester was a port of entry to the United States, although not as large or as active as Sodus Point. If Gehres was so inclined, he could take a local streetcar down to Rochester's nearby port of entry, located in the adjoining little seaport towns of Seabreeze and Charlotte at the mouth of the Genesee River on the southern shore of Lake Ontario. However, soon after arriving in Rochester Gehres found a new passion, aviation.

The search was on for a heavier-than-air, engine-driven aircraft capable of carrying passengers. Up to this time, the primary means of air transportation had been balloons, gliders, and dirigibles, none of which were efficient or practical in moving people on a timely basis to designated destinations. While the military used lighter-than-air craft and gliders, primarily for reconnaissance, they were considered of little value for combat and supply purposes.

But air technology was expanding rapidly. Local and national news media followed stories relating to the emerging role of engine-powered aircraft in both civilian and military environments.

The Wright brothers of Dayton, Ohio, had made several successful aircraft flights in 1903. They continued to expand their experiments in a small plant located in Dayton. Later, they would build larger plants at various locations.

Meanwhile, in nearby Hammondsport, New York, a little town along the south shore of Lake Keuka, a young man named Glenn Curtiss had been experimenting with heavier-than-air, engine-powered aircraft.[19]

Although he was building and flying both land- and water-based aircraft, Curtiss favored amphibious aircraft, in part because at the time there were more bodies of water capable of sustaining takeoffs and landings than there were airports.

The U.S. Navy had become aware of these experiments and indicated an interest. On June 20, 1911, the U.S. Navy assigned Lt. John H. Towers, a 1906 graduate of the U.S. Naval Academy, to observe and evaluate the Curtiss operations. Towers had a strong interest in aeronautics, especially in the design and airworthiness of engine-powered aircraft. He was also concerned about the future role of aircraft as worthwhile weapons of the U.S. Navy.[20]

In Hammondsport, Towers learned to fly several of the early Curtiss planes. As pilot number three in the U.S. Navy, he later obtained his official fighter pilot wings at the U.S. Naval Air Station, Pensacola, Florida. Towers made numerous trips to Hammondsport to observe and evaluate the aircraft produced at the Curtiss manufacturing establishment. He flew most of the Curtiss planes and offered advice on design, construction, and operation.[21]

Leslie E. Gehres read about Curtiss in the *Democrat and Chronicle* newspaper. One day, with his mother's permission and a day off from the Naval Militia, Seaman Gehres boarded the Baltimore and Ohio Railroad and headed south toward Bath, New York. This was a leisurely trip of less than two hours. From Bath, it was an hour's walk north to Hammondsport and the Curtiss plant. Arriving in the midmorning allowed Gehres several free hours to roam around Hammondsport and observe the Curtiss plant operation.[22]

Gehres always brought his lunch with him and usually ate it down by the waterfront. He generally had the afternoon free. However, he wanted to make sure that he returned to Bath in the early evening to take the last train to Rochester.

During his visits, Gehres may have met Lt. Towers. Gehres never got beyond the eighth grade and Towers was a U.S. Naval Academy graduate who was fourteen years older than Gehres. But Gehres and Towers had one outstanding commonality: their intense interest in the emerging field of aviation, and its future

# *Ships on Which Gehres Served Prior to Becoming a Naval Aviator*

*The USS* **Indiana**

*The USS* **Massachusetts**

***The USS* Jacob Jones**

***The USS* Aulick**

***The USS* Farenholt**

*Above, the USS* **Tingey**; *below, the USS* **Gillis..**

*The USS Salem*

role in the U.S. Navy. Later, the two would meet again as top-rated pilots serving together in the emerging carrier fleet. Here, Towers, as Gehres' superior officer, was in a prime position to observe the younger man's flying skills and leadership ability. Towers provided a strong role model for Gehres.

On April 6, 1917, the United States declared war on Germany. The New York State Naval Militia was mobilized. Gehres entered active duty in the U.S. Navy as an ordinary seaman. During the war, Gehres served aboard the USS *Salem*, USS *Indiana* and USS *Massachusetts*. These ships were assigned the duty of patrolling and protecting allied shipping and troop movements along the German U-boat-infested North Atlantic convoy route to Europe. [23]

After years of apparent aimlessness, Gehres applied himself as never before. He buckled down on his studies, reveling in the order and excitement of naval life. His size and intelligence soon attracted the attention of superior officers. A year after joining the fleet, Gehres was promoted to ensign, USNRF, on May 24, 1918. Later, in September 1918, after completing a short course at the U.S. Naval Academy, he was transferred to the regular U. S. Navy in the rank of ensign. Gehres was promoted to Lt. (jg.) USN in May 1919.

He reached full grade in June, 1922. During this time, he served aboard the destroyers USS *Aulick* and USS *Jacob Jones*. Later, Gehres would serve aboard the

USS *Farenholt* as its executive officer and aboard the *Aulick*, USS *Gillis* and USS *Tingey* as commanding officer.[24]

The *Gillis* would later be converted into a seaplane tender. It was assigned to Fleet Air Wing Four in the Aleutians from 1941 to 1943, under the command of Commodore Gehres.

Gehres' destroyer duty led to his courtship and marriage. His romance started in 1921 at the U.S. Naval Air Station, San Diego, California, where Lt. Gehres met Rhoda Rumsey shortly after her divorce. One evening while having dinner, he looked through his porthole and saw a beautiful blonde dining with another officer on a neighboring destroyer.

Gehres threw Hershey candy kisses to her through the porthole to get her attention. The story of how Lt. Gehres courted Rhoda is a family legend. The U.S. Naval Station, San Diego, was quite a distance from La Mesa, where Rhoda lived. Also, Gehres was at sea for extended periods. However, he continued to woo Rhoda for the next three years and made several unsuccessful proposals of marriage.[25]

Finally, after several months at sea, Gehres decided to propose to Rhoda just one more time. If she said no, he was going back to town and spend all his money on a good time. He phoned Rhoda and she accepted his invitation for a date.

Rhoda and her two children were living with her mother, stepfather and a stepbrother in La Mesa, about ten miles east of San Diego. To get to their home, Gehres had to take a ferry from Coronado and go across the bay to San Diego. From there, he had to catch a trolley to La Mesa. After arriving in La Mesa, he had to walk several winding streets, up a hill and take twenty more steps from the street level to Rhoda's family house. However, when he arrived, Gehres was told Rhoda was not home.

Gehres said, "This is final, it's all over."

He turned around and started walking back down the hill. When he got about halfway down the hill, a car came racing down the hill after him. In the car was Rhoda, her stepbrother, Bill, and his girlfriend.

Gehres climbed in the car and it took off. It appears that Rhoda said yes to Gehres' marriage proposal. They drove to Santa Ana, California, where, on June 16, 1923, they were married by Moffett Rhodes, minister of the M.E. Church.[26]

Gehres indicates on the marriage certificate that he was twenty-seven years old. But his birth certificate issued in Newark, New York, indicates his date of birth was September 23, 1898. One needs to remember that Gehres originally joined the New York State Naval Militia as an underage enlistee.

A few years after their marriage, the couple had a daughter, Leslie. During his years in the U.S. Navy, Gehres, Rhoda and their three children were a military family, living at several different locations. However, the San Diego area of California seemed to be their favorite location. After retirement, La Mesa became their permanent home.

After completing his sea service aboard destroyers in June 1924, Lt. Gehres was assigned to Pearl Harbor as the communications officer, U.S. Navy Yard. Following that tour of duty, in January 1927, he reported for pilot training at the U.S. Naval Air Station, Pensacola, Florida. It was a goal he had sought for years. On September 30, 1927, he received his pilot's wings, becoming a fully designated Navy aviator. Gehres would continue with aviation throughout his naval career.

*Gehres' marriage certificate*

*Gehres and his
new wife, the
former Rhoda
Rumsey.*

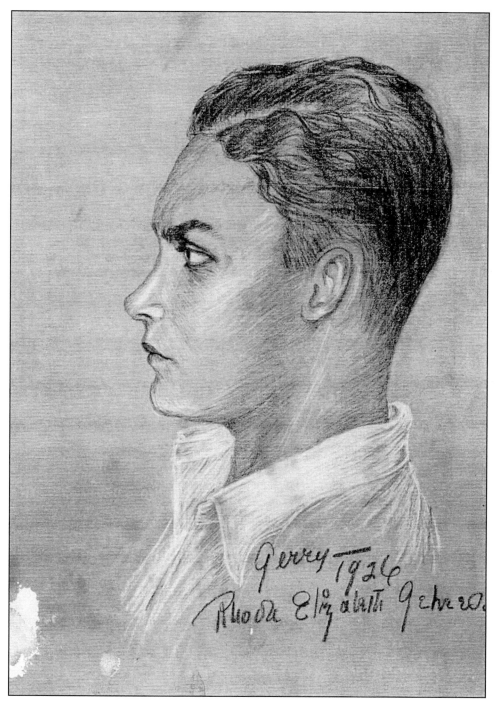

**Rhoda Gehres' portrait of her husband.**

# III
# Barnstorming Days, The Inter-war Years

*"To soar the limits of the sky and glide like the best of the winged birds, the maneuvering with twists and turns, and fly the course, makes for exciting and satisfying moments."*

**Charles A. Lindbergh**

On November 30, 1927, Gehres was assigned to Fighter Squadron One, based on the aircraft carrier *Langley*. Later, he was reassigned to the aircraft carriers *Saratoga* and *Lexington*. On these carriers, he held the positions of carrier combat pilot, flight officer, and operations officer.

Forerunners of today's Blue Angels, Naval Aviation's 'High Hats' thrilled the nation during the Roaring Twenties as they launched a legend for flight precision which still persists. At the 1929 Cleveland Air Races, awed fans watched the trio of Navy Boeing F2B's as they took off, looped, landed and taxied while tied together by short lengths of manila line. Cleveland team consisted of Lt. L. E. Gehres (RAdm. Ret.), Ltjg. F. N. Kivette (RAdm., ACNO) and Ltjg. F. O'Beirne (RAdm., ComCarDiv Three).

*Modern recognition of the founders of U.S. Navy aerobatics.*

***Charles Lindbergh with members of the High Hats.***

While stationed on the three carriers, Gehres organized, trained, and led the Nine High Hats, an aerobatic formation that performed a variety of stunts throughout the United States and in several foreign countries. One stunt was to tie a three-inch ribbon between three aircraft and perform a series of complicated maneuvers without the ribbon breaking. This was very dangerous as the planes were often less than ten feet apart. Sometimes banners and flags were attached to the ribbons. The act was one of the High Hats' show-stoppers and usually lasted for several minutes.

Frequently, Gehres' group of highly skilled fighter pilots performed aerial combat demonstrations. On at least one occasion, Charles A. Lindbergh joined the team. He was an excellent pilot and motivator, providing support and inspiration that the newer and younger pilots needed. He understood technical limitations and strengths of the era's aircraft.

Perhaps one of the most headline-grabbing experiences of the Nine High Hats was their performance in the movie *Hell Divers*, which was filmed in San Diego in 1930. The movie was a top-notch MGM production starring Clark Gable, Wallace Beery, Cliff Edwards, and Conrad Nagel. The Nine High Hats did the air combat scenes, with the piloting performed by Lt. Herbert Duckworth, Lt. E.P. Southwick and Lt. Jimmie Thach.[27] Gehres served as the technical adviser.

Many members of the Nine High Hats team went on to have successful careers in the U.S. Navy. Of the original members of the High Hats, both Leslie Gehres and Clarence McClusky achieved the rank of rear admiral. Jimmie Thach, a late arrival in the High Hats team, later became a World War II Navy air ace. He was credited with the development of the Thach Weave, a maneuver that enabled combat pilots to out-fly the more nimble Japanese Zeros during World War II. He became a full admiral as the commander in chief, U.S. Naval Forces, Europe.[28]

The Nine High Hats team had a rotation system of pilot turnover that provided a nucleus of highly qualified combat pilots. The highly motivated and skilled pilots challenged air science and technology in the early years of air flight. They developed advanced attack and evasive techniques. Remarkably, there is no evidence of accidents during the years that the troupe flew.[29]

The Nine High Hats were always a crowd favorite at the annual National Air Show in Cleveland, Ohio, and other locations where they performed. Two of the team's winning air-show trophies are on exhibit in the Rear Admiral Leslie E.

*The USS* **Langley**

Gehres Memorial Exhibit in Newark (New York) High School. They were won by the High Hats at the All-American Air Maneuvers in Miami, Florida, in 1930 and the Modoc Air Rodeo in Alturus, California, in 1931.

The aircraft used by the team were usually pursuit planes (which is what fighters were called), assigned to the aircraft carriers *Saratoga* and *Lexington*. Gehres continued to participate in the High Hats stunt team performances until shortly before World War II, when he was reassigned as the executive officer, Pearl Harbor, Hawaii.[30]

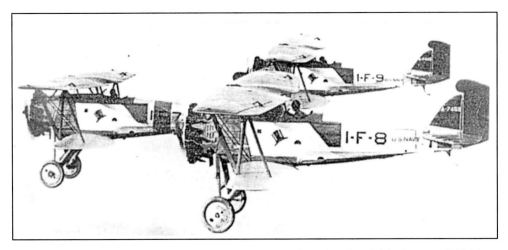

*Precision flying, courtesy of the High Hats, at the Cleveland Air Races of 1929. Note the group insignia just below the cockpit. Below, Gehres, at center kneeling, and the High Hats.*

*Lt. Commander Gehres, third from left, with executive officers at the commissioning ceremony of the USS Yorktown, 1937.*

*The USS* **Yorktown**

*Above, the USS* Saratoga; below, the *USS* Lexington

The Nine High Hats were involved in a variety of activities other than just national and international air shows. They also provided a positive public relations display, which undoubtedly increased the public's support for naval and military aviation.

Years later, as recently as 2002, the VFA Squadron, based at the U.S. Navy Air Station, Lamoore, California, flew F-14s that still carried the High Hat insignia. The Nine High Hats stunt team served as a prelude and an inspiration for the U.S. Navy Blue Angels aerobatic team, which was created in 1946.[31]

*Gehres, with his back to the camera, greets guests as his niece, Margaret, and a friend pose at Bailey's Lot in Newark, 1927.*

## Air Science and Technology

The world was fast changing after the turn of the 20th century, especially in the areas of transportation, communications, energy, and technology. The Industrial Revolution had brought an explosion of industrial, agricultural, and military development, which fueled keen competition for expanding markets at all levels. Carriers and naval aviation would soon be as essential as battleships for securing far-flung possessions of global trade.

In 1926, John H. Towers became executive officer and then captain of the aircraft carrier USS *Langley CV-1*.

**Admiral John Towers as commanding officer of the *Langley*, 1927**

Later, he became chief of staff and captain of the USS *Saratoga CV-3*. Towers, while captain of the USS *Langley,* was credited with renovating and upgrading the U.S. Navy's first aircraft carrier from an experimental platform into an efficient first-class fighting ship. Later, he also made many improvements on the USS *Saratoga.*[32] Shortly after Towers assumed command of the aircraft carrier USS *Langley,* Gehres was also assigned to the *Langley*. He later followed Towers to the *Saratoga*. During the time that Towers held these command positions, Gehres was a combat pilot, flight officer, operations officer, and executive officer. While serving on the *Langley* and the *Saratoga,* Gehres, with Towers' approval, organized, trained and led the famous Nine High Hats stunt team.[33]

The following seven shipboard improvements made on those two ships served as models for the construction of future American aircraft carriers. Lessons learned and implemented included:

- Launching and stopping carrier aircraft within the extremely limited area of the flight deck was a prime area of experimentation by Towers, who studied compressed air, explosives, steam pressure, and hydraulic technology.
- The USS *Langley* was designed without an island on its flight deck. Through an expanded and improved communication system, a more effective command and control protocol was established. Islands became standard on all future carriers.
- Introduction of color-coded uniforms for on-deck flight crews was initiated in 1930. This allowed crew members working under intense pressure to distinguish between ordnance men, handling crew, landing signal officers, etc. There were over sixteen different color uniforms implemented.
- A recommendation of extra armor plate in the construction of future aircraft carriers was made. The British armored their decks but the U.S. Navy did not.
- The British were the first to install radar on their ships. The United States bought this technology from the British and installed it in the early 1930s. It was a superior navigational aid capable of detecting enemy aircraft.
- Better fire control techniques and equipment were instituted.
- Well-trained crash and salvage control crews were created.[34]

***Gehres at the controls and J.M.F. Haase at the camera prior to
taking off to execute the Honey Lake experiment, 1930.***

***Haase, Gehres and W.A. McDonald.***

## *The Honey Lake Eclipse Expedition*

One of Gehres' more lasting contributions was in aerial photography. While Gehres was on duty at the U.S. Naval Air Station in San Diego, April 1930, he was assigned to fly for the U.S. Naval Observatory Expedition at Honey Lake, California. The purpose of the research assignment was to make aerial photographs of the moon's shadow on the earth during a total eclipse. Earlier attempts made in 1923 and 1925 to provide this information were not successful. The earlier photographs, taken from a dirigible at about 4,000 feet, were murky.

Two naval aircraft, a Sikorsky PS-3, and a Vought O2U-1, were secured for the expedition. The Sikorsky was used to transport people and equipment to Honey Lake. The Vought 02U-1 was equipped with an Akeley motion-picture camera for recording the eclipse shadow on film. Gehres flew the camera plane.[35]

He would only have a small window of opportunity to position his plane for successful filming. The goal was to use the findings to determine the exact centerline of the eclipse, which was needed to make corrections to the lunar almanac.

Isabel M. Lewis, a scientist at the event, shared her observations in the October 1930 edition of *Popular Astronomy*.

In addition to the photographs of the eclipse obtained on the ground, Lieutenant Leslie E. Gehres, U.S.N., and Chief Photographer J. M. T. Haase, U.S.N., in a pursuit plane at 18,000 feet obtained a fine film of the approach of the moon's shadow on the clouds at 12,000 feet elevation under most trying conditions. Lieutenant Gehres and Chief Photographer Haase reported upon their return from photographing the moon's shadow that they had seen it as "an elliptical, purplish-to-black spot on the clouds at an elevation of 12,000 feet above sea-level, darker than the surrounding dusk, and from one-half to three-quarters of a mile wide and that it had seemed to pass almost instantaneously across the clouds about one mile south of the predicted path." This difference in position was due to the fact that at an elevation of 12,000 feet above sea-level the altitude correction would shift the position of the path to the southeast. The calculated amount of the shift is nearly eight-tenths of a mile. The observed shift in position was stated to be about one mile. This gave a further check upon the correctness of the predicted path and the data upon which it was based.[36]

The expedition provided the first motion pictures of a total eclipse of the sun ever taken from an airplane.

During his long and distinguished U.S. Navy career, Rear Admiral Leslie E. Gehres' work, especially in the fields of air science and technology, was significant. This was finally recognized in 1969 when Gehres was awarded the Admiral John Henry Towers Memorial Award.

## The Boy Scout National Jamboree

On August 21, 1935, it seemed like the whole town of Newark, New York, was celebrating. Lt Commander Leslie E. Gehres, hometown hero, was due to make an early appearance. He was to arrive at about 9:30 a.m. flying an N2Y type aircraft

*Robert Palmer as a young Sea Scout.*

from the deck of the aircraft carrier USS *Saratoga*, located in the Annapolis area. This N2Y aircraft was formerly a scout plane for the rigid airship, *Akron*. After the 1933 loss of the *Akron* in a tragic air disaster,[37] the plane was serving as a utility aircraft aboard the *Saratoga*.

Gehres was to fly to Newark and pick up a young Sea Scout for an overnight on the *Saratoga*. The following day, Gehres was to fly the scout to Washington, D.C., where he would attend the first Boy Scout National Jamboree being held there August 22-30. Seventeen-year-old Robert Palmer had won this opportunity by submitting a winning essay titled "The Value of Worthwhile Merit Badges" in his Sea Scout troop's contest.

His Sea Scout troop was sponsored by the local Park Presbyterian Church. The trip had been arranged by the troop's scoutmaster, Lewis Van Huben, who was married to Bernice, Gehres' younger sister.[38]

This was a trip that Gehres was happy to make as he had a genuine interest in American youth. He was concerned about their having a firm understanding of

40

***Gehres in 1935 at the controls of a Grumman F2F-1 pursuit plane.***

American democracy and freedom. He felt that the American Boy Scout movement reinforced those values. Later, in retirement, Gehres would be a staunch member of the Freedoms Foundation of Valley Forge, which partners with the Boy Scouts in many projects advocating patriotism and pride of country.

At exactly 9:30 a.m., Gehres' plane was on the horizon There were no clouds in the sky. Approaching from the east, Gehres made a slow descent and landed at Newark's new airport. The Newark High School Band struck up several U.S. Navy tunes. A small crowd gathered as Gehres climbed from his cockpit to be greeted by a local welcoming committee. Included in the group were Stuart Hallagan, Karl Herman, and Eugene Morgan, all local businessmen. Hallagan and Herman were the only men from town who kept personal aircraft at the Newark Airport. They had been in the U.S. Army, while Morgan served in the U.S. Navy during World War I. Morgan had known Gehres from early school days in Newark. Morgan and Gehres were destined to meet and serve together in the Aleutian Islands in 1942 during World War II.[39]

Also in the group was Robert Palmer, the young Sea Scout who had won the prize trip. But shortly after Gehres arrived, a representative of the Boy Scout National Jamboree Committee notified Van Huben that, because of a polio epidemic throughout the United States, President Roosevelt had cancelled all large youth gatherings, effective immediately. This order included the Boy Scout Jamboree.

Bob Palmer realized that it was an opportunity lost forever. "I was quite upset at not being able to go," he said years later. "I really wanted fly in that U.S. Navy biplane." However, all was not lost, as Gehres took Palmer and some of his friends for short plane rides.

The experience stuck with Palmer. During World War II, he enlisted in the U.S. Army Air Corps and became an outstanding combat pilot, serving in both the Pacific and European theaters. Perhaps the airplane ride, along with the chance to converse with a genuine combat pilot, provided Palmer with the incentive to achieve that goal.[40]

## To Catch a Spy

Commencing in the early 1930s, relations between Japan and the United States began to deteriorate rapidly. Japan's militant government had begun a vast expansion program by conquering Manchuria and invading the northern provinces of China. The Japanese continued to enlarge their military forces in violation of existing arms-control treaties and agreements with various nations, including the United States.[41] As tensions increased, the Japanese established an extensive spy network in the United States. In 1937, Lt. Cmdr. Leslie Gehres helped smash one of these networks.

John Farnsworth was born and raised in Cincinnati, Ohio. He came from a middle-class family. Graduating with honors, he pursued his boyhood dream of entering the U.S. Navy. He made a good impression on his local congressman and he was appointed to the U.S. Naval Academy in June 1911.

*John Farnsworth*

Farnsworth graduated from Annapolis close to the top of his class. A brilliant student, he made an excellent officer and was sent to sea in various capacities, including destroyer duty in World War I. During this time, he became friendly with Gehres. Both Farnsworth and Gehres went on to complete flight training at the U.S. Naval Air Station, Pensacola, Florida. Farnsworth later taught at the air station, while Gehres went to the fleet as a combat pilot.

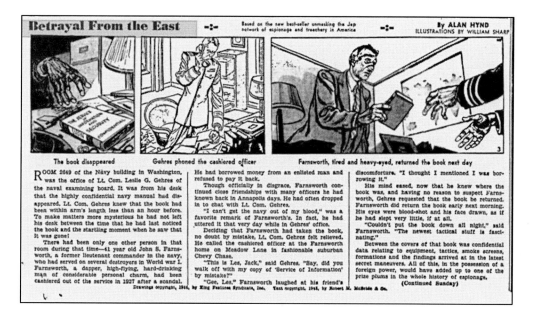

**Betrayal From the East** By ALAN HYND. ILLUSTRATIONS BY WILLIAM SHARP

Based on the new best-seller unmasking the Jap network of espionage and treachery in America

| The book disappeared | Gehres phoned the cashiered officer | Farnsworth, tired and heavy-eyed, returned the book next day |

ROOM 2649 of the Navy building in Washington, was the office of Lt. Com. Leslie G. Gehres of the naval examining board. It was from his desk that the highly confidential navy manual had disappeared. Lt. Com. Gehres knew that the book had been within arm's length less than an hour before. To make matters more mysterious he had not left his desk between the time that he had last noticed the book and the startling moment when he saw that it was gone!

There had been only one other person in that room during that time—41 year old John S. Farnsworth, a former lieutenant commander in the navy, who had served on several destroyers in World war I. Farnsworth, a dapper, high-flying, hard-drinking man of considerable personal charm, had been cashiered out of the service in 1927 after a scandal.

He had borrowed money from an enlisted man and refused to pay it back.

Though officially in disgrace, Farnsworth continued close friendships with many officers he had known back in Annapolis days. He had often dropped in to chat with Lt. Com. Gehres.

"I can't get the navy out of my blood," was a favorite remark of Farnsworth's. In fact, he had uttered it that very day while in Gehres' office.

Deciding that Farnsworth had taken the book, no doubt by mistake, Lt. Com. Gehres felt relieved. He called the cashiered officer at the Farnsworth home on Meadow Lane in fashionable suburban Chevy Chase.

"This is Les, Jack," said Gehres. "Say, did you walk off with my copy of 'Service of Information' by mistake?"

"Gee, Les," Farnsworth laughed at his friend's

discomfiture. "I thought I mentioned I was borrowing it."

His mind eased, now that he knew where the book was, and having no reason to suspect Farnsworth, Gehres requested that the book be returned. Farnsworth did return the book early next morning. His eyes were blood-shot and his face drawn, as if he had slept very little, if at all.

"Couldn't put the book down all night," said Farnsworth. "The newest tactical stuff is fascinating."

Between the covers that book was confidential data relating to equipment, tactics, smoke screens, formations and the findings arrived at in the latest secret maneuvers. All of this, in the possession of a foreign power, would have added up to one of the prize plums in the whole history of espionage.

(Continued Sunday)

Drawings copyright, 1944, by King Features Syndicate, Inc. Text copyright, 1944, by Robert M. McBride & Co.

*A syndicated column describing how Gehres caught Farnsworth.*

Farnsworth was later assigned to Norfolk, Virginia, where he commanded a squadron of fighter aircraft. Here, Farnsworth became a part of Virginia's high society, meeting and marrying into a wealthy family. The social strata in which they lived required an expensive home and lifestyle. The desperate Farnsworth borrowed money from an enlisted sailor, then refused to repay the borrowed money. The seaman made an official complaint and Farnsworth was court-martialed. He was found guilty and given a dishonorable discharge. Farnsworth's life fell apart and his wife divorced him. He was unable to obtain any employment because of his discharge.[42]

Japan offered him another option—obtaining important information from the U.S. Navy and secretly passing it along to a Japanese intelligence officer. His contact was Commander Yoshiashi Ichimiya, an intelligence officer in the Japanese Navy. In desperation, Farnsworth accepted the proposition and was soon flush with money. He remarried and moved into a luxury suite in the plush New Willard Hotel in Washington, D.C. He was often seen in the most expensive restaurants and nightclubs flashing $100 bills. He earned that money by providing important information about U.S. Navy vessels to the Japanese.[43]

He traveled the eastern seaboard, from Boston to Washington, D.C. obtaining information from his old friends still on active duty in the Navy. He would visit their homes and haunt their offices, telling them he was still loyal to the United States and hoped to be reinstated.

He would ask seemingly innocent questions about naval operations. This was not an uncommon habit among ex-service personnel, many of whom still had ties

*Lt. Cmdr. Gehres, 1939. Air officer aboard the* **Ranger.** *The inscription reads, "To my wife with love, L.E. Gehres, 10-21-39."*

to the navy. Through gossip, rumor, chit-chat and theft, if necessary, Farnsworth would gather information and documents for the Japanese.

When Farnsworth hoisted classified documents from his navy friends, he quickly had them copied by commercial firms, telling them that he was an active duty U.S. Navy officer.

But soon after Farnsworth visited the Washington office of his old friend, Lt. Cmdr. Leslie E. Gehres, then a member of the U.S. Navy Examining and Retirement Board, his spy game ended. After chatting a few minutes, Gehres had to leave his office. When he returned, he called his meeting with Farnsworth to an end, saying he had other duties that needed his attention. A short time after Farnsworth left, Gehres needed to consult a highly classified book titled, *The Service of Information and Security.* It had recently been distributed to a restricted group of officers.

Gehres made a thorough search of his office and questioned his staff. The document was missing. Then Gehres remembered Farnsworth's visit and telephoned him, asking if he had taken the document. Farnsworth said that he had inadvertently picked up the document by mistake while retrieving a folded newspaper he had been reading. He returned the document the next day.

However, Gehres did not recall any newspaper in his office. He had a feeling something was amiss. Therefore, he immediately made out a report of the incident and had it courier-delivered to the U.S. Office of Naval Intelligence (ONI).

Upon reading the report, Chief of ONI William Puleston, looked into Farnsworth's background. After reviewing Farnsworth's dishonorable discharge and unsuccessful search for work, Puleston decided to take immediate action.

Farnsworth was charged with espionage and tried by a jury in February 1937. Among other secrets stolen by Farnsworth were engineering and gunnery plans, including the blueprint of the model D-4 bombsight.[44]

Insisting he was innocent, he later changed his plea to "no contest." Farnsworth was found guilty and was sentenced on February 27, 1937, to four to twelve years in federal prison.

*The Franklin is floated out of her drydock after christening at the Newport News Shipbuilding and Drydock Company shipyard, Newport News, Virginia, on October 14, 1943, as a contingent of WAVES look on*

*This certificate testifies that the owner is an original crew member of the*
**Franklin.**

# IV
# The USS *Franklin* is Born

*"In this day, the task of the people is to save this nation and its institutions from disruptions from within and without."*

**Franklin D. Roosevelt**

The United States entered World War II with eight aircraft carriers. Before the end of the war, one hundred and thirteen additional carriers of various types had been built or were in the process of being built. During World War II, the United States lost five major carriers and six escort carriers.

The core of the U.S. Navy aircraft carrier fleet were the war-born *Essex* class vessels. The *Essex* squadrons were to become the cutting edge in the U.S. Navy's

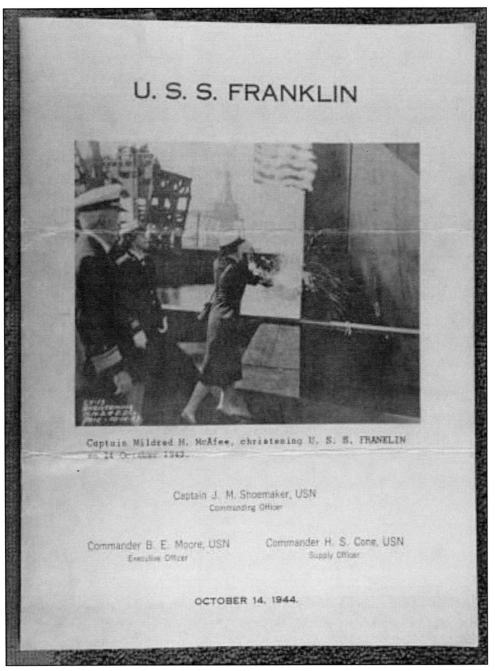

U. S. S. FRANKLIN

Captain Mildred H. McAfee, christening U. S. S. FRANKLIN
14 October 1943.

Captain J. M. Shoemaker, USN
Commanding Officer

Commander B. E. Moore, USN          Commander H. S. Cone, USN
Executive Officer                             Supply Officer

OCTOBER 14. 1944.

campaign to Tokyo. Without their massive power, victory over Japan undoubtedly would have been delayed.[45]

After the Coral Sea and Midway battles, it became evident that the aircraft carrier had become the dominant battle vessel of the U.S. Navy. The role of the traditional large battleship was beginning to fade. The aircraft carrier, with its ability to strike both land and sea targets with greater range than battleships or land-based air fleets, had emerged as the superior battle weapon.

Congress authorized money for the design and construction of the *Essex*-class carriers in 1939. *Essex CV-9*'s keel was laid on April 21, 1941 and it was commissioned on December 31, 1942. By November 23, 1946, twenty-four *Essex*-class carriers had been built and commissioned.[46]

Such an accomplishment was considered an assembly-line production miracle. Only through the inspired dedication of the American worker was this goal achieved. These huge aircraft carriers were impressive sights, massive complexes of welded and bolted steel components capable of delivering destruction to any enemy in its path on land or sea. The *Essex*-class carriers would prove their worth and contribute greatly to the successful conclusion of World War II. Not one of these carriers was lost in World War II. This is a tribute to the *Essex*-class design, which included a number of innovations. Some of the improvements incorporated in the design of these carriers were the result of experiments conducted by Admiral John H. Towers, Rear Admiral Leslie E. Gehres, Rear Admiral Carmon Briggs and other pioneer Navy aviators early in their careers.

The keel of the *Franklin* was laid in Shipway Number 11 at the Newport News Shipbuilding and Drydock in Virginia on December 7, 1942, precisely one year after the attack on Pearl Harbor. On October 14, 1943, Captain Mildred H. McAfee, Director of the U.S. Navy Women's Reserve christened the "United States Ship, the *Franklin*." In a record time of only ten months, the mainly completed hull of the USS *Franklin* was floated from its submerged shipway.

After the launching of the *Franklin*, it would take an additional three months to get its machinery fully operational and to train the crew. The *Franklin* was formally commissioned on January 31, 1944 with Captain James M. Shoemaker in command.[47]

The *Franklin* was the fifth *Essex* carrier. U.S. Navy engineers and over one thousand shipyard workers worked a seven-day around-the-clock schedule to complete the *Franklin*. The carrier displaced 27,200 tons with a length of eight hundred and sixty feet, and a beam of ninety-three feet with a draft of twenty-three feet. Its flight deck was eight hundred and twenty feet in length. Its engine room supported eight turbines producing over 150,000 horsepower operating four shafts. Its top speed was thirty-two knots. At fifteen knots, it had a range of slightly over fifteen thousand miles. Its fuel capacity was 6,330 tons of aviation-and fuel-oil.

This massive ship supported a crew of 3,421 sailors and officers. Included would be 740 Marine flight officers and crew members. The *Franklin* could carry up to a hundred fighting aircraft, both fighters and bombers. The completed

*Franklin* was truly an impressive sight to those that viewed this huge fighting lady of the sea.[48]

## The Shipyard Worker Remembers

U.S. Navy Captain Roosevelt "Rick" Wright Jr. provided a moving insight into the building of the *Franklin* at a ceremony in 2002 honoring Rear Admiral Leslie E. Gehres.

"I was born on July 24, 1943 in Elizabeth City, North Carolina, a historic U.S. Navy and U.S. Coast Guard community," he said. "My father, the late Roosevelt R. Wright Sr., was a civilian electrician who worked for the U.S. Navy during World War II. He made the daily commute from Elizabeth City to the Norfolk Naval Shipyard and also to the Newport News Ship Building and Dry Dock Corporation from 1942 to 1945.

*Roosevelt Wright*

"While I was growing up during the 1950s, my father used to joke that I was born on the USS *Shangri-La* or the USS *Franklin*. The *Shangri-La* was built at the Norfolk Naval Shipyard, and the USS *Franklin* was built at Newport News.

"Dad always told wonderful stories about his many work experiences with the Navy in building these two aircraft carriers. As an electrician, he wired electrical load centers, and connected various weapons systems electrical circuits. He also talked about working on the ship building ways and dry docks during the hot summer days and cold winter months, with much passion and love of the job.

"He also told me how dedicated the workers were, and how he had to get up early in the morning to take the forty-five-mile trip to the main gate of the Norfolk Naval Shipyard. Dad was always concerned about the plight of the young naval sailors who manned the ships he helped build. I will never forget how he told me the story of his heartbreak when he heard that the *Franklin* had been hit by the Japanese in the Pacific. He told me that the news brought the war home to our living room in Elizabeth City."[49]

## The Naming of the Franklin

*Edwin C. Bearss*

From the time of the launching of the USS *Franklin*, the carrier has frequently been referred to as "Big Ben." This was a nickname by its crew and others in the belief that it was named after Benjamin Franklin.

However, there are several conflicting explanations for the name. Part of the reason for the confusion is that carriers of the *Essex* class were named after previous Navy ships, famous battles and at least one mythical place. They included the USS *Essex, Yorktown, Intrepid, Hornet, Franklin, Ticonderoga, Wasp, Randolph, Lexington, Bunker Hill, Boxer, Hancock, Bennington, Bon Homme Richard, Leyte, Kearsarge, Oriskany, Antietam, Princeton, Lake Champlain, Tarawa, Valley Forge, Philippine Sea,* and *Shangri-La.*[50]

Of those twenty-four vessels three, the *Philippine Sea, Tarawa,* and *Leyte,* were named after World War II battles, although the *Leyte,* originally named for the Revolutionary War battle of Crown Point, was the third ship with that name.[51] At least one *Essex*-class carrier, the *Kearsarge,* was named after a ship whose namesake was a geographic feature, Mount Kearsarge in New Hampshire. The name honors the most famous *Kearsarge,* a Civil War Union Navy vessel that defeated the Confederate commerce raider, *Alabama.* Another, the *Shangri-La,* was named for the mythical place from which, President Franklin Roosevelt announced in jest, Jimmy Doolittle's raiders took off in 1942. But of all the *Essex*-class carriers, only the *Franklin's* name remains a matter of debate. Some historians credit the ship's name exclusively to the previous four *Franklins,* while others claim the carrier was named for the Revolutionary War-era statesmen. Respected scholar Edwin C. Bearss, historian emeritus, U.S. National Park Service, makes the best case for the ship being named after the Battle of Franklin.

The USS *Franklin,* CV-13, and her gallant crew perpetuated the memory of thousands of soldiers in the American Civil War, both the Grey and Blue, who were participants in the Battle of Franklin, Tennessee, which was fought on November 30, 1864. The linkage between the crew of the World War II USS *Franklin* and the soldiers of 1864 is particularly relevant as the Confederate charge at Franklin underscores the type of people who stood tall in defense of what they believed. The obvious comparison serves also to suggest that, like them, the officers and men on the *Franklin* stood tall in defense of the principles they believed, despite horrific experiences. The USS *Franklin,* CV-13 also commemorates the four ships of the United States Navy that preceded her with the venerable honored name of *Franklin.*[52]

More than forty accounts of the bloody Battle of Franklin have been published. Authors agree that it signaled the end of all hope for Confederate success. Confederate President Jefferson Davis, in his memoirs, conceded that the Battle of Franklin was the most frightful of the entire war.

In 1864, Franklin was a quiet and proud town in Williamson County along the banks of the Harpeth River, eighteen miles south of Nashville. It embraced a traditional southern lifestyle with a total population of about twelve hundred, of which about a hundred and fifty were slaves. In 1864, the community was primarily rural. Farming and small business operations were its mainstays. Tobacco and cotton were the main crops grown in the area. Also, there were a considerable number of grain fields producing for local consumption and cattle feed.[53]

The Battle of Franklin pitted two strong, well-qualified and battle-tried generals against one another. Commanding the Confederate army was General John Bell Hood. Major General John J. Schofield commanded the Union forces.

At about 4 p.m., General Hood's Confederate forces made the first of several frontal attacks on the Union forces and sustained heavy losses. The Confederate Army of Tennessee repeatedly charged the Union forces, which were entrenched in an arc around the southern perimeter of Franklin, anchored on either end by the Harpeth River. The Confederate army mustered a force of about 20,000 and sustained 1,740 killed, 3,800 wounded, and 702 missing. The Union forces numbered about 28,000 and lost 189 killed, 1,033 wounded, and 1,204 missing.

The nearby Carnton Plantation, home of Colonel John McGavock and his wife, Carrie, served as a field hospital during this encounter. A wounded soldier wrote to his wife: "The wounded were brought in by the hundreds during the battle, and

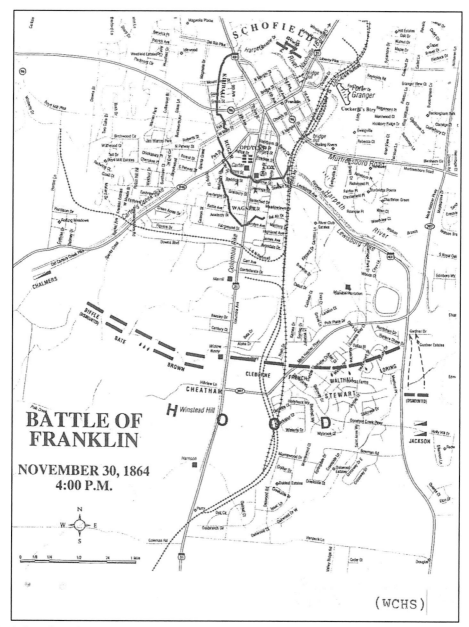

**BATTLE OF FRANKLIN**

NOVEMBER 30, 1864
4:00 P.M.

(WCHS)

all night after the battle. When this noble old house could hold no more, the yard was appropriated for the dead and wounded."

The Confederate Cemetery at the plantation was the largest privately-owned Confederate cemetery in the United States. Located there are 1500 separate Confederate soldiers' graves—a solemn portrait of supreme sacrifice. Almost all the men buried here were either killed or mortally wounded in the Battle of Franklin November 30, 1864.[54]

**McGavock Cemetery, Franklin, Tennessee.**

Schofield made his command post in the old Carter house residence, at 1140 Columbia Avenue, in Franklin. During the battle, the Carter family hid in the cellar. The many bullet holes in the exterior of the Carter House and its outbuildings are testaments to the intensity of the fighting.

A tragic footnote to the battle: Theodoric (Tod) Carter was born in the Carter House on March 24, 1840. He was educated in the local Harpeth Academy and he became a local attorney. In 1862, he enlisted in the Army of Tennessee. During the battle, he was mortally wounded about two hundred yards southwest of the Carter House. He was brought into his house by his family and died there on December 2, 1864.[55]

*Washington Star, May 19, 1945*

On October 8, 2002, the Franklin Board of Mayor and Aldermen held a special meeting to honor the USS *Franklin*, Captain Leslie E. Gehres and its crew. It also noted the naming of the USS *Franklin* to commemorate the Battle of Franklin.

Today, the Confederate and Union flags fly side by side, flowing in the gentle breeze over the last remaining ramparts of the Battle of Franklin. Every year on November 30 the flags are at half-mast in honor of all the brave soldiers who made the supreme sacrifice on that date. The killing fields of Franklin now lie quiet and are at peace.

*Gehres at his office in the Aleutians.*

# V
# Guarding the Gate: The Captain Assumes Command

*"There are no great men, only great challenges that ordinary men are forced by circumstance to meet."*

**William F. "Bull" Halsey**

On November 7, 1941, Commander Leslie E. Gehres received orders for his new assignment as commanding officer, Patrol Wing Four (PAW-4) based in Seattle, Washington. He left Hawaii one month before Japan attacked Pearl Harbor. The devastating attack left twenty-three hundred dead and many wounded. The strike damaged eighteen U.S. Navy vessels, including nine battleships and several other smaller craft. Also, there was considerable destruction of naval and civilian support facilities ashore. No aircraft carriers were involved as they were at sea. The United States declared war on Japan one day later.

In Seattle, Commander Gehres and his wife, Rhoda, settled into their new home at 4450 West Laurel Drive, Seattle. Shortly thereafter, Gehres reported to the headquarters of Patrol Wing Four at Sand Point, located in suburban Seattle, to assume his duties.[56]

A. A. Hoehling, former editor of the Congressional Research Service of the Library of Congress and author of *The* Franklin *Comes Home*, described Commander Gehres at the time as a six-foot-four, barrel-chested veteran of the First World War: "He was tough and 'reg' in the salty, crusty tradition of John Paul Jones, Perry and all of the Navy's hell-for-canvas no-nonsense immortals."

Hoehling said Gehres became a legend for his effectiveness as a pilot and fighting man, leaving a legacy of outstanding leadership and innovation. [57]

Patrol Wing Four consisted of four Catalina PBY squadrons. Its territory of responsibility included the west coast of the contiguous United States and the Aleutian Islands off the southern coast of Alaska. Its primary duties were reconnaissance and rescue missions. Occasionally, the PBYs hauled freight and ammunition and provided passenger services. While the PBYs could be equipped with considerable weaponry, it was not until later that they were refitted to perform long-range bombing missions. They were not considered front-line fighting aircraft.[58]

After the Pearl Harbor attack, PAW-4 made occasional sightings of submerged Japanese submarines. Upon detection , the submarines hastily retreated westward to safer waters.

The submarine threat was very real. As one writer states, "Over a seven-day period, from December 18 to 24, 1941, nine Japanese submarines positioned at strategic points along the U.S. west coast attacked eight American merchant ships, of which two were sunk and two damaged. Six seamen were killed. It was the only time during the war that more than one Japanese submarine appeared at the same time off the American coast."[59]

The four squadrons of Patrol Wing Four included Squadrons VP-41 and VP-42, which were stationed at Sand Point, and squadrons VP-43 and VP-44, which were based in San Diego. In July 1941, these squadrons stepped up the number of aircraft in its rotation program in the Aleutians. They also provided more reconnaissance flights over the western coastline of the United States. They operated particularly over high-risk sites such as the San Diego and San Francisco areas in California and the Bremerton, Washington, shipbuilding facilities.[60]

*Naval Air Station, Dutch Harbor*

Shortly before the attack on Pearl Harbor, the Joint Chiefs of Staff had recognized that an aggressive posture would be needed in the Aleutians. They saw these islands as potential bases from which to launch air attacks on the Kurile Islands near the northern Japanese mainland.[61]

Washington approved a dual-command organization led by Lt. General Simon B. Buckner, U.S. Army forces, and Rear Admiral Robert O. Theobald, recently promoted from captain. Major General William O. Butler, commanded the Army's 11th Air Force, and Commander Leslie E. Gehres would eventually lead the Navy's air group, Patrol Wing Four. Brilliant, but somewhat erratic, Theobald was saddled with a complicated command arrangement. General Buckner, who had seen his command stripped from him and placed under the U.S. Navy, and Theobald clashed repeatedly.[62] The naval patrol area had been extended to cover Alaska after Navy officials concluded that long-range navigation over bodies of water was their domain and not that of the Army.[63]

Based on the information received from Admiral Nimitz, Vice Admiral John H. Towers, ComAirPac, ordered Headquarters Patrol Wing Four to be moved immediately from Sand Point, Washington, to Dutch Harbor in the Aleutians. The move was ordered in anticipation of a possible attack and invasion of Dutch Harbor and other U.S. installations in the Aleutians. Increased weapons and additional bomb racks were hastily installed on all available PBYs. Additional PBY aircraft and two PV-1 Ventura bomber squadrons were assigned to Gehres' Patrol Wing Four (later Fleet Air Wing Four) for the Aleutian islands.

On May 25, 1942, newly-promoted Captain Leslie E. Gehres, Commander Patrol Wing Four, left Sand Point, Washington, with three staff members and four additional PBYs for Dutch Harbor in the Aleutian Islands. This was a permanent transfer of Patrol Wing Four headquarters to Alaska.

Gehres flew as copilot in a PBY-5 piloted by Lt. Commander James Russell, commander of Squadron VI-42. Gehres and Russell were good friends, having flown from the decks of aircraft carriers together during the late 1920s and 1930s. However, their personalities were quite different.

Russell exhibited a rather laid-back, quiet style of leadership while Gehres had a no-nonsense, hard-line manner. Russell was an excellent pilot and squadron commander. He was known for looking after his aircraft and crew members.

Russell was scheduled for promotion to commander. Upon completion of his promotion, Russell would be relieved as the commander of Squadron VI-42. Officers above the rank of lieutenant commander were not allowed to perform as squadron commanders. Later, on March 19, 1945, Captain Russell and Captain

*Aleutians command team*

Gehres would meet again under entirely different circumstances aboard the aircraft carrier, USS *Franklin* CV-13.

Recognizing that the Aleutian Islands assignment would be his first active and integrated combat command, Gehres knew that he would have to be cooperative and proceed carefully. Perhaps Gehres' most important concern was establishing a positive relationship with Rear Admiral Theobald, an old-school surface-ships sailor with little experience in naval aviation or intelligence. Gehres and several of the Aleutian military commanders would come to realize that some of Theobald's decisions lacked validity and were unproven by sound judgment.

Gehres' solution was to approach existing conditions in as aggressive and positive a manner as possible. By doing so, he was able to work effectively with Generals Butler and Buckner.

Gehres anticipated several major challenges. The first was the horrible weather prevailing in the Aleutian Islands and the difficulty of keeping aircraft flyable and in battle-ready condition in such an environment. He knew the weather forecasting and reporting system needed substantial improvement.

Another problem that faced Gehres and the other commanders in the theater was the threat of a Japanese attack and invasion of the Aleutian Islands. Captain

Gehres knew it was paramount that his personnel possess the necessary training for combat.

Captain Gehres arrived at Dutch Harbor in the late afternoon of May 25, 1942. He immediately went about setting up his headquarters in an abandoned wooden storage building adjacent to the local airport runway. Within hours, Gehres had established full communications with telephone, wireless, and teletype facilities fully functioning.

To better understand the genesis of the Aleutian campaign and Gehres' role in that struggle, it is necessary to examine the Battle of the Coral Sea and the Battle of Midway.

## The Coral Sea Connection

After Pearl Harbor, the Japanese moved its fleet to the western Pacific to reorganize and plan the next move. The bulk of the U.S. Pacific Fleet remained in Pearl Harbor completing repairs from the December 7th attack. Crews worked around the clock, as the U.S. Navy needed a combat-ready fleet to counter the anticipated return of the Japanese to the eastern Pacific.

The Japanese had a well thought-out plan designed by Admiral Isoruko Yamamoto. The initial goal of the Japanese was to capture Port Moresby in New Guinea and the surrounding islands, and thus control the Coral Sea and threaten Australia. Success would provide Japan with a protected route to move eastward and northward towards Midway and the Aleutian Islands. Also, it would provide bases for the invasion of the Hawaiian Islands and the west coast of the United States. The Japanese felt that controlling the Coral Sea area would deprive the United States of its remaining sea route to eastern Australia. The Japanese already had control of the sea routes to Western Australia.[64]

From CINCPAC (Commander in Chief, Pacific) headquarters in the Hawaiian Islands, Admiral Chester Nimitz ordered all available combat-ready ships that he could muster from the existing U.S. Pacific Fleet to proceed to the Coral Sea area to face the oncoming Japanese Navy.[65]

The U.S. Navy fleet was organized around three task groups in Task Force 17, commanded by Rear Admiral Frank Jack Fletcher. The task force consisted of two carriers (USS *Lexington* and *Saratoga,*), eight cruisers, twelve destroyers, an oiler, and a seaplane tender. However, no battleships were assigned to any of the task groups as most of them were either sunk or being repaired following the Pearl Harbor disaster.[66]

While the Coral Sea operation was designed by Vice Admiral Isoruku Yamamoto, Chief of the Combined Japanese fleet, the naval force was commanded by Vice Admiral Inouye Shigeyoshi, a battle-proven leader and the commander of the Japanese Fourth Fleet.

The Japanese fleet consisted of the new super-carriers, *Shokaku* and *Zuikaku*, which had joined in the attack on Pearl Harbor; an escort carrier, eleven cruisers, fifteen destroyers, plus additional support craft.[67]

The U.S. task forces rendezvoused in the general area south of Port Moresby in the Coral Sea on May 1 and 2. Contact was made between the two forces on May 3. However, in a hint of things to come, the contact was made not by conventional visual sighting from ship to ship, but instead by American and Japanese carrier aircraft on reconnaissance patrols. Thus, the Battle of the Coral Sea began. It would last for six days, from May 3 through May 8.

All engagements were fought in the air. The fighting was intense, with around-the-clock attacks by both American and Japanese aircraft. The United States lost the aircraft carrier *Lexington*, the destroyer *Sims*, and the tanker *Neosho*. In all, forty-six aircraft were lost. *Lexington* was the first American aircraft carrier lost in World War II. The Americans also lost almost six hundred men, according to official U.S. Navy records.

The Japanese lost the escort aircraft carrier *Shoho*, one destroyer and a hundred and forty-four aircraft. More than a thousand Japanese crew members were killed.[68]

The Coral Sea Battle was considered a strategic victory for the United States because it stopped Japanese plans to threaten Australia.

The *Yorktown* was severely damaged and had to leave the battle zone early to return to Pearl Harbor for emergency repairs. With the severe shortage of American aircraft carriers, it was essential that the *Yorktown* be repaired and returned to combat-ready condition as soon as possible. During the battle, the Japanese aircraft carriers *Shokaku* and *Zuikaku* were extensively damaged and would be out of service for over a year. While the Japanese had a considerably larger aircraft carrier fleet than that of the United States, the temporary loss of its two super-carriers would place the combined fleet at a serious disadvantage.

The loss of the *Lexington* was felt deeply by Gehres. He had served as a pilot and executive officer on the carrier from 1932 to 1934. Gehres had led many flights from the *Lexington*, including exhibitions of the Navy's aerobatic team, the Nine High Hats. During Gehres' tour of duty on the *Lexington*, Vice Admiral John H. Towers had been captain of the carrier.

The Coral Sea conflict was the first successful modern sea battle of the U.S. Navy. It was also the first ship-to-ship encounter in which opposing ships were not in actual visual contact. The introduction of the aircraft carrier as a superior fighting force presented an emerging political problem in the U.S. Navy. Many hardline battleship officers would not recognize the advantages of the aircraft carrier as a superior fighting weapon. They did not feel aircraft carriers would ever replace the battleship as the main component of power projection. The "battleship mentality" resulted in a lack of clear and specific roles and responsibilities for battleship and carrier commanders. It also cost the navy time and energy that could have been better used in the war.[69]

But as carrier power became more evident, the United States was to build twenty-four large *Essex-c*lass aircraft carriers, with twelve in service prior to the end of World War II. In addition, the United States would build one *Sable*-class, nine *Independence*-class and fifty-one *Casablanca*-class aircraft carriers, all of which would see service before the war's end. Together, these vessels would compose a large and formidable fleet of modern aircraft carriers. Nine shipyards located on both coasts of the United States, employing about fifty thousand men and women working twenty-four-hour shifts, were involved in this massive effort.[70]

The traditional role of the large battleship as the leading naval weapons carrier was over.

## Saving Midway

**General Jimmy Doolittle**

Five months after the Pearl Harbor disaster of December 7, 1941, Jimmy Doolittle led an air raid on Tokyo. His small fleet of sixteen Army B-25 bombers were launched from the aircraft carrier USS *Hornet* on the rainy morning of April 18, 1942. While the damage was minimal, the attack did much to uplift American morale. It also indicated that the Japanese mainland could be penetrated.

The Japanese reaction was a simultaneous invasion of Midway and the Aleutian Islands. This venture was also designed by Vice Admiral Yamamoto, a shrewd, old-line tactical officer who understood the power of the fleet's air arm. He felt that the attacks would lure the remaining capital ships of the U.S. Navy to sea for a battle of annihilation. Yamamoto's objective was the U.S. Naval Refueling Station and Airbase located in the Midway Islands archipelago, about 1,136 miles west of the Hawaiian Islands.[71]

The U.S. naval command had broken the Japanese code and regularly intercepted their messages. From these messages, U.S. naval leaders learned of the Japanese intent.[72]

Nimitz gathered as large a fleet as possible to confront the Japanese. The United States fleet consisted of two task forces. Task Force 16 was commanded by Rear Admiral Raymond Spruance and consisted of the aircraft carriers USS *Enterprise* and USS *Hornet*, six cruisers, and nine destroyers. Task Force 17 was commanded by Rear Admiral Frank Jack Fletcher and was made up of one aircraft carrier, the USS *Yorktown*, two cruisers, and six destroyers. There were twelve support ships assigned to the American fleet. Admiral Fletcher was in overall command of the American fleet.

Nimitz's orders were to seek out the Japanese fleet and force its withdrawal. His overall plan to force the battle by ambushing the Japanese and counterattacking as soon as possible proved to be successful.

The Japanese outgunned and outnumbered the American force. It was made up of eight aircraft carriers, eleven battleships, eighteen cruisers and sixty-five destroyers. In addition, there were twenty-six support craft. The overall command of this huge fleet was the responsibility of Vice Admiral Yamamoto, while the important task of commanding the eight aircraft carriers was assigned to Vice Admiral Chuichi Nagumo.

The confrontation occurred in the early morning of June 3, 1942 and lasted until June 8. As during the Battle of the Coral Sea, most of the fighting took place in the air. Both the Japanese and U.S. fleets made serious mistakes. Nagumo's decision to change his planes' bomb loads at a key moment offset the ineffectiveness of most of the American air attacks. But the American errors were not enough to offset Yamamoto's and Nagumo's strategic and tactical blunders. Despite a much smaller fleet, the United States forces were able to outfight and defeat the Japanese fleet.

The victory equalized the Japanese and United States naval forces. It allowed the United States to move from a defensive posture to a more aggressive role in the Pacific. In the Battle of Midway, the Japanese lost the aircraft carriers *Akagi*, *Kaga*, *Hiryu*, *Soryu* and one cruiser. Midway casualties were heavy. The Japanese lost over a hundred and forty-five aircraft; 2,512 sailors and airmen were killed and twelve hundred were wounded. The United States lost the *Yorktown* and the destroyer *Hammann*, along with two hundred and ninety-two aircraft. More than three hundred and forty Americans were killed and over seven hundred were wounded. The two hundred and ninety-two aircraft lost included not only aircraft carrier losses, but also Midway Island-based aircraft of the Navy, Army Air Force and Marine Corps.

***Rear Admiral Theobald***

One example of the intensity of the battle was the fate of Torpedo Squadron 8, based on the aircraft carrier *Hornet*. Of the fifteen pilots assigned to the flight only one, Ensign George Gay, survived. [73]

But the U.S. fleet suffered a major setback in the loss of the *Yorktown*. The carrier had been damaged in the Battle of Coral Sea, but was repaired in record time at Pearl Harbor, enabling it to fight again at Midway. The *Yorktown* was heavily bombed by aircraft from the Japanese carrier *Hiryu* and severely damaged.

The U.S. Navy later reported that while the *Yorktown's* crew was struggling to save their ship, a Japanese submarine, 1-168, was able to penetrate the protective circle around the *Yorktown* and release two deadly torpedoes below its waterline on June 6. The *Yorktown* reportedly sank with several crew members still aboard. But doubts still remain about the sinking of the *Yorktown*. Captain Gehres felt that if the captain of the *Yorktown* had remained on his ship, it might have survived. He made a pledge to himself that if he were ever in command of a U.S. Navy vessel damaged under similar circumstances, he would never abandon his ship and crew if there was a chance to sail it to a safe harbor.[74]

Gehres had once served as chief of staff of the carrier division to which the *Yorktown* was attached and had flown from its flight deck many times as a commander and pilot. The *Yorktown* was the second carrier lost in the series of Pacific sea battles, joining the *Lexington*, a casualty of the Battle of the Coral Sea.[75]

## *The Dutch Harbor Raid*

On June 2, 1942, Rear Admiral Theobald received a message from Admiral Nimitz indicating that a Japanese fleet under Rear Admiral Kakuji Kakuta was headed north for the Aleutian Islands and was expected to attack the Dutch Harbor area. This attack was the second wing of Admiral Isoruku Yamamoto's two-pronged plan for invading the Midway and Aleutian Islands.[76]

*View of Fort Mears from the Hog Island at some point during the attack on June 3rd. Below, first hit on the Navy dock; note settling water column in center of photo. Note also the huge fireball behind the spray column as the oil tanks at Rocky Point Tank Farm are hit.*

Admiral Kakuta had also been in charge of the air attacks on Pearl Harbor. One of his combat pilots, Lt. Janji Abe was the lead pilot in the Pearl Harbor attack and carried out the same role in the attacks on Dutch Harbor.

The initial attack on the Midway Islands occurred on June 3. Early that same morning, a prowling PBY from Dutch Harbor had located the Second Fleet Striking Force approaching the Aleutian Islands from the south. Despite heavy rain and fog, Gehres ordered all available aircraft to attack the approaching Japanese fleet. However, no American aircraft were able to locate the Japanese fleet. The Japanese were cloaked by the weather and constantly shifted their position, making contact impossible.

Weather also hampered the Japanese attacks. Early on June 4, illuminated by the Northern Lights, Admiral Kakuta's fleet reached a position about a hundred and sixty miles south of Dutch Harbor. At 3 a.m., the Japanese launched nineteen planes from the aircraft carrier *Junyo* for an attack on Dutch Harbor. Heavy rain, fog, and navigation errors forced the planes to return the *Junyo*.

At about 5 a.m., with the weather clearing, seventeen bombers and fighters took off from the aircraft carrier *Ryujo* and were able to reach Dutch Harbor. They bombed Fort Mears, the Army and Navy installations, several older fuel tanks, and an Army barracks. Admiral Kakuta was not satisfied with the results of the

*The **Northwestern** is hit and set ablaze.*

*Memo from Gehres to the Northwestern Sea Frontier command accompanying photographs of the Dutch Harbor attack.*

attack, so at about 9 a.m., he ordered another attack from the *Ryujo*. Inclement weather forced the planes back to the carrier.[77]

The bulk of Admiral Theobald's fleet was about five hundred miles away, leaving no U.S. Navy surface vessels to oppose the raid. Theobald had ignored naval intelligence and the advice of Gen. Buckner, and instead had assumed that the Japanese would attack near Kodiak. After missing the raid, he changed course from a south-southeast course to an eastern heading to rendezvous with several

**The Akutan Zero**

navy vessels, including two aircraft carriers, that Nimitz was sending north to enhance Theobald's small fleet.

However, because of new intelligence, Nimitz recalled this support group and commanded Theobald back to base.[78]

In the late afternoon of June 4, Admiral Kakuta refueled his fleet and headed west toward the island of Adak. Soon after he had started this journey, Kakuta's meteorologist informed him that the weather in the west was worse than in the east. Hearing this report, Kakuta headed back toward Dutch Harbor to recommence his attack. Returning to the Dutch Harbor area, he found the weather was good and his return unexpected. Immediately, *Junyo* and *Ryujo* launched twenty-nine bombers and fighters. These aircraft bombed and strafed the Dutch Harbor area, destroying or damaging a large aircraft hangar, a Dutch Harbor hospital wing, four new large fuel tanks, four PBYs moored in Dutch Harbor and the beached barracks ship *Northwestern*.[79]

## *Zero DI-108 Goes Down*

In the early morning of June 4, 1942, Captain Gehres sent Ensign Albert E. Mitchell, of Squadron VP-12, Fleet Air Wing Four, to deliver dispatches.

Two hours out, Mitchell's plane ran into a severe attack by six Zeros from the Japanese carrier *Ryujo*. One of Mitchell's gunners may have scored a hit on one of the Zeros. But Mitchell's plane was damaged so severely it soon crashed into the waters off Unalga Island. American soldiers stationed on a nearby island

*US Navy Lieutenant William Thies, left of Gehres, was the pilot of a Consolidated PBY-5A Catalina of patrol squadron VP-41, Fleet Air Wing 4 that discovered the Akutan Zero.*

watched in horror as the Japanese machine-gunned Mitchell and his crew as they attempted to escape their plane. There were no survivors. But, hours later, the PBY men were avenged.[80]

On June 10, a PBY piloted by Lt. William Thies on a routine reconnaissance mission located a downed Zero on Akutan Island. Gehres dispatched a salvage crew headed by Thies in an effort to examine and identify the fallen Zero. Thies reported the plane could be recovered and it was in repairable condition.[81]

By cooperating with the Seabee detachment on Dutch Island, Gehres was able to obtain the use of the needed heavy equipment and Seabee operators to recover the downed Zero. One of the Seabees assisting in this operation was EM 1/C

71

Eugene Morgan, USNR, who happened to be a friend and former classmate of Captain Gehres. Both had attended school and played baseball together in their hometown of Newark, New York.

Later, while on leave from the Aleutians, Morgan reported to his hometown that Gehres was already a legend in this northern outpost and praised his leadership by saying, "He is chasing the Japs out of the Aleutians."[82]

The wrecked Zero D1-108 was returned to the San Diego Naval Air Station in late July 1942, where it was repaired. The Zero underwent many simulated flights in an effort to determine its fighting and flying characteristics. The possession and testing of the Akutan Zero was a major intelligence accomplishment. Jim Rearden, author of the definitive account of the Akutan Zero, called the find a major prize for Allied technical intelligence.[83]

## The Battles Move West

In compliance with Admiral Yamamoto's recent orders, Admiral Kakuta began the movement of his fleet from the Dutch Harbor area to rendezvous with the remnants of the large Japanese fleet forming south of the western Aleutian island chain. The taking of Attu and Kiska by the Japanese immediately followed the attack on Dutch Harbor. On the nights of June 6 and 7, twelve hundred Japanese soldiers landed on Attu. There was no resistance, and forty-one islanders, mostly all Aleuts, were taken prisoner. The island of Kiska was occupied by a Japanese force of three hundred and fifty soldiers from a special landing force. On Kiska, a small U.S. Army staff assigned to the local weather station were taken prisoner. Again there was no resistance. The Japanese would substantially increase the number of occupying soldiers in the next few days. At their maximum buildup, the Japanese had about nine thousand tough, battle-tried and well-trained soldiers and fleet support.

Unfortunately, Theobald had positioned the fleet east and well south of the Aleutian Islands. Gehres' Fleet Air Wing Four and the U.S. Army's 11th Air Force tried to disrupt the nighttime Japanese troop landings, with only minimal results.

On June 11, CINCPAC sent a message to the Aleutians commanders. They were ordered to begin bombing the Japanese installations. The Army was expected to shoulder the load, but Gehres insisted on a role for his fleet air wing. Gehres showed his aggressiveness by developing a bombing rotation that, along with Army Air Force operations, kept up a constant harassment of the Japanese until they could be dislodged from the island.[84]

Gehres decided to use the PBYs and Venturas at his command as offensive weapons, a role for which they were not originally intended. His wing was a reconnaissance and patrol operation, and his use of the men and materiel in an offensive capacity has led to criticism. Some claim that he needlessly wasted men's lives by asking them to exceed the limits of their training and their equipment.[85]

However, that must be viewed against the intent and meaning of Admiral Nimitz's directive to Theobald to fight a war of attrition to reduce the Japanese fleet. One must also consider the political reality of the American forces leaving Japanese invaders lodged on American territory. Until the United States could develop an effective ground attack to evict the Japanese, bombing was the only answer.

But before the Americans moved against Kiska and Attu in force, CINCPAC had one more order for the commanders. After months of watching Admiral Theobald ignore advice from superiors and clash with his army counterparts, with disastrous results, the Navy had had enough. Nimitz replaced Theobald on January 3, 1943, with Vice Admiral Thomas Kinkaid.[86]

On March 18, 1943, Admiral Nimitz gave the go-ahead for the invasion of Attu and Kiska. The United States had assembled a large armada of almost a hundred navy vessels, and set sail on May 9. Aboard were 21,000 American and 5,300 Canadian troops.

The armada bypassed Kiska, and headed for the more important target of Attu. On May 11, the first wave of two thousand soldiers went ashore on the south side of the island. The Japanese garrison was concentrated on the eastern end of the island and soon made their presence known. Eventually, the Americans and Canadians would deploy about 21,000 more troops against the Japanese. Gehres' Fleet Air Wing Four and the Army's 11th Air Force provided air cover and softening up duties. The battle raged until May 29.

The battle ended with several thousand Japanese soldiers mowed down by the massive American and Canadian firepower. Of those who survived the battle, many chose suicide by pulling the pins from their grenades and killing themselves rather than being disgraced by capture. The U.S. casualties were six hundred killed and twice as many wounded.[87]

On the morning of August 16, 1943, American transports landed several thousand American and Canadian troops four miles south of the Kiska volcano. Patrols fanned out. Occasionally, the patrolling soldiers could hear gunfire, but encountered no Japanese soldiers. Unfortunately, the soldiers fired at one another by mistake. In one encounter, four Canadians soldiers and twenty American

*Navy crewmen thaw out a PBY.*

soldiers were killed. Overall, there were a hundred and twenty-one Allied soldiers wounded.

All the Japanese troops had been evacuated several days earlier on a dark night during a low heavy fog. The only living creatures on the windswept island were a few dogs.[88] An unknown American soldier wrote the following verse:

### Tales of Kiska

*You've heard the bloody tales of old,*
*of fearless knights and warriors bold,*
*But lo the muse pens tales of Kiska....*
*One hundred thousand men at muster,*
*Admirals, generals adding lustre;*
*Two hundred planes, as many ships,*
*All were bound for Kiska's Nips.*
*And now we come to know how and when*
*'Dog-day' got its name....*
*We searched volcanic craters vast*
*To catch a glimpse of one Jap at last.*
*It took three days before we learnt*
*That more than dogs there simply weren't...*

74

The islands now provided a sustainable base for American aircraft in the western Aleutians. The distance from Alexai Point, Attu, to northern Japan was about 1,500 miles round trip. The 11th Air Force bombers and the U.S. Navy's PBY and Ventura planes were capable of covering that distance. However, the PBY's extra range made it the preferred plane for such missions.[89]

## Weather, the Enemy

The weather conditions in the Aleutians were horrible. Fog, heavy rain, snow and ice, high winds, a wet mucky land base and extremely low temperatures played havoc with the daily operations of Fleet Air Wing Four. Keeping the aircraft in flying condition and able to complete their required missions was very difficult. Losses due to poor weather conditions exceeded those from enemy combat.

Providing timely and adequate maintenance in the inclement weather was difficult. Aircraft maintenance crews had to remove the oil from the plane's engines if they were parked outside for any length of time because of the possibility of the oil freezing or coagulating. To accomplish this difficult task in harsh weather, the crew drained the engine's still-warm oil into a large container and took the container into their barracks or tent, placing it beside the coal-burning stove in order to keep the oil liquid and ready for immediate use.

If the oil had been left in the plane's engine during freezing or inclement weather, a lengthy, cumbersome job of reheating the engine oil with primitive equipment would be needed. Sometimes the plane would have to wait for warmer weather for the oil to liquefy, a time-consuming process that took needed planes off the flight line.[90]

*Lt. Commander R.H. Maynard*

Captain Gehres was fortunate in having a well-established weather organization in operation when he took command. His friend, Lt. Commander R.H. Maynard, was in charge of the weather detachment at Kodiak, located at the eastern end of the Aleutian Island chain. At the time of Gehres' arrival, the weather retrieval and forecasting operations were adding several weather substations throughout the Aleutians. The work provided vital weather forecasting for the Army, Navy and their air forces.[91]

In 1945, an official U.S. publication, "Aerology and Naval Warfare: Fleet Air Wing Strikes" was published

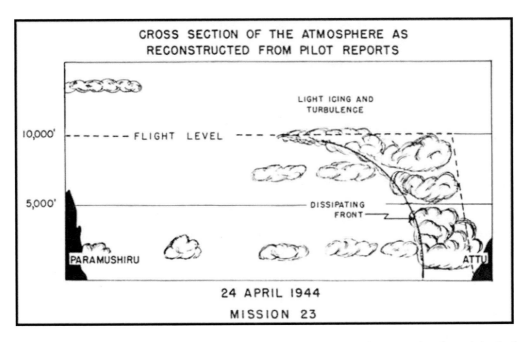

by the office of the Chief of Naval Operations. In its foreword, Vice Admiral Aubrey W. Fitch, deputy chief of naval operations (air), wrote "The primary objective of these analyses is to assist those officers who are charged with the responsibility for the planning and execution of similar operations."

Gehres wrote in its preface: "The whole thing was a joint operation and its success was the result first, of a determination not to accept the weather as

impossible, but to circumvent it and second, by all hands working all-out together to find the solution and make it work. Our Navy-trained pilots and aircrews, assisted and guided by courageous and devoted weather scientists, backed by an efficient ground organization, can and will tackle anything and surmount any difficulties to accomplish their assigned missions."[92]

Most of the existing substations scattered in the outer islands continued to operate well after the hostilities had died down. In later years, these stations have been improved and still provide weather forecasting services for the American and Canadian military services as well as commercial and private aviation services in the Aleutians.[103]

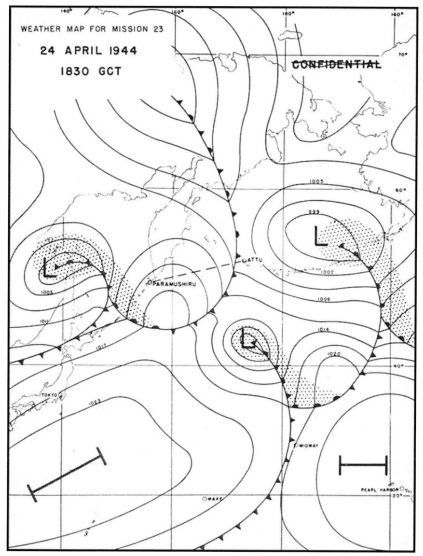

Accurate weather forecasting in the rapidly changing conditions of the Aleutians was critical, particularly during the long-range strikes from Attu to Paramushiro. Below is a portion of "Aerology and Naval Warfare: Fleet Air Wing Four Strikes," a 1945 report, along with two charts (above and next page), prepared by Gehres.

The necessity for accurate timing of the rates of movement and dissipation of frontal systems along the route and the benefits gained when this was accomplished can be illustrated by means of Mission 23.

Analysis of early synoptic weather maps showed that an occluded front had passed over the western portion of the Aleutian chain and that another center had developed well south of the west end of the chain. Regular Wing search planes were, however, unable to locate the center on the morning of 22 April. By the morning of 23 April, a weak cold front was known to be oriented northeast-southwest across the route but, except for this, conditions along the mission route were thought to be favorable. In the early afternoon, a special weather plane sent out to inspect the front was unable to pierce it or top it at 12,000 feet. Despite this, it was expected that a late take-off (i.e., after midnight) would allow sufficient dissipation of the front so that it could be topped with little icing and turbulence at mission flight level.

Accordingly, the Wing Commander ordered take-off for the night of 23 April but with the provision that no take-offs be earlier than local midnight. The point of added delay in allowing dissipation of the front was aptly proved. A strike group from a separate command took off the same night at about 2000 local time but was unable to pierce or top the front which they encountered 300 miles out. The front extended beyond the 13,000 foot level. Fleet Air Wing FOUR planes took off about five hours later as the other strike planes were returning. By the time that Fleet Air Wing FOUR planes intercepted the front they were able to pierce its thin top at 10,000 feet (regular flight level) encountering only light icing and turbulence. See map, page 16, and cross section below.

The four planes taking part in this strike all returned safely to base reporting with good pictures obtained in the target area. Bombing, too, had been satisfactory.

The success of the Alaskan weather service provided by the U.S. Navy remains a legacy of Gehres. It speaks to his ability not only to work with other branches of the American armed services but also to his foresight in understanding the importance of accurate weather information.

The U.S. Army Air Corps contingents based in the Aleutians were particularly appreciative of Gehres' work. A lieutenant in the Army Air Corps, Jacob W. Dixon, once wrote Gehres to thank him for his support. He enclosed a poem that read:

> *I don't have much use for the Navy,*
> *being an Army man,*
> *But I must take off my hat to some pilots*
> *of this sea-faring clan.*
> *These boys didn't give a damn for the weather,*
> *and Jap lead meant even less*
> *I've seen 'em fly thru storms aplenty,*

*their planes a riddled mess.*
*I'll always remember the way they informed us,*
*of the Jap's position at sea.*
*And how they told us almost to the minute,*
*the time the attack would be.*
*Then when we went on the offensive,*
*and flew with no land in sight,*
*We knew that in the clouds above us,*
*a rescue plane watched the flight.*
*They even patrolled where we were fighting,*
*to save us if we fell.*
*They hid in the clouds from the "Zeroes,"*
*and the ack-ack could go to hell.*
*So here's to those boys of the Navy,*
*a bunch of damn, good guys.*
*And especially to those great pilots,*
*who fly the PBYs.*[93]

## Increased PBY and Ventura Strikes and Payloads

Captain Gehres was now the commander of a considerably enlarged Fleet Air Wing Four, with increased responsibilities.

He felt that this position was the equal of his counterpart, Brigadier General William O. Butler, who commanded the U.S. Army's 11th Air Force, also operating in the Aleutian theater. Captain Gehres was promoted to commodore in July 1943, marking the first assignment of that rank to a U.S. Navy air officer.[94]

In the Aleutians, the PBY and Ventura fleets served Gehres well in performing routine reconnaissance, air search and rescue missions. They were also responsible for making frequent local and long-distance bombing raids on the Japanese-occupied islands in the Aleutian chain. Later, they also bombed northern Japan. [95]

With the expansion of World War II activities in the Pacific Theater, Commodore Gehres' Fleet Air Wing Four bombers were required to increase the number and severity of their bombing missions of the Japanese mainland. The flights to the Kurile Islands were long and dangerous. The Japanese defenses were well established, with up-to-date weaponry and combat interceptor aircraft. The losses on these missions by the Americans were high. The 1,500-mile round trip,

*A Ventura*

often in inclement weather, lasted sixteen or more hours. To provide for the increased bomber capability, Gehres devised improved technology to enable the planes to carry additional bomb loads and more fuel. Along with use of improved weather forecasting, and more accurate navigation instruments such as radio direction finders and radar, the operational range and capabilities of the aircraft were increased. Other improvements were in the areas of heavier armament and greater bomb-carrying capacity.[96]

By the end of 1943, the Japanese threat in the Aleutians was over and the number of military personnel in the islands had been reduced. The principle organizations remaining in the Aleutians were Fleet Air Wing Four and 11th Air Force. Gehres had moved most of his headquarters personnel and operations to the far western islands of Attu, Kiska, and Adak. Seabee and Army construction crews were busy on these islands constructing and repairing aircraft runways and building fuel storage tanks. Gehres also built new weather stations, communication facilities and introduced radar equipment to allow safer flights utilizing these airfields.[97]

The purpose of this movement and buildup was to provide a better location for making bomber runs targeting Japanese bases, army staging centers, and enemy airfields located in the Kurile and Paramushiro Islands. While no exact records

80

exist, it is believed that Fleet Air Wing Four made over three hundred bombing sorties during Gehres' tenure as the commanding officer.

At this time, the 11th Air Force had its number of aircraft reduced because all available U.S. Army aircraft were needed in other strategic locations throughout the Pacific Theater. This left Gehres with the primary responsibility of continuing and increasing the bombing missions. The Japanese made sporadic attacks on the outer Aleutian Islands in the early fall of 1943 causing only minimal damage. They made their final raid on October 13, 1943. The PBYs and Venturas of Fleet Air Wing Four under Commodore Gehres established a regular bombing schedule in the northern Kurile and Paramushir Islands. The Japanese naval forces in home waters were eventually forced to retreat to safer harbors farther south along the coast of Japan. [98]

On Tuesday, February 15, 1944 Gehres had an interview with Mel Meadows, a reporter for the Seattle-based *Post-Intelligencer* newspaper.

Gehres insisted that full credit go to the pilots and their crews. Commodore Gehres told of "terrific beating" taken by these airmen on the fifteen-thousand-mile round trips, among the longest over-water missions being conducted in the war.

After sitting, waiting sometimes for hours or days for a 50-knot or more wind to clear the field, the pilots take off bucking strong turbulence, icing and below zero weather on a thirteen-and-a-half-hour mission," he said. "Sometimes, over Paramushiro, they run into heavy flak, and occasionally night fighters come up. The first plane may draw twenty bursts from the ground gunners, while the second plane may be bounced around with about two hundred bursts. It's a mighty tough fight.[99]

But there were still battles to be fought to subdue a strong and active Japanese military establishment. The United States was no longer on the defense, but was the aggressor. Nimitz's orders continued to be simple and clear in indicating to his naval units that they were to seek out, attack and destroy the enemy.

## Bomber 31's Last Journey

In the early morning of March 25, 1944, Lt. Walter S. Whitman and his six crewmen embarked on a bombing run. Bomber 31, PV-1 Ventura, was overloaded with a full crew, more than three thousand pounds of munitions, and topped-off fuel tanks. It departed from an icy, fogbound runway in bitterly cold weather on

Attu to begin a fifteen-hundred-mile journey on a bombing mission to the Kurile Islands in northern Japan.

Prior to the departure of bomber aircraft on such long and dangerous missions, Commodore Gehres assessed weather conditions and flight preparations. He was usually in the flight operations office providing final approval for the flight, checking the proposed route, weather reports and approving final mission instructions. As the crew members walked to their planes, Gehres shook each man's hand and wished him a safe journey.

Gehres' farewell remarks were often blunt and honest. He was known to have told waiting crews that possibly their flight just might not make it, and that they needed to be prepared for the worst. Such remarks were not always well-received. However, the crews undoubtedly understood the impression Gehres was trying to make.

Bomber 31 was part of a five-plane group that would embark on this mission. However, of the five Venturas that departed, one crashed on takeoff, two returned to Attu because of severe weather conditions, and one completed the mission. The fifth plane, Bomber 31, flown by Lieutenant Whitman, seemed to have vanished.

Radio contact was lost shortly after takeoff. After the plane failed to return, Bomber 31 and its crew were declared missing in action. The fate of this plane and its crew remained a mystery until recently, when some American officials received photos revealing an American bomber's mangled remains scattered about on a remote, snow-covered mountainside on Russia's desolate Kamchatka Peninsula. It was believed by the examining authorities that the wreckage was that of the missing Bomber 31.

However, the evidence was not totally conclusive. The remains of the plane indicated it had been hit by weaponry. The exact source of such an attack was not determined but was believed to be Russian. The examining authorities found a few very small human bones scattered near the wreckage. It was felt that possibly they were the remains of some of the crew members of Bomber 31. From this evidence, investigators decided to use DNA testing to determine the identities of the remains. But the Navy was unable to find relatives of the flyers for the genetic testing.

When private investigator Shirley Ann Casey, from Deerfield Beach, Florida, heard of the problem, she accepted the challenge of trying to solve this mystery that had stumped United States Navy officials. Through extensive research, she located a relative of Whitman. The relative agreed to provide a blood sample. The blood test proved to be a positive match and the mystery was solved. It was concluded that the wreckage was that of the lost Bomber 31. Had it not been for

*Capt. Gehres presenting Distinguished Flying Cross to Lt. Gibbs.*

Casey's determination and dedicated investigative work, Bomber 31 might never have been identified.

However, some facts relating to the lost bomber still remain to be solved. What exactly caused Bomber 31 to crash? Was the bomber shot down by the Russians or possibly the Japanese? Could there have been a mechanical problem, such as an engine failure or a fuel line leak? What happened to the crew members? Were they killed or injured in the crash, or were they killed after the bomber crashed? Did they die from starvation, injury, or illness after the bomber crashed? Regrettably, the story of the lost Bomber 31 is not complete.[100]

## The Price of Battle

Most of the U.S. Army and U.S. Navy personnel who died in the Aleutians are buried in the American Cemetery on Attu. It is in a beautiful setting, next to a small waterfall at the top of a small knoll in a quiet pastoral setting.

There is another smaller American cemetery located on Attu at Holtz Bay. In addition, scattered around the Aleutian Islands are numerous single and small

***Above, a cartoon showing the nerve center of Gehres' Aleutians operation.***

grave sites, most identified, others not. Most of the Japanese soldiers killed were committed unceremoniously to large common graves.

Both the American and Japanese forces lost men to accidents, disease and exhaustion. The largest number of noncombat fatalities resulted from trench foot, caused by the lack of adequate foot gear. The total monetary cost to support the Aleutian campaigns for both the Americans and the Japanese was estimated to be about two billion dollars.[101]

Overall, Gehres' Fleet Air Wing Four lost a total of 66 PBYs and PV-1 Venturas. His total loss of naval personnel consisted of approximately 1,100 combat and non-combat deaths.[102]

Prior to Gehres' departure to accept his new assignment, Vice Admiral Frank J. Fletcher, who had recently been named commander of the U.S. Navy forces in the Aleutians, presented the medal of the Legion of Merit to Gehres on January 19, 1944.

He said: "When the history of this war is written," he said during the presentation, "I am confident that Commodore Leslie E. Gehres will be credited more than any other officer with the defeat of the Japanese in the Aleutians,"[103]
The proclamation read:

THE SECRETARY OF THE NAVY WASHINGTON. The President of the United States takes pleasure in presenting the LEGION OF MERIT to COMMODORE LESLIE E. GEHRES, UNITED STATES NAVY for service as set forth in the following CITATION: "For exceptionally meritorious conduct in the performance of outstanding services to the Government of the United States as Commander of a Patrol Wing and later as Commander of a Fleet Air Wing in action against enemy Japanese forces in the Aleutian Islands. Despite extremely unfavorable weather conditions and limited communication facilities, Commodore Gehres directed the operations of his planes with such excellent tactical skill and sound judgement as to enable them to locate, attack and destroy hostile ships and installations, and to provide our forces with vital weather data and detailed information of enemy activities. The expert professional ability and valiant devotion to duty of Commodore Gehres greatly contributed to the success of his command in frustrating Japanese plans for invasion of the eastern Aleutians." For the President, (signed) Frank Knox, Secretary of the Navy.

Vice Admiral Frank Jack Fletcher's full remarks were as follows:

It has been my privilege and my pleasure to present decorations and awards on a number of occasions. None has given me more satisfaction than in the case of the officer who is awarded this decoration. When the history of this war is written, I am confident that the recipient of this medal will be credited more than any other officer with the defeat of the Japanese in the Aleutians. When a commanding officer is awarded a decoration, it is the reflection and reward for an entire command. No one knows better than you men of Fleet Air Wing FOUR how much cooperation and teamwork mean to the success and conduct of war. An effective combat unit depends upon the complete performance of duty of every man from the lowest rating to the highest rank. The outstanding performance of Fleet Air Wing FOUR proves that every man in the organization has carried on with the complete devotion to duty not only through fog but through ice, wind, and snow, in addition to the perils of combat.

Gehres was criticized for his relentless bombing campaign, which was conducted in arduous conditions at a high cost.

*Vice-Admiral Frank J. Fletcher presents Gehres with the Legion of Merit.*

***Belleau Wood, left, and Franklin after being hit by kamikaze planes during the
Battle of Leyte Gulf.***

But the offensive served its purpose, tying down Japanese men and materiel that
might have been used elsewhere.[104] His behavior in the Aleutians was a precursor
of the style he would bring to his next command.

Although Commodore Gehres was not required to fly dangerous or combat
missions, he would sometimes fly as the lead pilot or observer on reconnaissance
and combat missions. His leadership style was viewed as blunt, tough, and
autocratic but fair. However, under his hard crust, he possessed a genuine
sensitivity that was seldom expressed. Gehres took the loss of aircraft and flight
crews personally, with deep sadness and respect. He could often be seen in the
flight operations office waiting long hours for the planes that never returned.

Commodore Gehres had requested a new assignment, preferably as
commanding officer of an active aircraft carrier. By then, Vice Admiral Towers
had been ordered to Hawaii to assume command for naval air forces in the Pacific.
Gehres soon got the assignment he wanted; he was to replace Captain J.M.
Shoemaker as the commanding officer of the relatively new *Essex*-class aircraft

***Sailors assess damage to the* Franklin *at Bremerton.***

carrier, the USS *Franklin* CV-13 located in the Pacific Theater. Gehres had to accept a reduction in rank from commodore to captain, as no vessel in the U.S. Navy could have a commanding officer with a rank above captain.[105]

The transfer was scheduled to take place in early November 1944. In early October 1944, Gehres was given leave. He returned to his permanent home in Seattle with his wife, Rhoda, while waiting to begin his new assignment. Shortly after the first of November, Gehres left Seattle by navy aircraft for the island of Ulithi, a U.S. protectorate located on the Caroline Islands chain. The Ulithi Lagoon provided a large protected staging area for the U.S. fleet. The *Franklin* had recently arrived in Ulithi for repairs after a kamikaze attack on October 30. The suicide plane hit the flight deck and crashed through to the galley deck, killing fifty-six and wounding sixty.[106]

On November 9, Captain J. M. Shoemaker relinquished his command of the USS *Franklin*. Six days later, Captain Leslie E. Gehres took command. Gehres then sailed the *Franklin* east to the Bremerton Shipyard, Puget Sound, Washington, for repairs.

*Captain Gehres on the bridge of the* **Franklin.**

# VI
# From Pearl Harbor to Battle Zone

The transition from Captain James Shoemaker to Captain Leslie E. Gehres was much more than a change of leadership. Shoemaker's style had been more informal than that of his successor. Gehres was a by-the-book, activist captain, labeled a martinet. One of the most positive depictions of Gehres upon taking command is that provided by A.A. Hoehling.

"He brought with him to the *Franklin* an athletic coach's *esprit de corps* and heartiness combined with an overriding zeal to mold all aboard into at least the stereotype of a sailor. This sparked acutely mixed reactions from the pilots, who never really thought of themselves as part of a ship's company."[107]

Aboard the *Franklin*, the younger crew members had been given to Gehres' care to train and nurture into dedicated and skilled crew members. His final challenge was to return these young men back to their homes in one piece. However, the crew was used to a different sort of discipline. Admiral Ralph Davison, who would again serve on the *Franklin* during her fateful March 1945 cruise, remarked upon the crew's behavior following his first tour on the carrier:

My duty on the *Franklin* has been very pleasant and I am proud of her fine work. And, of the excellent spirit of the ship's company. There is one thing, however, which mars the pleasure of being aboard. A thing which you too, would find unpleasant in your home. I mean the silly and senseless use of profane and obscene language.

Profanity and obscenity are not indications of manliness; they are really the opposite of this, for they are used chiefly by little boys writing on fences, or degenerates scribbling on the walls of latrines. If you want to be considered adolescent or queer, by all means keep on using them; if you want to be respected as a man, cut them out of your conversation."

***Admiral Charles Pownall***

Shoemaker's replacement by Gehres was part of an effort by the naval command to winnow out officers who, for a variety of reasons, were not effective in combat operations. This was an ongoing process, as war brought out qualities which in peacetime may have not been as obvious.

In November 1942, for example, Admiral Frank Jack Fletcher was removed from command in the Pacific after criticism for his handling of the fleet during the Battle of the Eastern Solomons.

Admiral Theobald was sacked in January 1943. A month later, Carrier Division 3 Commander Admiral Charles Pownall was forced ashore for a lack of aggressiveness.[108]

So aggressiveness combined with experience in carrier aviation soon became essential prerequisites for combat leadership in the Pacific. Gehres' attitude and experience made him well-suited for the front.

One of his first acts upon assuming command was to issue the following memo to the crew:

Captain Leslie E. Gehres
THE NEW CAPTAIN
As I know a ship's company is always curious about a new captain, here follows a brief sketch of my naval career to date.
Nov. 1914 – Joined Naval Militia of New York State.
April 1917 – Mobilized and mustered into Navy for World War I.
April 1918 – Commissioned Ensign, U.S.N.R.
Sept. 1918 – Commissioned Ensign, USN(T).
During World War I served on board various battleships engaged in patrolling the north Atlantic convoy routes.
Commissioned Lt. (jg), USN May 1919, Commissioned Lieut., USN June 1922.
From May 1919 to June 1924 served in destroyers, Pacific Fleet, during which period I was Executive of the USS FARENHOLT and commanded the USS TINGEY, USS AULICK, and USS GILLIS.

Juno 1924 to November 1926 – Communication Officer, Navy Yard, Pearl Harbor.

January 1927 to September 1927 – Student Naval Aviator, Pensacola.

October 1927 to December 1929 – Pilot and Flight and Operations Officer in Fighting Squadron ONE. On board Carriers LANGLEY, SARATOGA, and LEXINGTON. Led the "Nine High Hats" stunt team at National Air Races, Cleveland, 1927.

January 1930 to May 1932 – NAS, San Diego.

June 1932 to July 1934 – Executive Officer, Fighting Squadron SIX and Fighting Squadron FIVE. (USS SARATOGA and USS LEXINGTON)

January 1934 – Commissioned Lieutenant Commander, U. S. Navy.

June 1934 to September 1935 – Navy Department – Aviation member of Naval Examining and Retiring Board.

September 1935 to July 1936 – CO, VF Squadron, NAS, Pensacola.

July 1936 to July 1937 – OinC, Corry Field, NAS, Pensacola.

July 1937 to July 1938 – Chief of Staff, ComCarDivTWO, USS YORKTOWN (No. 1) and USS ENTERPRISE.

July 1938 to June 1939 – Assistant Air Officer, USS RANGER.

July 1939 – Commissioned Commander, U. S. Navy.

June 1939 to December 1939 – Air Officer, USS RANGER.

January 1940 to November 1941 – Executive Officer, NAS, Pearl Harbor.

November 1941 to September 1944 – Commander Fleet Air Wing FOUR.

May 1942 – Appointed Captain, U. S. Navy.

July 1943 – Spot appointment to Commodore, U. S. Navy,

September 1944 – Re-appointed Captain – to take command of FRANKLIN.

During the first six months of World War II, I commanded Fleet Air Wing FOUR operating from Dutch Harbor to the California border. From May 1942 until September 1944, the Wing was engaged in the campaign in the Aleutian Islands and against the northern Kurile Islands of Japan.

Hold World War I ribbon with star, and for this war, the National Defense ribbon with star, North American Area ribbon, Asiatic-Pacific Area ribbon with two stars, the Purple Heart, the Distinguished Flying Cross, and Legion of Merit.

HOBBY: Being a Naval Officer.

LIKES: The Navy and the people in it.

AVERSIONS: Japs, lazy people, dirty people, noisy people, and smarty-pants boots who imagine they are being "salty" by showing off ashore, or who snub me by not saluting and thus preventing me from saying "Good Morning" to them.

IMMEDIATE AMBITION: To get the FRANKLIN clean, repaired, and back into action.

NOTE: Only within the limits of the quarterdecks do I want officers and men to remain at attention when I am about. In other parts of the ship, only those men within six paces of me need rise and salute – and they may carry on as soon as I have passed them. Men actually working will continue their work unless I stop and speak to them. You have all seen how big I am, so you can realize I really need gangway in the narrow passageways and on ladders, and captains are usually in a hurry.[109]

Such a message did little to endear Gehres to his crew. Relations were strained even more by his by-the-book style and repeated drills as the *Franklin* completed its shakedown cruise. The clash in leadership styles and crew attitudes would reap a bitter harvest in the months ahead and leave scars that would last for lifetimes.

With the completion of maneuvers, the *Franklin* slipped out of Pearl Harbor during a blackout. Early the next day, Captain Gehres announced to the crew that they were headed for Ulithi where they would join Task Force 58, the mightiest U.S. Navy striking force in the history of naval warfare. Task Force 58, when fully formed and in place at its destination off the eastern coast of Japan, extended more than fifty miles across the Pacific Ocean. It was so large that it had to be split into four divisions. It consisted of over one hundred surface vessels and sixteen aircraft carriers, including powerful *Essex* class vessels.[110]

**Admiral Marc Mitscher**

Vice Admiral Marc A. Mitscher was in command of Task Force 58. He was a pioneer in U.S. naval aviation, having piloted one of Commander John Towers' NC-1 planes during an attempt to fly the Atlantic in 1919. The commander of the Third Fleet, of which Task Force 58 was the largest component, was Admiral William F. Halsey. The commander of Task Force 58-2, to which the *Franklin* was assigned, was Rear Admiral Ralph E. Davison, a

1916 U.S. Naval Academy graduate. Mitscher and Davison had served together in the same positions in Task Force 38, the precursor of the new armada.[111]

On Thursday, March 15, 1945, the *Franklin* quietly slipped its moorings in Ulithi Lagoon and departed on a northeast course plotted by Commander Stephen Jurika, the ship's navigator. The *Franklin,* part of Task Force 58-2, was headed toward the waters off the Japanese home island of Kyushu. The task force's objectives were to seek out, attack, and destroy enemy mainland naval installations.

By Sunday, March 17 the *Franklin* was pushing northeast to the island of Kyushu. There were no enemy planes in sight or on the radar

***Admiral Ralph Davison***

screen. Father Joseph T. O'Callahan and his counterpart, Protestant Chaplain Grimes "Gats" Gatlin, held religious services in two separate locations on the hangar deck.[112]

***Cmdr. Stephen Jurika***

The *Franklin's* crew had been at General Quarters since moving northward from Ulithi. For the crew, the alert level meant very long stretches of boring watch duty along with little relief and no decent meals. Gehres practiced various drills of crew training in a variety of areas, such as fire control, gunnery practice, emergency and escape procedures, medical instruction, basic shipboard indoctrination, aircraft and flight training. To some crew members, such frequent training sessions seemed to be excessive.

In the early morning of March 18, 1945, as the *Franklin* was approaching Kyushu, the *Franklin* sent up a squadron of Corsair fighters to draw out enemy aircraft. They encountered a much larger group of Japanese combat aircraft. In the ensuing engagement, the *Franklin* lost four Corsairs. One pilot was rescued by a submarine; another was captured. The other pilots were lost. Gehres, in announcing the loss to the crew, noted that more losses could occur. [113]

By midmorning March 18, most of Task Force 58 had already arrived within sixty to seventy miles of Kyushu and the target area around Kagoshima. The *Franklin* was continuing to move northeast at about twenty-five knots.

**Franklin** *pilots from Squadron VT13.*

The weather was getting colder and the seas were quite rough. The *Franklin* still had about a hundred combat aircraft battle-ready for its upcoming strikes on Kagoshima and other nearby targets. But as the carrier moved closer, it entered a killing zone.

Rear Admiral Davison frequently went on routine walks around the decks and visited work stations throughout the *Franklin*. Davison was an easy person to talk to, and he enjoyed interacting with the *Franklin's* crew members at all levels. On the evening of March 18, as Davison walked among the crew, several men complained about their lack of sleep and decent food.

Early on March 19 there was an abundance of different alert levels. Captain Gehres had ordered General Quarters, which is battle preparedness, when he returned from a short nap to the bridge at about 03:36 a.m. At 03:39 he set material condition ZEBRA.

However, he was soon confronted by his executive officer, Commander Joe Taylor, and Rear Admiral Davison, who had been walking the decks and talking with the crew. They suggested to Gehres that the crew was tired, hungry, in need of food and rest. They suggested lowering the alert level. Captain Gehres agreed.

***Commander Joe Taylor,***
***Executive Officer,* Franklin**

At 06:01, Gehres lowered the alert level to Condition 3, except at the gun batteries and fire control stations, which remained at effective operating levels.

All three officers agreed the alert levels assigned were sufficient to meet any anticipated emergencies.

Crew members on the hangar deck complained that their workplace needed more ventilation. Davison indicated that he understood these complaints to be valid, so he contacted Commander Joe Taylor, the executive officer, and explained the situation to him.[114]

Commander Taylor was a popular officer and a 1927 graduate of the U.S. Naval Academy. He had already seen considerable combat in the Coral Sea and Guadalcanal, where he had been awarded two U.S. Navy Crosses.

Davison felt that the large outside doors on the hangar deck should be opened to allow increased ventilation and that the crew members should get more sleep and better food. Taylor felt it best to discuss this situation with Captain Gehres. Gehres listened to both Davison and Taylor and agreed that lack of sleep and food does not make the most battle-ready sailor. He lowered the alert to Condition 3.

Taylor, along with other officers and petty officers, devised a rotation system whereby at least some of the more tired crew members could get some sleep. The galley picked up the slack in the food operation by providing more sandwiches and plenty of hot coffee for the crew. Taylor also arranged to have the outside doors in the hangar deck opened to provide increased ventilation.

Taylor made certain that all guns had sufficient crews to properly function if the *Franklin* were attacked. The large forward hatch on the flight deck was open, as it was necessary to allow uninterrupted movement of battle-ready aircraft and supplies from the hangar deck to the flight deck. These actions seemed to placate most crew members.

The Japanese had laid an extensive magnetic minefield. Fortunately, the *Franklin* was degaussed against electrically triggered mines. However, when a mine was sighted, it made good target practice for the *Franklin's* gunnery crews.[115]

In order for the *Franklin* to arrive at its assigned anchorage on time, the ship's navigators and skipper had to plot a careful zigzagging course, with changes along the way, through the dangerous mine field. At about 6:30 p.m., the *Franklin* arrived at its designated location and dropped anchor. The *Franklin* was safe from the minefields, but not from Japanese submarine and air attacks. Here, the *Franklin* would remain at anchor for several hours until Mitscher ordered Task Force 58 into attack position.

On the evening of March 18, few aboard the *Franklin* knew exactly what lay ahead. Life's journey would end for nine hundred and ninety-eight crew members the next day, and more than four hundred men would be seriously wounded. Shortly after midnight, Mitscher gave the order to move Task Force 58 out into the upcoming battle zone, about fifty miles east of Kyushu. At about 2:30 a.m., the *Franklin* moved into its position as the flagship in Task Force 58-2.

# VII
# The Battle for Survival

*Abandon? Hell! We're still afloat!*

***Captain Leslie E. Gehres, March 19, 1945***

Captain Gehres arrived on the bridge at about 3 a.m. on March 19, replacing Commander Joe Taylor. As there was considerable enemy air activity, Gehres decided to upgrade combat readiness to General Quarters. He began issuing orders, using his handy megaphone and standby messengers.

At 7:03 a.m., some fifty miles off the east coast of Japan, the *Franklin*'s duty officer and navigator, Commander Stephen Jurika, received a scratchy message from the carrier *Hancock*, indicating that an enemy plane was closing on the *Franklin*. Jurika immediately notified Captain Gehres. Unfortunately, the *Franklin*'s radar did not pick up the intruder. Apparently, the pilot had been cruising high above the clouds, occasionally diving through the overcast sky in search of a prize target. This time, he found one in the middle of Task Force 58-2, a 27,200-ton aircraft carrier named the *Franklin*.

The Japanese pilot put his "Judy," a Yokosuka D4Y Suisei, into a fast dive. He dropped two five-hundred-pound, semi-armor-piercing bombs on the *Franklin*. The first bomb dropped just aft of the large forward elevator, exploding in the hangar deck, knocking the thirty-two-ton elevator off its pinions and blowing upward through its open hatch in a massive sheet of flame. The bomb also caused further huge explosions, fires and destruction on the hangar and on the second and third decks.

The second bomb fell aft of the tower island on the flight deck and tore through two additional decks, causing more fires and explosions. There were fifty-three parked combat planes waiting their turn to take off. The *Franklin*'s other combat planes were not aboard the carrier; they were either on sorties attacking mainland Japan or helping to defend Task Force 58-2 from enemy aircraft.

Captain Gehres, who was on the bridge, was knocked off his feet. Rising, still dazed, he watched a column of flame roll skyward into one tremendous detonation.[116]

Father Joseph T. O'Callahan, a Jesuit chaplain who would receive the Medal of Honor for his heroism during the *Franklin*'s battle for survival, recalled Gehres' leadership.

The smoke hid the island and its bridge completely from my view. Then a rift in the cloud gave a view of Captain Gehres on the bridge, firm and stern. Behind him was Steve Jurika, navigator. "Why don't they leave the island before they're trapped completely?" When the smoke closed in again, they were still there. Again a rift—the same sight, the same question, and again they didn't leave. Then an explosion. I think I was thrown to the deck. I know I saw shrapnel, entire airplane engines, and untold smaller chunks of steel shooting through the air—hurtling up, then pelting down. More smoke. Was the island still there? Another glimpse of the bridge and of Captain Gehres. This sequence continued intermittently. Each time the smoke lifted, those on the forward flight deck had a glimpse of Captain Gehres; each glimpse giving the ship the courage born of brave example.[117]

S2/c Jackson Toon, V6 USNR, who was born and raised in Franklin, Tennessee, considered the namesake of the carrier, recalled his experience aboard on that eventful day.

"I wasn't at my regular station that morning. I was working on a balky side-gun turret at another location. That is what saved my life. I was ordered to report to another battle station as something had gone wrong with a gun there. As for my own gun station, well, after the attack it was only a smoking twisted wreck."

Toon recalls that the Japanese Judy came in fast and unexpectedly, and he doesn't remember any defensive rounds of anti-aircraft fire sent up.

"It felt like the whole ship was falling out from under me. That is about all I remember about the first terrible instant after the Japanese dive bomber had released two 500-lb. armor-piercing bombs. One hit near the flight deck elevator and ricocheted aft into the parked aircraft awaiting take off. The bomb seemed to wait for the second bomb, its companion, to explode. The second bomb penetrated into the bowels of the ship where they both exploded at about the same time. In a few seconds, the *Franklin* had become a roaring inferno and in danger of sinking."[118]

*S2/c Jackson Toon*

Warren L. Baumann of North Fort Myers, Florida, was on the carrier's main deck when the attack came.

At about seven o'clock, I was standing in front of one of the island shacks watching the planes take off. Out of a clear sky, I heard two explosions that rocked the ship and blew me into the shack on top of a lot of other fellows. The *Franklin* at that time was not on general quarters, so most of the watertight hatches were open and chow was being served. I thought we were going down for sure.

As soon as we got to our senses, one of our fellows, Mucklow, yelled "Let's get the hell out of here and go forward." However, heavy black smoke engulfed us, and although we couldn't see any flames, we could sure feel the heat. Jack Richardson and I ran forward. We had no idea where we were, but we had to get out of the smoke and fire.

For some nutty reason, we tried to get down to the hangar deck, but bent hatches, smoke, and fire blocked that. About this time, things started exploding, carrying us off our feet. Jack and I got panic stricken, and we were scared. We now decided that the safest place on the ship would be the forecastle deck. As we decided to move, the explosions continued and I don't know how we missed so many holes in crossing the forward deck. The fellow next to Jack was hit with something from the explosions that blew off his back. He was dead, so there was no sense trying to save him.[119]

*Smoke and flames roars from the Franklin as a rescue ship nears.*

Another sailor, John E. Frajman, recalled the horror on the flight deck.

On the flight deck there was general confusion. As the first bomb had fallen near the tower island, it had killed thirty crew members and wounded about fifteen more inside the control room. The ship was not only on fire and exploding but had taken on a serious list of about 13 to 15 degrees. Crewmen were busy trying to correct this problem. The list caused the parked planes to shift about. Some went overboard, frequently taking their crews with them. Brave crew members died pushing burning planes overboard. Many planes that still remained on deck were on fire and exploding, their engines often still running. Of the remaining men, some were burned or injured by whirling propellers. Others were seriously injured and needed attention. Those men who could not find a safe haven usually jumped overboard or were blown off the ship by explosions. [120]

Toon, who was shielded from the twin blasts by the gun, joined a group fighting fires on the flight deck. But as the fires and explosions approached, his position became untenable. Because of his precarious position, he felt he had no other alternative than to go overboard. He found a rope ladder, and lowered himself into the cold water of the Pacific. He was only in the water a short time

***The burned out hangar deck, looking toward starboard.***

when Captain Gehres, using a megaphone, called for all the overboard sailors to come back aboard the *Franklin*. Upon hearing the captain's order to return to the *Franklin*, Toon soon located a rope ladder and climbed topside. He said later that despite the carnage, he was glad to be back aboard his ship again.[121]

The hangar deck, where the first bomb had made a hit, reeked of death and fire. One of the surviving crew members called the scene Dante's *Inferno*. Fifty planes, mostly Hellcats, were parked on the deck. Most of them had been recently equipped with the new Tiny Tim rockets. This weapon weighed over a thousand pounds and was encased in a ten-foot-long metal tube with a diameter of almost twelve inches. This rocket was a formidable weapon. It gave a group of Hellcat fighters the equivalent firepower of a full division of U.S. Navy cruisers. The blast caused many of them to fire, ricocheting through the hangar deck and exploding. Other ammunition and gasoline aboard the planes exploded, causing even more devastation. Few crew members on the hangar deck escaped unscathed.[122]

Warren Baumann described what he saw when he and a friend ran down to the deck to help.

Jack and I got to a point of the catwalk where we could look back and see what was happening. There wasn't much to see, except smoke, fire and explosions. It looked like a gala Fourth of July celebration. At this point, we were tired of just standing around and trying to dodge the smoke and fire, so we began to go down to the hangar deck and help with the fires.

We went down from the catwalk and grabbed a hose. There wasn't over ten men on the whole hangar deck manning hoses. No one seemed to care if the *Franklin* survived or sunk. The pressure in the hoses was low, which didn't help.

The deck was littered with burned airplane parts, engines, wings, tails and bodies. It was like a morgue—a total wreck. We worked there as long as we could.[123]

*Julius F. Payak, USMC*

Julius F. Payak, USMC, assigned to the *Franklin* from Johnstown, Pennsylvania, told a story of brotherhood that resonates years later.

My first thought upon rising was to get to a place of safety on the top deck. I first tried using the ladder in the marine department, but it was full of flame and dead bodies. My next attempt was through the officers' mess hall passageway. But, it was also full of flames and thick smoke. Then, I tried several other ways to reach the top deck, again blinded by heavy smoke and flames, without success. Finally, I got down to the mess hall, after walking over many dead bodies. There, I met a shipmate who wanted to come along with me. We finally made it top side, after four-and-a-half hours. At first I thought the ship was being scuttled, so as we were about to go overboard, we heard a loud voice shouting, "Don't jump!" I noticed it was my mess sergeant. He told us to go to the flight officer's quarters and get some dry clothes.

The next day, a black shipmate came up to me and thanked me for saving his life. I said, "Forget it; you would have done the same thing for me."

That is the first time that I realized that he was a black person. It goes to prove, that we all are brothers, regardless of the color of our skin. I had thought the shipmate that I had picked up along the way, was just another white sailor that had been through hell.[124]

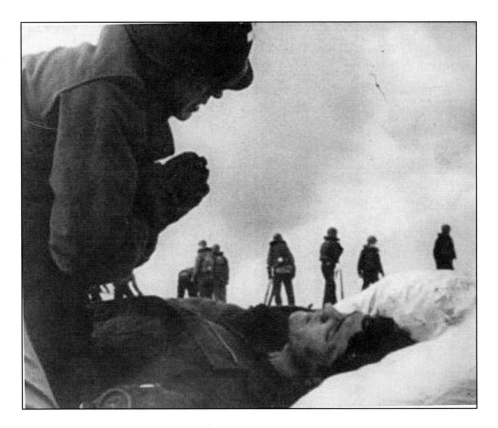

*Iconic image of Father Callahan tending to Robert Blanchard March 19,
1945 on the fiery deck of the USS Franklin. Blanchard, overcome by smoke
inhalation would live to 90 years old.*

Fire control and medical personnel responded as soon as possible. However, some crew members witnessing this grim scene found it difficult to initially participate in its cleanup. But competent leadership, including that of Commander Taylor, Chaplain O'Callahan, and a couple of hard-nosed petty officers, moved the cleanup work along quickly and without complaint. Remains of fallen crew members were carefully prepared for burial at sea. *Franklin's* two chaplains, O'Callahan and Gatlin, performed appropriate burial services, with a number of crew members attending. Then, they were laid to rest overboard, to repose forever in God's hands in the blue waters of the Pacific Ocean.[125]

Identification and removal of the remains were difficult. However, the crew recognized the need for these tasks to be performed in an honorable and dedicated manner. Gehres was pleased, and complimented the work crews for a job well done. Gehres claimed that he was not a very religious person. But years later, in describing the battle for the *Franklin's* survival, at one point in the worst of it, with bombs going off, hell breaking loose all around him, he said he had heard a strange voice.

"This is something that I have not told anybody before," he said. "In the midst of all that, I suddenly I heard a voice inside of my head repeating the Twenty-third Psalm . . . *The Lord is my Shepherd. . .* which I hadn't thought about since I was a kid."[126]

Toon was concerned about his hometown friend, James Harper, with whom he frequently talked about old times back home. The two would reminisce about hiking in the hills of Williamson County, or swimming and fishing in the Harpeth River. Toon made a search of the battered *Franklin* for Harper, but was never able to find him. So, he once again went back to fighting fires.

S2/c James Albert Harper, V6, USNR, Toon's hometown friend, had entered the Navy after begging his parents to consent to his enlistment in the Navy. He needed their permission because he was underage.

"He was determined to somehow get in the Navy," his mother said. "Young Harper had a mind of his own. He had a mind set and a will of his own, that boy."

Harper enlisted in Nashville, Tennessee, in late October 1944. After completing his basic training at the Great Lakes Naval Training Center, he was immediately assigned to the *Franklin* in February 1945, which was being refitted in Washington State. Harper had served for less than a month aboard the *Franklin* when he disappeared during the attack and fire.

"Jim was a good friend of mine and I never knew exactly what happened to him, or how he died," Toon said. "We were on routine half shifts when the bombs bored in. I think he was deep down in the belly of the ship, where one of the bombs exploded."

Toon continued fighting fires without much food or rest. The *Franklin* was listing badly, and he was concerned about the possibility of the ship capsizing and sinking with many crew members still aboard. The *Franklin* was dead in the water and being towed by the cruiser *Pittsburgh*.

"After a few hours, the *Franklin* was able to continue under its own power, and we were able to cut the flames down to merely smoldering. Then, we knew that our ship would survive."[127]

As the morning wore on, the super-human effort by all levels of *Franklin*'s highly trained crew in fighting the fires and tossing overboard unexploded ordnance began to tell. A large number of seriously wounded crew members aboard the *Franklin* needed immediate medical attention. They were treated as

**The USS Santa Fe's *Capt. Harold Fitz boldly moved his ship alongside the* Franklin.**

soon as possible by the *Franklin*'s depleted medical staff, but they had to be transferred to better medical facilities aboard another ship. Captain Harold C. Fitz of the cruiser USS *Santa Fe* (CLAA60) came to *Franklin*'s rescue and moved his ship alongside the listing starboard side.

This was a dangerous maneuver, which Fitz and his crew performed in an outstanding manner. Fitz asked Gehres if his ammunition magazines were flooded. The response was yes. Fitz then put several lines aboard the *Franklin* and started to take aboard some wounded. The *Santa Fe*'s water pumps were soon helping the *Franklin* to quench its massive fires. As the transfer was taking place, a five-inch shell storage magazine exploded aboard the *Franklin*, sending flames and smoke over two thousand feet in the air.[128]

Large pieces of debris were thrown all over the *Santa Fe*. Two sections of fire hose were broken. But, no *Santa Fe* crew members were injured or lost. The *Santa Fe* was in a dangerous position, so Fitz ordered all remaining lines attached to the *Franklin* removed. He then ordered his cruiser to back away and stand by, allowing him time to plan his next move.

Admiral Mitscher, noting the precarious position of the *Franklin,* directed his signalman aboard the USS *Bunker Hill* to transmit a routine message to the *Franklin* granting permission to abandon ship. Captain Gehres ordered his signalman to reply "Abandon? Hell, we're still afloat!"[129]

A short time later, Captain Fitz decided to batter his way back through enormous amount of debris to help the distressed *Franklin* and continue the transfer of the wounded. Seizing the opportunity, the *Santa Fe* moved in at about twenty-five knots. The *Santa Fe* hit the side of the *Franklin* pretty hard, toppling one of *Franklin's* radio masts and knocking out a couple of gunnery positions, along with chewing up much of the port side of the *Franklin.* The carrier shuddered under the blow. While the seas were rough and the decks were pitching, the *Santa Fe* and the *Franklin* were now firmly hitched together, making it possible to walk or easily jump from one ship to another. This position made it easier to transfer the wounded from the *Franklin* to the *Santa Fe.* It also allowed other crew members the opportunity to abandon ship, although there was never a general abandon ship order issued.[130]

John E. Frajman (AA) (T), described the confusion that ensued as men ran across to the cruiser, leaped overboard, or were blown off the *Franklin* by the recurring blasts.

> I immediately started down the starboard passageway. I got as far as the canteen, when a horde of sailors was coming down the passageway yelling that we had been hit forward. I did an about face and headed for the nearest hatch to the fantail. When I reached topside there were a lot of smoke and high temperatures.
>
> When I got to the fantail, there were many sailors there before me. A short time later, the explosions started. I was on the starboard side of the fantail. There was a life raft in the water roped to the ship. The raft was killing sailors that were abandoning ship forward. Rufus Gentry yelled to cut the raft loose. I took out my sheath knife and was about to cut the line of rope, when a young officer drew his .38 revolver and said he would shoot the first man that cut the rope. Rufus stepped up between me and the officer and told the officer, "Put that gun back in your holster or I will shove it up your ass." I barely touched the rope with my knife and it sounded like a rifle shot when it parted.[131]

Men were making life-and-death decisions under horrific conditions, and some of those decisions would come back to haunt many of the sailors. As Frajman wrote:

About this time, Sgt. Major Manco yelled to man the 40 mm AA on the fantail. We were about to pass the ammunition to him when the explosions intensified. He then realized it was our own munitions that were exploding, so he ordered all 40 mm ammunition to be thrown over the side, I was standing by the lifelines looking aft when CWT AAT Proccasio approached me and asked what I was going to do. I told him that if I had a life jacket, I would go over the side. A short while later there was a violent explosion on the port side aft. The next thing I remember, I was in the ship's wake, churned to the point where I could not distinguish between up or down. My lungs were bursting, so I tried to breathe. A short time later, I tried again . . . . At about the same time, I broke the surface and breathed in a lung full of smoky air. I was treading water when an unknown shipmate gave me a five-inch powder can to keep me afloat. A short time later, I swam to a life raft. The first person I recognized was Rufus Gentry. He took charge of the life raft. There were so many in the life raft, it submerged. He made all able-bodied men with life jackets get into the water, and he moved the disabled into the raft. He kept order on and off the raft, continuously assisting the disabled, until boarding the rescue vessel, the USS *Hunt*.[132]

Gentry's bravery, however, would later earn him censure from Gehres. Baumann, who was authorized to leave the *Franklin*, recalled how welcome the *Santa Fe* was to him and many other survivors of the carnage.

About this time, the light cruiser *Santa Fe* came along side and the crew was busy rigging lines to take aboard the wounded. The *Santa Fe* was only able to take aboard several wounded men and a few other departing sailors. Because of the many close-by explosions, placing the *Santa Fe* in jeopardy, it pulled away.

The faithful *Santa Fe* continued to stand by, awaiting the opportunity to move in again and help the *Franklin*. We went back to the forecastle, choking from the smoke. Now we were told go to the Flight deck for the purpose of boarding the *Santa Fe*.

From the flight deck, we saw the *Santa Fe* circle and come up on our starboard and ram the *Franklin* side, locking her deck with our gun sponson. The crash shook the whole ship. Now it was possible to step aboard from one ship to another.

Commander Hale, the air officer, was in charge. He ordered that all wounded men would be taken off first. Many were carried over in stretchers along with others that could walk. Everyone was quite calm. Next, Hale ordered the pilots and air crews off. After them went the air department. The V-l and V-2 (air squadrons) were also ordered off.

I crawled down the radio antenna. Other crew members were climbing down rope lines, with others either stepping or jumping aboard. As we pulled away, I could see the *Franklin*'s skipper observing from the bridge. He must have kept Commander Hale informed on how to direct the operation and when to end it. It all went quite smoothly.[133]

*John Caruso, Sm1c,* **Santa Fe**

The crew of the *Santa Fe* provided welcome relief to the tired *Franklin* firefighters and burial details. They helped with the cleanup of the debris and aided the *Franklin*'s medical staff in treating the wounded and sick prior to transferring them. Seaman 1/c John A. Caruso, from Land-O-Lakes in Wisconsin, was stationed aboard the *Santa Fe*. Caruso gave up his berth to a *Franklin* sailor who was critically wounded. He believed the *Santa Fe* took aboard over eight hundred wounded, sick, and able-bodied *Franklin* crew members. Caruso felt

that *Santa Fe*'s crew, especially the medics, did their best in caring for these crew members.

He had high praise for his skipper, Captain Fitz, in his skillful maneuvering of the *Santa Fe* when in close proximity with the *Franklin* and in directing onboard operations during the rescue mission. Fitz continued to take aboard *Franklin* crew members until Captain Gehres told Fitz that it was time for the *Santa Fe* to pull away.[134]

*Irvin (cut) Foster, Rdm3c,*
**Hancock**

Irvin (Cut) Foster, Rdm 3/c from Millinocket, Maine, was a sailor aboard the USS *Lewis Hancock* (DD 675). He later retired to Englewood, Florida.

The *Lewis Hancock's* assignment was to stand by to perform rescue and protection support for the battered Franklin. Foster recalls standing with his shipmates along the rails of the *Lewis Hancock*, staring in awe at the *Franklin*. The carrier had taken on a thirteen-degree list and was burning furiously, with flames shooting hundreds of feet to the air.

He described an amazing story of a *Hancock* sailor who had appendicitis, and was transferred earlier to the *Franklin's* superior medical facilities for surgery. After the attack, Foster said, a *Hancock* lifeboat found the young sailor floating in the icy waters. Once aboard, he was placed in a warm berth and given a little liquid nourishment. Needless to say, he was happy to be back aboard his ship.[135]

The *Franklin* was dead in the water and slowly drifting toward the Japanese mainland. Arrangements had been made by Rear Admiral Davison and Captain Fitz for the heavy cruiser, USS *Pittsburgh* CA-72, to take the *Franklin* in tow and remove it from the battle zone. A little before noon on March 19, Fitz advised Mitscher that the fires aboard the *Franklin* had diminished and were under control, and that the list was stabilized at thirteen degrees with a skeleton crew aboard. Fitz further radioed, "If you will help save the *Franklin* by providing air and submarine coverage from the Japanese, we can save the *Franklin*."

Mitscher replied, "Tell the *Franklin* we appreciate your message, and we will do all we can."

Fires still raged on the *Franklin,* and it seemed like a doomed ship, in danger of capsizing and sinking with many crew members still aboard. Rene N. Gauthier F/1c from Plainville, Connecticut, described the *Franklin's* precarious situation:

***Rene M. Gauthier, F1c,* Franklin**

Horrific fires, smoke, wounded and death were everywhere. It was a horrific scene, nothing like I had ever witnessed before. We were about fifty miles off the eastern coast of Japan, and slowly drifting towards the Japanese mainland. The Japanese were still attacking the *Franklin* from the air. They really wanted to finish off the *Franklin* and make sure it would sink to a watery grave. The *Franklin's* guns were responding as best they could. However, our aircraft and the guns from our surrounding safety net were aggressively keeping the Japanese at bay, and the *Franklin* safe.[136]

*John L. Wisse Sm2C*

Captain Gehres had sworn earlier that he would never abandon any ship he commanded if there were crew members still aboard. He could never forget the death of the *Yorktown* after the Battle of Midway, when the carrier was sunk, reportedly with crew members still aboard, after extensive battle damage.[137]

There were many heroes on March 19, 1945. Mistakes were made, many lives were lost, and many were saved. Stout sailors lost their lives; others were left with physical and mental scars that would last a lifetime. But what could have been the most tragic sea disaster in the history of the U.S. Navy became its most outstanding story of heroism. The spirit of the crew and the help of other task force vessels was the difference between disaster and survival.

John L. Wisse SM2C, of Rotonda, Florida, was aboard the USS *Hickox* (DD673). He recalled how his destroyer raced into danger to help the men of the stricken carrier.

After the bombs were dropped on the *Franklin*, it became an instant inferno. I saw sailors blown into the air from the concussion of the explosions, others burned to a crisp in the fire. Many others jumped overboard to escape death by immolation.

Our skipper ran the bow of our destroyer under the stern of the carrier. I could see there were about twenty crew members still trapped on the stern deck. Lines were rigged from the *Franklin* to the *Hickox's* five-inch gun and two stretcher cases were brought aboard the *Hickox*. Some of the remaining crew members jumped onto the deck of the *Hickox*. The *Hickox* put out a whaleboat, which I went aboard.

I was rewarded by a handwritten letter fifty years later from (a rescued survivor) James M. Stuart Y2C, from Dayton, Ohio.[138]

*A high order detonation on port side. Note debris in air and firefighters running to escape. Note topmast broken at radar platform level.*

The USS *Franklin* was labeled as "The Ship That Wouldn't Die." The story of its survival rings strong and clear. But some parts of that story still remain untold, perhaps because of the horror. Baumann recalled a grim sight he witnessed from the deck of the *Santa Fe*.

The *Santa Fe* was following directly behind the *Franklin*. Some of the *Santa Fe's* crew noticed that the *Franklin* was tossing remains overboard. For them, it was a gruesome sight. They felt they were being thrown overboard without any decent final burial service.

Captain Gehres and the chaplains aboard the *Franklin*, when informed of this situation, responded by saying that all burials performed at sea were in full accordance of official U.S. Navy regulations. However, they admitted there were problems sometimes in identifying remains and sometimes it was impossible. But nevertheless, the chaplains claimed that there was always a decent burial service conducted, even under the most difficult circumstances. Captain Gehres said that they would continue to do the very best they could, and that was going to be it.[139]

The spectacle of the *Franklin* fighting for its survival while engulfed in fire, smoke and explosions was a terrifying sight. It paralyzed many of the viewing crew members from the neighboring ships of Task Force 58. In a successful effort to ward off attacking aircraft and submarines, the remaining twenty ships in Task Force 58-2 formed a protective circle around the wounded *Franklin*.

Donald E. Fowler, a sailor from Englewood, Florida, who was aboard the aircraft carrier USS *Bennington* CV-20 of Task Force 58-1 observed the battle from a distance.

Fowler remembers seeing the *Franklin* on the horizon, belching smoke from its fires and explosions. The *Bennington* was not in a position to help the *Franklin*. Fowler noted that the *Bennington's* crew was too interested in saving their own ship from the relentless bombing and strafing attacks by the Japanese Air Force to be concerned about the *Franklin's* battle.[140]

The *Franklin* was a roaring furnace of heroism, death, and injury. From a distance, flames and explosions seemed to encompass the ship. Many observers from other nearby ships didn't believe that the *Franklin* would survive. Quartermaster 1st Class Casey Kraft from Sarasota, Florida, who witnessed the disaster from the USS *Halsey Powell* commented:

> Oh, she was badly damaged. We saw her not long after she was hit. She was smoking and had a list. It was kind of scary to see. Any sailor who has gazed at a burning, sinking ship understands what is happening to their fellow sailors on deck—the panic, the screams of the dying, the hopelessness. You try not to think about it too much. In many ways you just seem to accept the things of war after a while. You ignore it; you're a fatalist is what it amounts to. Still you realized, looking at her, that this could happen to you, too.[141]

Sometimes, there were other causes for fires and explosions. Distracted crew members would find a need to light their cigarettes, or use matches to help light up dark passageways aboard the *Franklin* in an area that was reeking with gasoline fumes or leaking gasoline tanks. The results were often tragic.

Gauthier still pauses as he remembers the grimmest task left to the survivors: "Of necessity, work details were continuing to clean up the ship. We picked up bodies that had drowned in the lower compartments, where they had suffocated and boiled to death. It was a gruesome task. The only way we could bury them was to pick them up in shovels and put their body parts in trash cans, then the chaplains blessed the remains, which were then relegated to their watery grave."[142]

Lt. j.g George K. Leitch, an ensign at the time who was an aide to Commander Taylor, was given the assignment of obtaining volunteers to go two decks below the hangar deck on a cleanup mission. The men found a berthing area where all of the occupants, about sixty men, were dead. Undoubtedly, most of the crew members appeared to have died from suffocation. In preparing the corpses for burial, most of the dead were not wearing dog tags, making identification difficult.[143]

Captain Gehres had once told Lt. Commander Robert E. Wassman, assistant navigator and "N" division officer aboard the *Franklin*, that the navigator knew the ship blindfolded. Wassman recalled:

> Therefore, I made a pledge that I would somehow rescue several shipmates trapped below in the steering engine room. Accompanied first by quartermaster Gilbert Abbot and later by quartermaster Virgil Verilek, I set out from the bridge for steering aft on the morning of March 19 in search of several shipmates trapped in the stern engine room. We held battle rescue lanterns to find our way underneath the blazing hangar deck. We went from one flooded compartment to the next, unlocking bulkhead doors through heavy smoke and darkness.
>
> Finally, we reached the sealed hatch leading to the steering engine room. We cleared away the debris and proceeded aft to the steering engine room to open a corridor from which the trapped men could escape. On our return to the bridge from the fantail, we found a badly wounded crewman. Using a blanket, we dragged and carried him forward over the burning and jagged-edged flight deck, where we saw the medics busy treating the wounded.
>
> Once back on the bridge, we gave the men in steering aft instructions on how to move out to a safe location. All five men were finally released from what could have become their tomb because of a failing oxygen supply. It was a great thrill![144]

While there were many heroes aboard the *Franklin* on March 19, 1945, two examples of courage stood out.

One hero was Lt. j.g. Donald A. Gary, a veteran of twenty years in the Navy who, like Gehres, had come up through the ranks. Four times Gary went down to the *Franklin*'s galley area through various ventilating shafts to lead over three hundred crew members to safety. He later received the Medal of Honor for this heroic act.

*Tow lines are secured.*

Another officer, Jesuit priest and senior chaplain, was Lt. Commander Joseph Timothy O'Callahan. He was everywhere on the ship helping and administering to the wounded and dying. He was also very active in providing leadership in helping to jettison ammunition overboard. At times, he led rescue parties below decks. Crewmembers willingly followed him. Commander Taylor described O'Callahan as a soul-stirring sight:

"He was everywhere, giving extreme unction to the dead and dying, urging the men on and himself handling hoses, jettisoning ammunition and doing everything he could to help save our ship," Taylor said.

Gehres recommended both Gary and O'Callahan for the Medal of Honor, which was awarded to both men by President Harry Truman on January 23, 1946.

Shortly before noon on March 19, the *Pittsburgh* pulled into place and waited to attach a very heavy steel cable to the *Franklin*. Since there was no power aboard the carrier, the ship's capstan was not working; the task of attaching the cable to the *Franklin* would require substantial human effort. Captain Gehres called upon a large group of mess men, all of whom were black. The men turned to the task. First a hawser was thrown across the *Franklin*. Then the men began their back-breaking pull, chanting old work songs to a steady beat as they tugged. With

*The* **Pittsburgh** *backs into place to pass a tow cable to the* **Franklin***.*

songs, sweat and muscle, the cable was pulled aboard and attached to the anchor chain. [145]

Once the anchor chain was attached to the *Pittsburgh's* cable, the *Pittsburgh* could take the *Franklin* in tow. However, a lone Japanese Judy decided to attack the *Franklin*, which was a sitting target as it was dead in the water. A large armor-piercing bomb missed the *Franklin* by about a hundred and fifty yards off the port bow and exploded. The explosion shook the *Franklin* and slowed the towing operation. However, by 12:20 p.m. the *Pittsburgh* had pulled up the slack in the cable and was beginning to move the *Franklin* out of the battle at about two knots. The seas were rough and the winds were strong and steady which hindered *Franklin's* movement. But nevertheless, the *Franklin* was now headed for Ulithi, in the Caroline Islands.[146]

Crew members were busy working to correct the list. At about 9 p.m., the engine room personnel were able to light one boiler. As the hours wore on, some of the more-necessary functions were restored. They mainly included electrical service to power the water pumps, communications, ventilation, limited shipboard lighting, and some engine power. Gauthier, who worked in the boiler room of the stricken carrier, described the superhuman efforts to contain the raging fires while getting the vessel underway.

From fighting the fires, our dungarees were soaked with salt water, and when dried, stiff as a board. Our shoes were rotted from the salt water, and our feet were very cold and broken out with fungus. My feet were swollen up to my knees and thighs chafed and bleeding. Later, at Captain Gehres' request we found replacement clothes. We now had dry dungarees, rubber boots and heavy woolen socks—what a relief.

Later, Captain Gehres ordered our engine-room crew back to the engineering department location. Here, we found that number three fire room was our best bet to get working, so we fired up the first boiler and were successful. This allowed for the operation of some electric generators, fresh water evaporators, water pumps and later to slowly begin to move the main engine screws and provide a slow under way.[147]

By noon the next day, four boilers and two engines were in operation. The *Pittsburgh* was able to cast off and the *Franklin* was making fourteen knots under its own power. With basic communications restored, radio and wireless messages were being sent and received. The following messages were received:

20 March 1945
To:      Captain Gehres USS *Franklin*
From:    Captain Fitz USS *Santa Fe*
MSG Captain Gehres. Congratulations on heroic work and outstanding efficiency of yourself and men in getting your ship underway and saving her. It is an example we will never forget.

20 March 1945
To:      Captain Gehres USS *Franklin*
From:    Captain Highet USS *Hickox*
From Captain and executive officers. Our sympathy and congratulations on your superb courage.

20 March 1945
To:      Captain Gehres USS *Franklin*
From:    Rear Admiral Low COmTaskUnit 58.2.9
My compliments on your fine performance and bringing your ship through.

At the end of the day March 20, the *Franklin* was surrounded by several cruisers, including the *Santa Fe, Guam, Pittsburgh* and *Alaska,* as well as two destroyers, all of which had to continually fight off attacking Japanese aircraft.

The next morning, March 21, 1945, Captain Gehres ordered the crew to muster on the flight deck for a head count. At least two hundred and eight-six officers and enlisted men stood roll call. Other shipboard personnel say the number was somewhat less.

Gauthier came up with the figure of two hundred and ninety-six officers and enlisted men.[148] In any event the number was small; the original total crew of officers and enlisted men exceeded three thousand before the attack. As the ship progressed on its homeward journey, there was confusion about an accurate headcount. After the assembly, Gehres read a message from Admiral Marc A. Mitscher, Commander Task Force 58:

> 21 March 1945
> To:　　Captain Gehres USS *Franklin*
> From Admiral Mitscher CTF 58
> You and your historic crew cannot be too highly applauded for your historic and successful battle to save your gallant ship in spite of the difficulty the enormity of which is appreciated. Deep regards for your losses which we feel as our own.

Gehres continued: "Yesterday, we were given up for lost. Today we are hailed as heroes. I am a proud man, proud to say that I served with you. But I am also a very stiff-necked officer. The watchword will be work and more work from now on. If there is a man who thinks he cannot stand up to such a schedule, let him say so now and I will transfer him to another ship. When we get home, I will see that each of you gets a well-deserved rest."

Our first and most important task is to find, identify and bury dead. Then we will clean up the ship. I will not have a dirty ship. Secure from quarters and hop to it."

Gehres and Joe Taylor kept the crew members busy and their minds off the events of March 19. Two days later Joe Taylor found a workable mimeograph machine and on a tired typewriter wrote a simple plan for the coming days. It read in part:

BIG BEN BOMBED, BATTERED, BRUISED AND BENT, BUT NOT BROKEN

The plan read:

PF#2093: +01:15:44:18

***Capt. Gehres addresses the remaining crew of the Franklin during a memorial ceremony shortly after the attack.***

1. All hands will wear dungarees, blue eyed hats, black shoes to quarters. Chin up, chests out, and tails over the dashboard.
2. Gun crew will wear helmets. All usable gun batteries will be manned.[149]

During the night, the crew quenched the last fires aboard the ship. The following day, they began the grim task of cleaning up the ship, searching for the dead, and burying their former shipmates. It was always hard work, and at day's end, the men were exhausted and very dirty. The burial details were usually carried out and headed by one of the chaplains, a few officers and mostly enlisted crew members. As time went on, most of the men on these burial details became hardened to their assignment. However, the chaplains found it necessary to watch all the men closely, especially the young, for fear that their minds would be stressed to the breaking point.[150]

The burial crew did not devote all their time to the task of burying the dead. Several times, the burials were interrupted as men scrambled to rescue trapped crew members. Several men were found, often badly burned or injured. Some of the search parties required special skills to enter compartments where the entrance

119

*A wounded seaman being transported by breeches buoy from the Franklin to the* **Santa Fe**

doors were severely jammed shut and could not be easily opened. Chaplain O'Callahan came across an old-time sailor, Bosun Frisbee Bow, who was desperately working to open a jammed door sealed by an explosion. Frisbee had considerable experience in opening jammed doors. O'Callahan went up to Frisbee and gave him some words of encouragement. Frisbee stopped for a few moments and replied:

"OK, I'm tough and hard: I can do rough work and I think that I have guts. But men like me didn't save this ship. The man up there on the bridge, he saved the ship. He's got character. He's a leader. I take my hat off to the old man."[151]

That night the crew had a hot meal, the first since hostilities had begun. Saxy Dowell and his band struck up the music, which became a nightly occurrence until the *Franklin* reached New York. A new ship's motto had been created: "A ship that won't be sunk can't be sunk."

On the morning of March 22, Gehres received two more messages. After breakfast, he read the messages to the crew.

22 March 1945
To: Captain Gehres USS *Franklin*
From: Rear Admiral Davison
I am at a stranger's doorstep. But I claim you again with pride. Battered though you may be you are still my child. Great work.

22 March 1945
To: Captain Gehres USS *Franklin*
From: Rear Admiral Garner ComCarDiv 7
Msg to Captain Gehres. Congratulations on booting home the long shot.
To you and your great gang we touch our scorched forelock.

On March 24, 1945, the indomitable *Franklin* carefully maneuvered into the Ulithi Lagoon in the Caroline Islands. Saxi Dowell's band struck up the tune of "The Old Gray Mare," and the crew sang. But the chorus was a little different.

> *Oh, the old Big Ben,*
> *She ain't what she used to be,*
> *Ain't what she used to be,*
> *just a few days ago*
> *Bombs in the hangar deck!*[168]

As the *Franklin* was pulling into Ulithi Lagoon, the faithful *Santa Fe*, which helped to guard the *Franklin* from the battle zone, passed to the starboard, and dipped its flag in a true expression of respect for the *Franklin* by Captain Fitz and his crew. The *Santa Fe* then moved out ahead of the *Franklin*. In a spurt of speed, it immediately pulled alongside of the hospital ship *Bountiful*. Here, *Franklin's* wounded, and distressed crew members were transferred to the best medical facility available.

The *Franklin* would rest in Ulithi for a few days, then head for Pearl Harbor. During the three days, some salvageable material, including bombs and airplane parts, were shipped ashore. With the help of other ships and equipment obtained from local supply depots, the *Franklin* was fast becoming sea fit again. Nearby ships also assisted in making the final pumping out of the *Franklin*. Now the *Franklin* was mechanically ready to proceed to its next port of call—Pearl Harbor.

When the *Santa Fe* arrived in Ulithi, Baumann and other survivors were transferred to a troopship that was being used as a receiving ship. The men who had already been rescued and the men brought in on the *Santa Fe* had a grand reunion, Baumann recalled.

We went from compartment to compartment, looking for our friends. When we met, we put our arms around them and kissed them. This was a very common sight, one that reflected genuine friendship.

The *Franklin's* remaining crew was transferred to the TJSS *Oneida* P.A. 233, an attack transport, which brought us back to Pearl Harbor. Here, we

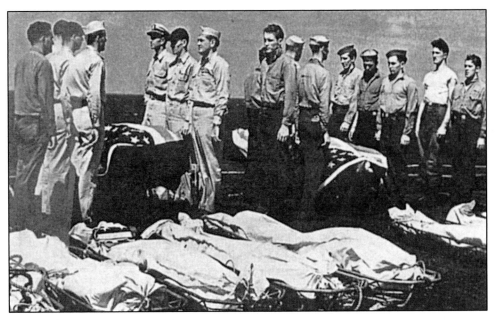

*A grim burial detail aboard the* **Franklin.**

were permitted to go aboard the *Franklin*, that had already arrived, and we were given fifteen minutes to retrieve our gear that remained aboard. I was given a sea bag to carry such gear, but when I left the ship, I gave it back. I had nothing. Our compartment had about eight inches of water in it, and everything had been burned out. Going by the hangar deck on the way out, it looked like a junkyard. Well, from that time on, 'til now, I never saw the *Franklin* again.[152]

Only one more task needed completion. Gehres recognized that he would need additional crew on the next leg of his homeward journey. But there was not enough room aboard the damaged ship. Storage space was almost non-available. The ship's latrines were few and frequently did not function. The ship was a plumber's nightmare. Fresh drinking water was scarce, and bathing facilities on board were usually a salt-water operation. The main galley was heavily damaged, and the preparation of several hundred extra meals would be extremely difficult, perhaps impossible.

Crew members for the journey home would be chosen on the basis of the skills needed aboard the *Franklin*. However, two groups were given priority for boarding.

*Capt. Gehres and Lt. jg Donald Gary examine damage on the hangar deck. Below, the* **Franklin** *under the watchful eyes of the fleet.*

*Rescued sailors from the* **Franklin** *rest aboard the* **Santa Fe.**

*Sailors on the fire-blackened Franklin cheer as the ship steams into Ulithi.*

The first group consisted of those officers and a few enlisted men who were accused by Gehres of disobeying an order not to abandon the *Franklin* during its battle for survival. Gehres planned to court-martial them once the *Franklin* had made homeport at the Brooklyn Navy Yard in New York. The second group demanding priority was the marine detachment aboard the *Franklin*. The commanding officer bluntly told Gehres that his men were coming back aboard, and he wouldn't support any attempts to charge them with desertion.

Some *Franklin* sailors still bristle when they recall Gehres' decisions in the aftermath of the tragedy. John E. Frajman (AA) (T), wrote the author with an example of the rancor caused by Gehres' behavior.

Upon arriving in Ulithi, the survivors were put aboard a U.S. Army transport bound for the United States. Before we were settled in, word was passed around that we were to be transferred to the *Franklin*. We came aboard via a Jacobs's ladder rigged to the port side of the *Franklin*. After coming aboard, we were lined up in ranks on the hangar deck. Captain Gehres welcomed us aboard by addressing us as deserters. Rufus Gentry stepped forward and requested to be transferred to another ship if he was going to be branded as a deserter. I do believe if the captain had known all the facts of our abandoning ship that his choice of words would have been different. I'm sure that Rufus bore this stigma to his grave. In my judgment, he should have been decorated for heroism instead of being branded a deserter. One of the purposes of this letter is to pay tribute to Rufus Gentry, a hero, and a great shipmate and to clarify that my shipmates who abandoned the Franklin on March 19, 1945 were not deserters.

Although Captain Gehres agreed to Rufus Gentry's request, Gentry never transferred. He remained aboard for the *Franklin*'s return to the United States. Gentry had a reputation aboard the *Franklin* as a mentor of younger crew members. He said that regardless of his experiences on the *Franklin*, it still was his favorite ship to have served on. He achieved the rank of chief bosun's mate, and retired in Portland, Oregon, after twenty years' service.

The *Franklin* took aboard four hundred and eight additional men for a total of seven hundred and four. This number was just about the maximum the *Franklin* could accommodate. Because of extensive damage, the sleeping quarters were cramped and the kitchen and galley space were limited.

The *Franklin*'s crew now had a day off. For many crew members, this allowed them a free day of rest and recreation on the tiny island of Mog Mog, located in the Ulithi Lagoon. Mog Mog was a sixty-acre recreational island where men could rest and relax by swimming, playing baseball and basketball, drinking beer for the enlisted men and liquor for the officers in their segregated lounges.

On Wednesday, March 28, 1945, it was time for the *Franklin* to weigh anchor and continue its homeward journey to Pearl Harbor and beyond. The *Franklin* slipped quietly and slowly out of Ulithi Lagoon, passing Point Able at about 6:30 p.m. heading eastward toward its next destination, Pearl Harbor.

During the relatively quiet evening of March 28, Gehres read three more messages praising the crew of the *Franklin*

24 March 1945
To: Captain Gehres USS *Franklin*
From: Captain Potter USS *Stephan*
Our hats off to you. The Japs can't beat the spirit you have displayed.

24 March 1945
To: Captain Gehres USS *Franklin*
From: Lt Commander Johnson USS *Miller*
Please permit me to express the unbounded admiration for all hands. From all hands on board the *Miller* for you and your gallant ship. We are proud to have been associated with her.

25 March 1945
To: Captain Gehres and all ships in Task Force 58
From: Admiral Spruance TF 58
The courage fortitude and ability of you and your crew in saving and bringing back the Franklin for future use against the enemy cannot be too highly praised.[153]

Soon after leaving Ulithi Lagoon for Pearl Harbor, the *Franklin* was cruising about twenty-four knots. Gehres kept his pledge to keep the crew busy. There was still much cleaning and disposing of enormous amounts of trash, as well as painting, to be done. Also, there were occasionally dead bodies locked in compartments that needed to be opened and the men buried. This routine would continue until the *Franklin* arrived in New York. The last burial detail took place only a few miles out to sea before entering New York harbor.[154]

When the *Franklin* arrived in Pearl Harbor on the morning of April 3, it received a heartwarming welcome. The *Franklin* could muster only about four hundred crew members who could be spared from their duties. Actually, because of the condition of the flight deck, that was about all it could safely support.

The *Franklin*, with Captain Gehres at the helm, came in on a wide swing at an above-average speed, smashing into the dock and damaging both ship and pier. A group of WAVES poised to welcome the ship with song had to run for their lives. On a second try, the *Franklin* docked without incident.[155] After the ship made fast, the WAVES burst into song. Also, several military and civilian dignitaries spoke briefly, congratulating the crew of the *Franklin* for their courage and skill in saving the *Franklin* and the lives of many shipmates. While most of the crew was still amassed on the flight deck and many visitors were remaining on the pier, Gehres made an announcement that he had received three more messages of praise.

3 April 1945
To:      Captain Gehres USS *Franklin*
From:   Vice Admiral Murray ComAirPac
   The indomitable fighting spirit and the sacrifice made by Officers and men of the Franklin saved a gallant ship under the severest conditions. Commander Air Force, Pacific Fleet extends deepest sympathy for your losses and high praise for success. Well done.

3 April 1945

To:    Captain Gehres USS *Franklin*

From:   The Commander in Chief Pacific

   Fleet Headquarters at Pearl Harbor

   May we add our congratulations to those of CINCPAC.


3 April 1945

To: Captain Gehres USS *Franklin*

From: The Captain of the HMS *Patroller* (British)

Captain to Captain, May I offer my congratulations on your superb effort in bringing her safely home.[156]


The crew was afforded a short shore leave to visit their favorite haunts, including Vic's, the Manhattan Inn, and the Kaimuki Inn. Others chose a calmer atmosphere at the Army Recreation Center. By the time the *Franklin* arrived at Pearl Harbor, most of the several hundred crew members had already arrived from Ulithi aboard a variety of transports. About seven hundred had arrived on the *Santa Fe*. These crew members were placed in a pool at several replacement locations to await further reassignment.

They asked Captain Gehres for permission to come aboard and retrieve any personal effects that they may have left behind when they had to flee the burning *Franklin*. Permission was granted and they were allowed twenty minutes to seek any items that could be located. However, most of their belongings had been lost, scattered, or thrown overboard in the cleaning process.

A number of crew members expressed disappointment over not being allowed to return to the United States aboard the *Franklin*. They felt that as crew members on the *Franklin* they had saved not only their ship, but also the lives of many shipmates. On this basis, they believed it was their right to return to New York and enjoy the recognition and celebrations that they expected would take place. Gehres claimed there was just not enough room to take them aboard the *Franklin* for the long trip back to New York. Many of *Franklin*'s crew members would languish in the replacement depots at Pearl Harbor.[157]

A nephew of Captain Gehres, Leslie Van Huben, was stationed in Hawaii, and Gehres invited him aboard the *Franklin* for a short visit. The visit was mainly a walk through what Van Huben described as damage beyond belief—the ship was in shambles. He wondered how the ship ever survived and how it would make the voyage back to New York. In examining the crew's quarters, he noted they were dingy and extremely limited in size. He wondered how seven hundred and four crew members could ever function in such cramped quarters.[158]

*Home port, seen through the wreckage of the* **Franklin** *as New York Harbor comes into view.*

After four days in port, the *Franklin* departed in the early evening of April 7. The journey from Pearl Harbor to the Panama Canal was mostly uneventful. The days were filled with the work of continuing to clean the wreckage and continue burying crew members' bodies discovered in the ship. But the conditions were relatively good, and the food was most of the time above average.

At sunset on March 27, the *Franklin* departed on its final leg of its return voyage to the United States. Once a doomed ship, it now was moving homeward at between twenty-two and twenty-four knots. During the voyage home, Gehres continued to push the crew. The burial details were still at work as other crew members cleared the ship of wreckage. The paint detail was always busy. When the *Franklin* arrived at the Panama Canal, one watch went ashore at Panama City and the other at Colon.[159]

After leaving the Panama Canal, the *Franklin*'s destroyer escort reported a German submarine contact off the coast of Florida. The contact was soon lost, and the *Franklin* proceeded unscathed north toward New York. At about the same time, on April 12, the flags on the USS *Franklin* were lowered to half-mast. The president and commander-in-chief, Franklin D. Roosevelt, had died.

Two days later, Gehres wrote to his wife, Rhoda. After commenting on the death of President Franklin Roosevelt, he opened up to Rhoda: "If you aren't in New York when I arrive there, I am going to be absolutely heartbroken. But you'll be there, I know. I couldn't have gotten the fires out, the ship underway, wreckage

**HEROIC OFFICERS BRING BATTERED CARRIER HOME**

Senior surviving officers of the U.S.S. Franklin as they appeared at press conference in New York, after their long voyage home with only a skeleton crew. Left to right: Cmdr. Joe Taylor of Danville, Ill.; Capt. Leslie E. Gehres, Coronado, Calif., and Cmdr. Henry H. Hale of Gary, Ind.

*Lt. Cmdr. Henry Hale, on right, would replace Gehres as captain of the* **Franklin.**

cleared, flooded holds pumped out and steamed thirteen thousand miles from Japan to New York and you not be there to meet me . . . You just have to be there."[160]

The letter was a rare glimpse into the soul of a man responsible for the lives and deaths of thousands. It showed a side of Gehres the crew could never see: the anguish of a skipper who had to make hard choices in a stoic manner to save his ship and crew.

On April 26, five weeks after the battle off the coast of Japan, the *Franklin* quietly slipped into New York's outer harbor and dropped anchor in Gravesend Bay. All available hands, in clean dungarees, were called to muster on the forward flight deck at quarters for entering port. They could observe an inspiring view, the New York City skyline and the Statue of Liberty. Two days later, on April 28, the *Franklin* weighed anchor, continued up the East River almost unnoticed, and docked at pier number 12 at the Brooklyn Navy Yard.

Years after the epic voyage, men still singled out Gehres as the man responsible for guiding the *Franklin* to safety.

"As I went among the boys, I began to realize the weight of the responsibility for all the lives aboard the USS *Franklin* which rested on Captain Gehres' shoulders," Father O'Callahan recalled. "His ability to evaluate all factors and then make a decision and stand by it unless other factors appeared to change the situation, his strength of character, his willingness to assume great responsibilities firmly, calmly and confidently, influenced my own behavior."

Lt. Donald A. Gary said later: "Captain Gehres was on the bridge shouting orders through a megaphone to save his ship and crew, although he had orders prepared to abandon ship. Teamwork and drills taught our fighting Captain to act and pass along orders. Teamwork and drills are what brought other ships to our rescue. Teamwork and drills saved the lives of many crew members and our ship. Teamwork and drills enabled the remainder of the crew to bring Big Ben home. And it was teamwork and drills that enabled our navy to fight a hard war to a victorious ending . . . A busy mind is a wonderful cure for most ills, and our Captain kept all hands busy."

Julius Payak, USMC, who was Captain Gehres' orderly, wrote the author that without Gehres' leadership, the ship and a large portion of its crew would have been lost. After interviewing Payak, the author invited him to a ceremony honoring Gehres. Payak, who was in ill health, sent his regrets and a heartfelt message:

"I thank Captain Gehres for saving my life."

*May 1945 awards ceremony on the Franklin.*

# VIII
# Final Assignments: Newark's Hero Comes Home

The miraculous story of the *Franklin*'s fight for survival was kept classified until May 11, 1945. Once the story hit the national and local publications and radio shows, it made instant heroes of Captain Gehres and his crew. Newark, New York, was well aware of its hometown hero. Newark, the self-anointed rose capital of the world, was busy planning its annual gala Rose Festival for June 16, 1945. Gehres was the logical choice to be grand marshal of the event.

Arthur N. Christy, a businessman and chairman of the Rose Festival Committee, was an old friend of Gehres. He invited Gehres and his wife, Rhoda, to participate in this special event. Gehres said that June 16 was a busy day for him, but that he would cancel several other commitments to be able to spend the day in Newark. It would be a homecoming, when he and Rhoda could celebrate their twenty-second wedding anniversary with Gehres' family and friends.

A busy day was planned. Gehres was scheduled to make two major speeches and be interviewed by a number of local and national news reporters at the event. This was the first chance that the news media had to hear firsthand the story of *Franklin's* ordeal. Captain Gehres held about sixty journalists and other guests spellbound as he described in gripping detail the disastrous bombing of the *Franklin*. He also told how the carrier and many men's lives were saved by the monumental efforts of a highly skilled and dedicated crew.

Gehres was asked about the war with Japan. In replying, Gehres asserted that he believed that the Japanese were a tough foe and would stop fighting and surrender only if enough of them were killed. Gehres said that it would take the United States about three more years to defeat Japan.[161]

The United States dropped the first atomic bomb on Hiroshima on Aug. 6, 1945 and followed with a second atomic bomb on Nagasaki on August 9, 1945. These bombs killed over a 115,000 Japanese, along with injuring another 150,000. Such huge losses fulfilled Gehres' prophecy that a large number of Japanese would have to be killed before they would surrender. On August 14, Japan agreed to surrender, and on September 2, Japan formally signed a surrender agreement. Captain Gehres was never required to return to another battle assignment in the Pacific.

While Gehres' presentation was primarily concerned with the tragic *Franklin* disaster and the story of its survival, it did not lack a little humor. He told interesting tales about his youthful adventures while living in Newark. It would appear that Mark Twain's Huckleberry Finn and Gehres had a number of similar adventures. Gehres wasn't bashful in reminiscing about his lack of interest in his local school agenda. Gehres did have one strong interest in his school's activities, and that was in sports, especially in baseball and basketball. It was the highly structured academic curriculum that he found dull.

In talking about bygone days, Gehres recalled the times when he returned to Newark and performed aerobatics over downtown Newark. However, his favorite maneuver was to fly his plane low and buzz Newark's Washington School, where his academic records languished.

Captain Gehres concluded his speech with a single strong quote by John Quincy Adams: "I live my life for my country, serving with an abundance of pride, loyalty, courage and integrity."

Later, Newark's Mayor Elzufon was able to draw Gehres aside for a final bit of conversation. Elzufon said later that Gehres was easy to talk to. Elzufon said it was a conversation he never forgot.

*President Truman awards the Medal of Honor to Commander Joseph T. O'Callahan and Lt. Commander Donald A. Gary, January 1946.*

Captain Gehres and Rhoda spent the next several days visiting with relatives and friends in Newark and the surrounding area. They also visited Newark's North Main Street cemetery where Gehres' father, mother, and brother are buried.

Gehres proposed organizing a club known as the "Big Ben 704 Club." The club would present each member with a signed card of membership, in hope that in the days of peace that would follow, the club members would be able to meet again on a regular basis in paths that would be in happier times. It never succeeded for lack of crew members interest and support. The idea spurred resentment among crew members who had been refused permission in Ulithi or Pearl Harbor to re-board the *Franklin*.

## *After the Fire*

There was one piece of unfinished business for Gehres. Shortly after arriving at the Brooklyn Navy Yard, he had initiated court martial proceedings against crew members charged with abandoning the *Franklin*.

He felt that a small number of *Franklin's* officers and crew had knowingly abandoned their assigned positions during the March 19th attack on the *Franklin* without any official abandon-ship order being issued.

There were many reasons why they had left the ship. Communications aboard the *Franklin* were chaotic during the attack and fires. Crew members frequently had no option but to jump overboard when dangerous fires and explosions were closing in on them. In some situations, crew members were blown overboard. Most of the crew members who voluntarily abandoned the *Franklin* sincerely believed that an order to abandon ship had been issued and simply fled to the *Santa Fe* or other rescue ships that were standing by.

The defense, team headed by Lt. Cmdr. Samuel Wolf and Lt. (jg) Randall Creel, spread the rumor that if the lower ranks were to be court-martialed for leaving the *Franklin*, so would brass hats such as Admiral Davison. The potential embarrassment led the Navy to convince Gehres to drop the charges.

The Navy stipulated that both Captain Gehres and Lt. Commander (Chaplain) Joseph T. O'Callahan were to receive the Medal of Honor at the same time, on January 23, 1946. Unfortunately, the U.S. Navy Decorations Committee withdrew support for his award. O'Callahan said that if Gehres could not be awarded the medal, then he would not accept it either. The Navy then offered O'Callahan the Navy Cross instead of the Medal of Honor. O'Callahan refused, for the same reason.

Captain Gehres went before the Decorations Board and withdrew any further attempt to receive the Medal of Honor. He said that he was only doing his duty as the captain of *the Franklin*, and his job was to save his ship and the lives of as many crew members as possible. Lt. Commander O'Callahan was then awarded the Medal of Honor.

## U.S. Naval Air Station, San Diego

In July 1945, Captain Gehres received a new assignment as the commanding officer of the U.S. Naval Air Station, San Diego, California. This was a significant post. The final and formal surrender of Japan did not take place until September 2, 1945. But after World War II, the Russians continued to maintain a large naval fleet and several army divisions in the upper Pacific area. Both China and Russia advocated the expansion of the Communist doctrine throughout the western Pacific. These factors weighed heavily in recognizing the need for the United States to continue a strong naval presence in the Pacific.

The U.S. Naval Air Station, San Diego, had a storied history. In 1911, Glenn Curtiss conducted the first successful seaplane flight by the U.S. Navy from the base. Curtiss had experimented with and had flown water-based aircraft earlier from his aircraft and engine manufacturing plant located on Keuka Lake in Hammondsport, New York. However, to obtain U.S. Navy approval and funding for his aircraft operations, Curtiss had to provide satisfactory seaplane flights meeting U.S. Navy specifications at an approved naval location, such as the North Island base. This was the same Glenn Curtiss who had befriended Gehres years ago.

In 1914, Glenn Martin, then an unknown aircraft builder and pilot who would later build an aircraft company bearing his name, demonstrated at North Island a pusher type of aircraft. During the flight, a ninety-pound civilian woman named Georgia "Tiny" Broadwick made the first successful parachute jump in the San Diego area. Martin had to select a lightweight person for the jump beccause the plane could not have accommodated anyone heavier. The first midair refueling operation also took place at the base.

Shortly before the air station was commissioned, Glenn Curtiss, as a certified U.S. Navy pilot, also trained the first group of Japanese aviators at his North Island flying school. Among his Japanese students was a young lieutenant, Isoruku Yamamoto, who would later become the renowned head of the Japanese Naval aviation operations during World War II.

In 1923, the base sponsored the first transcontinental flight across the United States. In 1927, Charles A. Lindbergh took off from the base for New York and onward to Paris. Lindbergh's plane, *The Spirit of St. Louis*, was built in San Diego.

***North Island in 1935, with the Langley at lower right.***

In the early 1920s, the coal collier *Jupiter* was converted to an aircraft carrier and renamed the USS *Langley*, becoming the first official aircraft carrier in the U.S. Navy. In 1924, the *Langley* was posted to the base. That began a continuous use of the North Island location as the home port of the Pacific Fleet carriers, along with providing support services and training for the carrier fleet personnel.

By 1935, North Island was home to all U.S. Navy's carriers, the USS *Langley*, USS *Lexington,* USS *Saratoga,* USS *Ranger,* USS *Enterprise,* and the USS *Yorktown*.

Gehres had served aboard each of these carriers, beginning from the time of his duties as a fledgling fighter pilot aboard the *Langley* and on to his service as chief of staff aboard the *Yorktown*, when the Navy based them at North Island.

The base played a vital role in successfully maintaining the Pacific aircraft carrier fleet during World War II. At one time during World War II, it supported eighteen large aircraft carriers as well as a number of smaller carriers. It also supported foreign aircraft carriers in an emergency.

During World War II and thereafter, North Island and South Island's naval facilities comprised the major continental U.S. bases supporting the U.S. military and naval operations in the Pacific. In addition to the carrier fleet, this massive military complex supported the U.S. Coast Guard, Army, Marines, and Seabees.

*Al Slotnick*

The nearby city of Coronado, located on South Island, became home for thousands of U.S. Navy factory workers and their families.

## *Franklin—A Haunted Ship?*

After the war, the *Franklin* remained assigned at the Brooklyn Navy Yard until February 17, 1947, when it was decommissioned and mothballed at Bayonne, New Jersey.

At the Bayonne location, it was still necessary for the U.S. Navy to provide security and maintenance for its mothballed fleet. Helping to provide this necessary security was a young 19-year-old sailor named Al Slotnick. Sixty years later, he related some unusual experiences that he had while serving aboard the *Franklin*.

It seemed that the *Franklin* was a haunted ship. For example, while on duty on a dark, lonely night he received an emergency call from the hangar deck. To the best of his knowledge, no living person should have been at that location. Once Slotnick was on the hangar deck, he heard voices from people down below. They were laughing, as though a party was taking place. It sounded like they were playing cards.

"Looking up I saw a Marine with a .45-caliber weapon shooting at another person on a yardarm who was waving to him," he said. "Upon investigating the scene, there was no one there. Also, I heard moaning from the stored rafts, called camels in the navy."

To Slotnick, the voices seemed to be real. Again, in probing the source, the rafts were empty. Slotnick and his navy buddies experienced a number of similar incidents. For a young man doing duty on dark, lonely nights, such occurrences were scary. Some civilian maintenance workers would refuse to work at night because of the fear of being confronted with these mystical encounters.[162]

*Vice-admiral Fitch awards Captain Gehres the Navy Cross, May 1945.*

On October 1, 1952, the *Franklin* was recommissioned for active duty as an attack aircraft carrier. It is not known if any subsequent crews heard the mysterious voices.

## Journey's End

The *Franklin* never made it back to the war. After its renovation, the *Franklin* was as good as or better than any other carrier on active duty. But with the war winding down, the ship did not have an active schedule. Captain Gehres was no longer the commanding officer and captain of the *Franklin*. Commander Henry H. Hale, the former air officer, was selected to replace Gehres. After the war, the *Franklin* was opened to the public for Navy Day celebrations. On August 8, 1953, it was designated an antisubmarine warfare carrier. On May 15, 1959, the *Franklin* was again designated as an aircraft transport. On October 1, 1964, the *Franklin* was struck from the U.S. Navy register.

In 1966, the *Franklin* was removed from the mothball fleet and sold to the Peck Iron and Metal Co., of Portsmouth, Virginia. The ship had cost over $66 million to build and was sold for $228,000. However, the U.S. Navy soon repossessed her due to an urgent need for the use of her four turbo generators in another newly constructed aircraft carrier. Ultimately, the *Franklin* was again sold for scrap to the Portsmouth Salvage Co. on July 27, 1966.

On the evening of August 1, 1966, the *Franklin* departed U.S. Naval custody, towed by the Red Star Towing Co. to Portsmouth Salvage's scrap yard where it was finally torn apart and, ironically, its steel sold to Japan.[163]

Before the *Franklin* was totally dismantled, NBC made a documentary of the ship's heroic battle for survival. The documentary is titled *The Ship That Wouldn't Die: USS Ben Franklin*. Gehres played a significant role in the film. Gene Kelly, who narrated the film, invited a small group of former *Franklin* officers and enlisted men to the salvage yard to witness and take part in the documentary. Several of the former crew members wept at the sight of the dismantling of the *Franklin*. It had been their home, where they had shared many interesting shipboard experiences. For years, the crew had worked and fought together for a common cause. As they walked the deck of the *Franklin* for the last time, many of the former crewmen recalled their longest day: March 19, 1945.[164]

## *Naval Officer Procurement Office*

Captain Gehres' final tour of duty was his assignment as the director of the Naval Officer Procurement Office, Los Angeles. This assignment required either an admiral or a high-ranking captain as director.

After only nine months of duty, Rear Admiral Gehres retired from the U.S. Navy and entered a new and untested lifestyle as a civilian. Upon retirement, Gehres and his family lived in Coronado, California. Later, they moved to more familiar surroundings in La Mesa, near San Diego, where he lived for the remainder of his life.

# IX
# A Civilian Career of Service:
# 1949-1973

*"What is the use of living, if it be not to strive for noble causes and to make this muddled world a better place for those who will live in it after we are gone?"*
***Winston Churchill***

Shortly after his retirement in 1949, Gehres entered local politics. By 1962, he had become San Diego's leading Republican and was elected chairman of San Diego County's Republican Central Committee. [192]

He approached politics with the same enthusiasm and rigor that he had embraced the navy. Republican Congressman Bob Wilson said about Gehres, "I kicked him early out of the Navy into politics. I ran Gehres' campaign for Congress in 1950, and he lost. In 1952, he ran my campaign and I won."[193]

Pete Wilson, a former governor of California and a protégé of Gehres, offered an anecdote about Gehres' gallantry and old-fashioned sense of honor. He wrote:

> I was walking behind him as we left the Cow Palace at the end of a session of the Republican National Convention in 1964. About two steps ahead of him, a teenage girl was enthusiastically marching along carrying a campaign placard. Suddenly a scruffy, unshaven man in his mid-thirties stood scowling in her path, knocked the placard from her hands, and he thrust his face into hers, shouting an obscenity at her. Les was then in his late sixties, wearing glasses and a stylish straw fedora. But he was a big man, burly and powerfully built. In two lightning fast strides, he was suddenly between the young girl and the shouting man, had pinned the man's arms against his sides, lifted him and slammed him down on the hood of the nearest parked car.

"I ought to break your neck, you gutless thug!—"

The gutless thug was not only gutless, but speechless and plainly scared witless, as he stared up at Les, unable to move. Neither he nor I were in any doubt that the strong, very angry man holding him pinned to the car hood could in fact break his neck if he decided to. His eyes grew round with fear the next instant when Les picked him up, grabbed him by the scruff of his neck and the seat of his pants and yelled at him, "Now get the hell out of here before I change my mind and do it!"

With that, Les gave the thug a mighty shove that sent him flying. He just managed to keep his feet. When he was about fifteen feet away, he turned, red-faced and scowling, and yelled, "You old bastard!" Les took a quick step in his direction and the coward turned and ran like a rabbit . . . It was not the last time I would see that same instinct in Les, the proper action in almost instant response to a threat to a person or cause he cared about. . . [193]

Gehres turned out to be a sound, shrewd politician. Wilson said the San Diego Republican organization was built around Gehres' ideas and personality. Representative Sinclair "Clair" Burgener (R-Rancho Santa Fe), described Gehres as a "truly great American patriot . . . In any association I had with him, I always came away with a greater love of my country . . . I was proud to be his friend."[194]

Eleanor Ring of Coronado, a member of the Republican Central Committee and also a former national committeewoman, said that Gehres' work in opening the GOP to the young was among his greatest accomplishments.[195]

California has continued its growth of the Young Republican movement. California's success with this program has motivated other states to follow suit. Today, in most states, there are many Young Republican clubs. [196]

Gehres led local Republican campaigns for President Eisenhower, President Nixon, Governor Ronald Reagan, Senator William Knowland, and Senator George Murphy. He also fostered Republican candidates at the local level.

## Community Service

In 1950, Gehres became the executive vice president of the Constitutional Foundation Inc. of San Diego. This was an organization dedicated to rebuilding faith and devotion to the principles of loyalty to the United States and supporting Americanism and patriotism.

Gehres made many speeches throughout the United States, including his home territory of upstate New York, during an era in which the Communism was seen by many as a major threat to American values and capitalism. The Freedoms

Foundation of Valley Forge awarded him seven George Washington Honor Medals for his work. [197]

He also published opinion pieces in many national and local newspapers, including his hometown newspapers, the *Newark Courier Gazette* and the nearby *Rochester Democrat and Chronicle* and the *Geneva Times*.

Rear Admiral Gehres was active, held office, and participated regularly in a number of local community service organizations including the American Legion, the Legion of Honor, the Military Order of Wars, the San Diego YMCA, the Boy Scouts of America, the Hearing Aids Society, and the National Conference of Christians and Jews.

Gehres was the past president of the San Diego Kiwanis Club and the Junior Achievement organization of San Diego. He was active in the local Rotary Club, the San Diego Chamber of Commerce, and the Governing Board of the National California Maritime Academy.

## Business Associations

In 1954, Gehres took a position as the manager of personnel and security for the Ryan Aeronautical Co. He stayed with that organization until 1961, when he met financier C. Arnholt Smith, who headed the Westgate-California Corp., a large consortium of local and regional businesses. In late 1961, Smith appointed Gehres general manager of the National Marine Terminal Co. Gehres also ran Smith's local tuna fishing and tugboat companies.

When Gehres was the head of the tugboat company, he annually made his tugboat fleet available to children of San Diego for a free half-day's excursion around the city's bay. He provided a tour guide for each boat and a free picnic lunch. During this time, Gehres was sent to San Francisco to reorganize Smith's newly acquired Yellow Taxi Company. In late 1963, Gehres was named industrial relations director and later became the vice president of Smith's primary company, the Westgate-California Corp. Gehres entered into his second retirement in 1973.[197]

Rear Admiral Gehres continued to be active in his community organizations. However, in 1975, at the age of seventy-six, Gehres had a fall and was hospitalized. During a routine physical examination, doctors discovered he had cancer, from which he never recovered.

***Descendants of Gehres. Daughter Leslie is on the second row, far left.***

Leslie E. Gehres' life's journey ended when he died in the Balboa U.S. Naval Hospital on May 15, 1975. Rear Admiral Gehres was given a full naval funeral service, with burial in the Glen Abbey Memorial Park.

At his funeral and in the newspapers, people from all walks of life spoke and wrote of the many contributions this outstanding citizen had made to his country and to them. One such article appeared in the *Rochester Democrat and Chronicle* on May 21, 1945. The article was written by Patricia MacGregor, a niece of Rear Admiral Gehres. In the highlights of the article, she said:

> After his retirement from the U.S. Navy, he turned to business, in which he made a successful career in California. He was very active in the Freedoms Foundation and campaigned for President Eisenhower and Governor Ronald Reagan.
>
> I am very proud of his service to this country and know that his God has now taken him home. He was all those 'square' things—loyal, honest, true, faithful, hard-working and made his way up the ladder on his own.
>
> I believe that the Stars and Stripes will fly a little higher and brighter this Memorial Day, especially in the eyes of his family and God.[198]

Rear Admiral Gehres was survived by his daughter, Leslie G. Girard; a stepdaughter, Mrs. Rhoda Wells, and stepson, retired U.S. Navy Captain Dexter C. Rumsey, and eight grandchildren.

# USS Franklin—Its Legacy

The dictionary definition of legacy is simple: ". . . anything that is handed down—something that comes from the past." Other more specific explanations complement the formal definition by noting that something of value needs to be included. The term *value* has many meanings, including the principle or ideal of intrinsic worth or actions that are human rather than material. Value can imply the worth of those qualities of mind, character and moral excellence.

War creates several outstanding sources of legacy in leadership, where an individual's example inspires generations of fighting men and women. Army Generals Douglas MacArthur and George Patton, Navy hero Admiral George Dewey, and Marine air ace Lt. Commander Gregory Boyington are in this category. There are many others.

In the U.S. Navy there is also a legacy of vessels, such as that of the USS *Constitution*, "Old Ironsides." However, one ship in the U.S. Navy history has a legacy that will never die. The aircraft carrier *Franklin*. The *Franklin* left a legacy of success in battle. Its crew became the most decorated fighting unit in the history of the U.S. Navy.

A new generation of fighting men have come to honor the *Franklin*'s legacy. One young sailor, Kristopher Mitchell, when home on leave from frigate duty, said the tale of the *Franklin* was passed along by senior petty officers. It is the author's hope that others will draw strength from the legacy of the *Franklin* and the brave sailors who manned her.

The story of the *Franklin*'s battle for survival is a significant legacy of U.S. Navy history that is still alive today. It is a remarkable story that continues to serve as a model of dedication, leadership, skill, heroism, and survival.

Years after the critical events of March 19, 1945, Rear Admiral Gehres was approached by his grandson, Peter. The young man asked his grandfather why he chose to stay with the *Franklin* instead of abandoning ship.

He turned his face away and thought about it, Peter Gehres Girard recalled, then turned and spoke softly. He was terribly haunted by the thought that if he had abandoned the ship, he would have been abandoning men who could not escape.

# Epilogue

Rear Admiral Leslie E. Gehres' is a tale of one man's ability to rise above his humble beginnings through perseverance, honest effort, courage and outstanding leadership. His accomplishments were many, but he has yet to receive his due.

Rear Admiral Gehres' most significant contribution to his country was his thirty-two years of noteworthy U.S. Navy service. Gehres was a big man both in size and character. He complied with his superior officers' orders and expected the same from subordinates. To officers and enlisted men under his command, Gehres appeared to be a harsh and severe taskmaster. However, he possessed a sensitivity of responsibility and concern for the well-being of his men. Gehres' style of leadership produced well-run and highly prepared commands, but it also generated resentment.

Rear Admiral Gehres' route to success in the U.S. Navy was not without its obstacles as he progressed from the lowest enlisted rank to rear admiral. He was able to rise above the old-boy network of Annapolis graduates to become the first enlistee to command a U.S. Navy aircraft carrier. His naval career was a commendable and rewarding journey that should be an inspiration for others of all ranks.

Ironically, although many considered Gehres unbending and conservative, his career paralleled the most dramatic changes in naval doctrine since the introduction of iron ships and steam power. That he remained at the forefront of the revolution in naval aviation speaks to his flexibility and willingness to embrace new ideas.

He embraced naval aviation early and matured as that powerful wing of our armed forces grew. Gehres came of age at the birth of naval aviation, when he, like John Towers, visited the Glenn H. Curtiss Aircraft and Engine Co. factory in Hammondsport, New York. And Gehres was there at the height of naval air power in World War II when a mighty fleet of carriers took the Pacific War to the home waters of Japan.

Gehres entered U.S. Navy flight training in January 1927 and graduated as a fighter pilot in September 1927. Gehres was assigned to the first American aircraft carrier, the USS *Langley* where he served at the flight officer of Fighting Squadron One. He also served aboard the USS *Lexington* and the USS *Saratoga* as executive officer of Fighting Squadrons Five and Six, respectively. During Gehres' early career he founded and led the Nine High Hats stunt team, the U.S. Navy's first aerobatic stunt team, created at a time when military and naval aviation advocates depended on aerial exhibitions to gain support from the public and Congress.

Gehres trained the best and brightest of the young pilots, many of whom grew to become leaders in navy aviation during and after World War II.

As commander of Fleet Air Wing Four in the Aleutians, Gehres transformed his reconnaissance mission into one of offense. He expanded the defensive and reconnaissance capabilities of his Venturas and PBYs to include offensive operations, solving the problem of long-range bombing in treacherous weather that had frustrated the Army Air Force.

Yet he eased the difficult inter-service relations by working closely with his counterparts in the Army. His pioneering work in both weather forecasting and the weatherization of the airplanes in his command helped maximize the fighting efficiency of his forces.

Vice Admiral Frank J. Fletcher acknowledged Gehres' unheralded role by commenting, "When the history of this war is written, I am confident that [Gehres] will be credited more than any other officer with the defeat of the Japanese . . . "

Gehres' final sea command was as the captain of the powerful *Essex*-class aircraft carrier USS *Franklin*, CV-13, with a crew of more than thirty-four hundred officers and enlisted men. Early in the morning of March 19, 1945, the *Franklin* was severely attacked and damaged by the Japanese. With the ship in danger of sinking, Captain Gehres and his dedicated and skillful crew saved the *Franklin* and many lives that would have been lost if the ship had been abandoned.

The *Franklin* was named "The Ship That Wouldn't Die" after its thirteen-thousand-five hundred-mile journey home to the Brooklyn Naval Yard for repairs. The crew of the *Franklin* became the most decorated crew for a one-day battle in the history of the U.S. Navy. The story of the *Franklin's* survival is a part of American naval lore and a reflection of the indomitable spirit of Leslie Gehres. He did not give up the ship.

In May 1949, after thirty-two years of dedicated U.S. Navy service, Rear Admiral Gehres retired. Gehres, who never forgot a lesson and learned from every endeavor, fought as a politician to defend the freedoms many take for granted. Gehres became an active member of the Republican Party in southern California, organizing campaigns for both local and national politicians. He also joined the Freedoms Foundation of Valley Forge, , which is dedicated to the furtherance of American principles of patriotism and citizenship

On September 28, 2002, almost a year to the day after the 9/11 tragedy, a memorial exhibit honoring Rear Admiral Leslie E. Gehres was dedicated. The memorial was organized by the author and his wife, Eleanor. It contains memorabilia from Gehres' years of service, a replica of the *Franklin*, and other artifacts that illustrate Gehres' career. It includes Gehres' dress uniform, a portion of the *Franklin*'s deck planking, ship citations, and other items of historical significance. The display is housed in Gehres' hometown at the Newark, New York, High School.

During the dedication ceremonies, a host of dignitaries paid tribute to Gehres. They included New York Governor George Pataki, who spoke by phone, Congressman James Walsh, Newark Mayor Fred Pirelli, State Senator Mike Nozzolio, and others. Ten members of Gehres' family attended the dedication.

*Newark Central School District Superintendent Matt Cook, who was instrumental in restoring the Gehres memorial, joins Stewart's descendants Will Snyder, Grace Murphy, and Jamie Murphy as they present mementoes to the memorial.*

Gehres, who never went beyond the eighth grade, was awarded an honorary high school diploma by Newark High School Principal Tom Miller. Rene Gauthier, a survivor of the *Franklin*, drew a standing ovation when he spoke. Roosevelt Wright, a Syracuse University professor and Navy captain, told the moving story of how his father helped build the *Franklin* and mourned its tragic fate. The museum, like this book, represents a permanent effort to honor Gehres.

There are many routes to leadership. Family ties, wealth, and influence often ease such journeys. Gehres' road was much rockier. He had little money or influence; he rose through sheer tenacity and intelligence. So the life of Rear Admiral Gehres is an American story, a fulfillment of America's promise that anyone with the will to work hard can succeed. Gehres succeeded, and in doing so he made America stronger. He merits the thanks and acknowledgement of the nation.

# Acknowledgments

During the several years that it took to write this biography, I received considerable valuable assistance, input and encouragement from many sources. I give my sincere thanks to each of these sources. Unfortunately, there are some contributors that I may have overlooked. To each such individual or organization, I wish to extend a genuine apology.

First, I want to recognize and thank my wonderful wife, Eleanor M. Stewart, for her support and encouragement, which has inspired me to complete this book in a proper manner. She has also frequently offered perceptive suggestions and has been a diligent proofreader. I thank my editor and publisher, James M. Abraham for his wise, compassionate, and challenging expertise in helping to make this a better book in each phase of its writing.

I am especially indebted to Rene Gauthier for his many involvements and contributions to this biography and to the Rear Admiral Gehres Memorial Exhibit. Also, I want to thank Robert St. Peters, president of the USS Franklin CV-13 Association, Inc. for his support and contributions to the Rear Admiral Leslie E. Gehres Memorial Exhibit and his helpful suggestions in writing the Gehres biography.

Rear Admiral Gehres was Newark's hometown hero. My father and mother, along with a number of older Newark residents, knew Gehres as schoolmates and friends. I was also acquainted with a number of his relatives living in Newark and its surrounding areas, including Bernice Van Huben, Gehres' sister, and her family. Gehres' uncles Elliot and Erwine Thomas were neighbors of my parents. My grandmother, Kate Merson, was a good friend of Gehres' mother, Phebe Thomas Gehres.

I was also fortunate in obtaining many interesting insights into Gehres' life from his daughter, Mrs. Leslie Girard and her sons Leslie and Peter Girard.

The following individuals and organizations were instrumental in helping create the Rear Admiral Leslie Edward Gehres exhibit in Newark, New York.

Robert V. Christmann, former superintendent, Newark Central School District, who helped organize the 2002 tribute to Admiral Gehres and helped launch the memorial exhibit; former Mayor Peter M. Blandino; Fred J. Pirelli; John Strait,

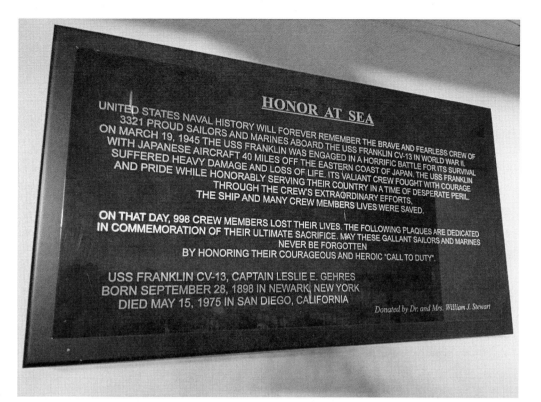

**HONOR AT SEA**

UNITED STATES NAVAL HISTORY WILL FOREVER REMEMBER THE BRAVE AND FEARLESS CREW OF 3321 PROUD SAILORS AND MARINES ABOARD THE USS FRANKLIN CV-13 IN WORLD WAR II. ON MARCH 19, 1945 THE USS FRANKLIN WAS ENGAGED IN A HORRIFIC BATTLE FOR ITS SURVIVAL WITH JAPANESE AIRCRAFT 40 MILES OFF THE EASTERN COAST OF JAPAN. THE USS FRANKLIN SUFFERED HEAVY DAMAGE AND LOSS OF LIFE. ITS VALIANT CREW FOUGHT WITH COURAGE AND PRIDE WHILE HONORABLY SERVING THEIR COUNTRY IN A TIME OF DESPERATE PERIL. THROUGH THE CREW'S EXTRAORDINARY EFFORTS, THE SHIP AND MANY CREW MEMBERS LIVES WERE SAVED.

ON THAT DAY, 998 CREW MEMBERS LOST THEIR LIVES. THE FOLLOWING PLAQUES ARE DEDICATED IN COMMEMORATION OF THEIR ULTIMATE SACRIFICE. MAY THESE GALLANT SAILORS AND MARINES NEVER BE FORGOTTEN BY HONORING THEIR COURAGEOUS AND HEROIC "CALL TO DUTY".

USS FRANKLIN CV-13, CAPTAIN LESLIE E. GEHRES BORN SEPTEMBER 28, 1898 IN NEWARK, NEW YORK DIED MAY 15, 1975 IN SAN DIEGO, CALIFORNIA

*Donated by Dr. and Mrs. William J. Stewart*

former president of the Newark Central School District Board of Education; and *The Newark Courier-Gazette*.

Also: Brenda Pittman, Newark Central School District, public relations, who wrote several articles on the exhibit; Superintendent Matthew Cook of the Newark Central School District; Thomas Roote, Newark High School principal; Stacy Schultz, assistant to Superintendent Cook, who worked with the exhibit since its inception; Jackie Miller, Newark High School library media specialist; Bob Adams, display case designer and builder.

Diane Allerton, Arcadia town clerk, who contributed Admiral Gehres' birth certificate; Marshall Bowes, who shared research information, including Admiral Gehres cartoons; Mark Braunlich, who provided considerable information and pictures of Lt. Gehres' participation in the Nine High Hats stunt team's performance at the Cleveland Air Races in 1929. These photos are from Braunlich's private source and were made by a friend of his great aunt.

The Glenn H. Curtiss Museum, Hammondsport, NY, which was instrumental in gathering material about John H. Towers; The Carter House, Franklin TN, a museum dedicated to the relics and history of the Battle of Franklin and its association with the *Franklin*.

James Crider, past commander of American Legion Post 113, Rotonda West, FL, who furnished sailor-oriented poems; Else Quirk Public Library, Englewood, FL and its research information and web site input.

Emil Buehler, Navy Aviation Library, National Museum of Naval History, Pensacola, FL; H. MacDonald, librarian, who assisted with background information and tapes relating to the *Franklin* and Gehres. Robert Hoeltzel, Newark-Arcadia historian; Cecillia E. Jackson, Arcadia historian; Rev Timothy Johnson, Presbyterian minister, who presented a sermon on Dr. William J. Stewart's biographical work on Gehres.

Lt. Cmdr. R.H. Maynard, who served with Commodore Gehres in the Aleutian Islands; Donald Moore, newspaper reporter, *The Sun*, Port Charlotte, FL, who assisted in locating Franklin survivors; Martifacts, Inc., Jacksonville. FL, which provided museum materials for the Rear. Admiral Gehres Memorial Exhibit.

Newark-Arcadia Historical Society, which provided pictures of early Newark, NY and other information courtesy of John Zornow; David and John Murphy of Newark Granite, who procured the granite monument for the Rear Admiral Leslie E- Gehres Memorial Exhibit

Newark Public Library, which offered related research material and web site assistance; Nick and Janette Nickson, who gave background information relating

to the Rochester, New York area; Ontario County Records and Archives Center of Hopewell, NY, which provided early background information on Ontario County and Newark-Arcadia; Patriots Point Naval and Maritime Museum, which gave museum objects for the Rear Admiral Leslie E. Gehres Memorial Exhibit, courtesy of E.L. Wimett.

Gene Procasky, research; Allan Slotnick, for several original objects from the *Franklin* that are located in the Rear Admiral Leslie E. Gehres Memorial Exhibit;

Ron Reeves, who provided related letter facades of U.S. Navy aircraft carriers; Sodus Bay Historical Society, Sodus Point, NY, which provided pictures of early Sodus Point, NY courtesy of Eugene E. Seymour.

Suncoast Engraving, Venice, FL, which designed and constructed permanent wall plaques for the Gehres exhibit; Mrs. Jackson Toon, who provided a letter and information relating to her husband, Jackson Toon, a crewmember aboard the Franklin.

Margaret Turcotte, Gehres' niece, who provided background information relating to Rear Admiral Gehres; John and Kim Walker, who furnished background information on the relationship of the Franklin with Franklin, TN; William and Louise Walker, who gave information about Franklin, TN and the Franklin, initiated meaningful contacts with interested local individuals and organizations, and furnished relevant information pertaining to Jackson Toon and James Harper.

Wayne County Historian's Office, Lyons, NY, which gave background information relating to Peter Gehres, Admiral Gehres' grandfather; Williamson County Museum, Franklin, TN, which provided background information on Jackson Toon and the Battle of Franklin; Michelle Vair, who designed the Gehres exhibit located in the Newark, NY High School; and David Morgan and Andrew (AJ) Morgenthal, research assistance.

Through the dedication of Newark School District Superintendent Matthew Cook, the Gehres exhibit created in 2002 was updated in 2016. Superintendent Cook moved the display from the lobby of the high school to the library. He oversaw the creation of bright, well-lit display cabinets and arranged to have the exhibit curated and maintained by the school district.

Under his dynamic leadership, the display is now located in a central area of the high school, where students and guests can appreciate the life and times of Rear Admiral Leslie Gehres.

Recently several of Dr. Stewart's descendants honored the school board of Newark with new additions to the display. Grace Murphy, Jamie Murphy, and William Snyder presented Gehres' Navy Cross, Victory Medal, and a photograph of the admiral receiving the Navy Cross, the Navy's highest award, from Admiral Aubrey Fitch. Also in 1916, the family awarded an annual scholarship endowed by Dr. Stewart to the winning student who wrote an essay on patriotism in today's society.

The legacy of the *Franklin* and Admiral Gehres is being preserved for posterity.

# Appendix

A number of relevant documents, because of their length, could not be placed in their entirety in the narrative portion of this book. Care has been taken to reproduce photographic copies of many of these documents so as to ensure their authenticity. The following documents are included:

Awards given to personnel aboard the U.S.S. Franklin for action on March 19, 1945

Excerpt of the "Deck Log - Remarks Sheet" of the *Franklin* for Monday, March 19, 1945.

Letter from E. Robert Wassman

Letter from Robert Bartlett

Letter from Rene Gauthier

Letter from Edward J. Harkin

Oral History: Attacks on Japan. By Lt. Commander Samuel Robert Sherman, MC, USNR, Flight Surgeon, USS *Franklin*.

Oral History: As I Saw It. By Lt. (jg) George K. Leitch, USMR, USS *Franklin*.

Service record, Rear Admiral Leslie Gehres.

Particle Memorandum: Statement and Log Entries—USS *Hickok* D 673. Furnished by John L. Wisse, SM2c, USS *Hickok*.

Oral History: Rear Admiral Leslie E. Gehres, by former California Governor Pete Wilson.

Announcement: September 28, 2002: Leslie Gehres Day, Furnished by *Newark, (N.Y.) Courier-Gazette*, 2 September 2002 Memorial Tribute to Rear Admiral Leslie E. Gehres Ceremony, 28 September 2002.

Ceremony program: Furnished by Newark, N.Y., Central Public School District.

Speech by Captain Gavin D. Lowder, USN Retired, ROTC University of Rochester, Rochester, N.Y.

Statement by New York State Governor, George Pataki, 28 September 2002.

Statement from Gordon R. England, Secretary of the Navy, 16 September 2002.

Letter from Edwin C. Bearss, Chief Historian Emeritus, National Park Service, Washington, D.C., 9 October 2002.

Letter from Donald Rumsfeld, U.S. Secretary of Defense, 13 September 2002.

## Awards given to personnel aboard the U.S.S. *Franklin* for action on March 19, 1945

ABAGON Angel (n) CST(AA) Letter of Commendation (Ribbon)

ABBOTT Gilbert P. QM3 Silver Star Medal

ABELLON Placito CCK Bronze Star Medal

ADELSON Albert (n) WT3 Letter of Commendation (Ribbon)

AIZPURU Joe Lt.(jg) Bronze Star Medal

ALBRECHT William R. S2 Bronze Star Medal

ALBRITTON Jr. Jesse M. Lt. Bronze Star Medal

ALEMIDA Arthur S. AOM3 Bronze Star Medal

ALLEN Edward T. Pfc. Bronze Star Medal

ANDERSON Willie 'B' StM2 Letter of Commendation (Ribbon)

ANDREWS Robert Frederick EM1 Letter of Commendation (Ribbon)

ANTALL Richard Charles S1 Letter of Commendation (Ribbon)

ARTZ Harry Woods Lt. Letter of Commendation (Ribbon)

ASTORIAN Gerald E. S1 Bronze Star Medal

BAKER William Latta CMM Letter of Commendation (Ribbon)

BARNABY Donald R.E. Lt.(jg) Bronze Star Medal

BARNES Franklyn Ralph MM3 Letter of Commendation (Ribbon)

BARR John B. Lt. Bronze Star Medal

BARRY Ralph (n) WT1 Bronze Star Medal

BARTLEY Albert (n) StM2 Letter of Commendation (Ribbon)

BASHAM John Russell RM3 Letter of Commendation (Ribbon)

BERESKA Paul (n) MM1 Letter of Commendation (Ribbon)

BERGER David LCDR. Silver Star Medal

BERGIN Kyran Francis AMM2 Letter of Commendation (Ribbon)

BERGMAN Earl Allen Mus2 Letter of Commendation (Ribbon)

BILLINGTON Donald G. Lt. Letter of Commendation (Ribbon)

BIRCH George Bobby WT1 Letter of Commendation (Ribbon)

BLACKWELL Ralph (n) F2 Letter of Commendation (Ribbon)

BLANCO Jr. John Eliss BM2 Letter of Commendation (Ribbon)

BOLOPUE Herman Carl F1 Letter of Commendation (Ribbon)

BONINE Donald Leander S2 Letter of Commendation (Ribbon)

BOULTON Ulysses (n) StM2 Letter of Commendation (Ribbon)

BOWMAN Alex E. Y3 Bronze Star Medal

BOWMAN Marvin K. Lt.(jg) Bronze Star Medal

BOYCE Joseph Walton S1 Letter of Commendation (Ribbon)

BOYD Robert L. S1 Bronze Star Medal

BRENNER William Ernest WT3 Letter of Commendation (Ribbon)

BROOKS Floyd (n) StM2 Letter of Commendation (Ribbon)

BROWN Charles (n) CK1 Letter of Commendation (Ribbon)

BROWN Don Graviel StM2 Letter of Commendation (Ribbon)

BROWN John Franklin Y2(T) Bronze Star Medal (Post)

BROWN Paul W. S2 Bronze Star Medal

BROWNING William L. SM3 Bronze Star Medal

BRUMFIELD James I. WT1 Bronze Star Medal

BRUNDIGE Maurice M. Lt.(jg) Bronze Star Medal

BRUNN Wilby Francis S2 Letter of Commendation (Ribbon)

BRYANT Mathew William F2 Letter of Commendation (Ribbon)

BUJA John Michael GM3 Letter of Commendation (Ribbon)

BURKE Russell Emmett S1 Letter of Commendation (Ribbon)

BURTON Edward Arthur S2 Letter of Commendation (Ribbon)

BURTON Vernon Luke RM2 Letter of Commendation (Ribbon)

CALDWELL Charles Guy BM1 Letter of Commendation (Ribbon)

CALDWELL William Bowles EM3 Letter of Commendation (Ribbon)

CARR Charles Lt. Bronze Star Medal

CARTWRIGHT John E. GM3 Bronze Star Medal

CATT Harold Raymond S2 Letter of Commendation (Ribbon)

CESAR John Norman GM3 Letter of Commendation (Ribbon)

CHAMBERS Patrick A. WT3 Bronze Star Medal

CHARNSTROM Lloyd E. Pfc. Bronze Star Medal

CHASE Jr. Frank T. S2 Bronze Star Medal

CHASSE Richard Damasse F1 Letter of Commendation (Ribbon)

CHENEY Frank C. Lt. Bronze Star Medal

CHENEY Jr. George W. Lt. Bronze Star Medal

CHRISTMAN Frederick William S2(GM) Letter of Commendation (Ribbon)

CLINGERMAN Kermit Gene S1 Letter of Commendation (Ribbon)

CLOSE Jr. Hugh W. Lt.(jg) Bronze Star Medal

COBB James (n) StM2 Letter of Commendation (Ribbon)

CODY Charles Lewis S2 Letter of Commendation (Ribbon)

COFFIE Thomas (n) StM2 Letter of Commendation (Ribbon)

COLE Frederick Thomas F2 Letter of Commendation (Ribbon)

COLE Russell Edgar S2 Letter of Commendation (Ribbon)

COLLINS Arthur L. F1 Bronze Star Medal

COLLUM James Harold F2 Letter of Commendation (Ribbon)

CONNOLLY Robert Thomas Lt.(jg) Letter of Commendation (Ribbon)

COOK Ralph Marcello ART1 Letter of Commendation (Ribbon)

CORLISS Wayne Albert S1 Letter of Commendation (Ribbon)

COSTA Laurentino E. MM3 Silver Star Medal

COX John James RM3 Letter of Commendation (Ribbon)

CROFF Donald Eugene F1 Letter of Commendation (Ribbon)

CROWTHER Thomas Dwight GM2 Letter of Commendation (Ribbon)

CULBERSON Leonz (n) StM2 Letter of Commendation (Ribbon)

CULLEN Charles Albert S2 Letter of Commendation (Ribbon)

CURTIS Thomas Franklin MMS2 Letter of Commendation (Ribbon)

CUSICK James J. Letter of Commendation (Ribbon)

DARRINGTON Keith Olsen S1 Letter of Commendation (Ribbon)

DAVIS Lewis F. LCDR. Bronze Star Medal

DAY Robert Wayne S2 Letter of Commendation (Ribbon)

DE ROCHE Edward Thomas GM3 Letter of Commendation (Ribbon)

DEFILLIPO Michael Vincent MoMM3 Letter of Commendation (Ribbon)

DENNIS Jeff (n) StM2 Letter of Commendation (Ribbon)

DICKERSON Leslie J. StM1 Letter of Commendation (Ribbon)

DICKSON Robert C. S/Sgt. Bronze Star Medal

DODARO Louis (n) RM3 Letter of Commendation (Ribbon)

DOWELL Horace Kirby Mus1 Letter of Commendation (Ribbon)

DOWNES Robert B. LCDR. Navy Cross

DRESSELL William Richard F1 Letter of Commendation (Ribbon)

DROLSON James Hilo S1 Letter of Commendation (Ribbon)

DROUIN Leo Willie WT3 Letter of Commendation (Ribbon)

DUDIAK Peter Paul S1 Letter of Commendation (Ribbon)

DUNN Charles Rex EM2 Letter of Commendation (Ribbon)

DUNNE James Louis WT3 Letter of Commendation (Ribbon)

DURR Charles G. Lt. Bronze Star Medal

DURRANCE Benjamin Myron CSF (AA) Bronze Star Medal (Post)

DYER Joseph Arthur F1 Letter of Commendation (Ribbon)

DYICKANOWSKI Andrew (n) MM2 Letter of Commendation (Ribbon)

EDDINS Lewis R. Ch.Carpenter Gold Star in lieu of Second Bronze Star Medal

EDE Jr. George Mach. Letter of Commendation (Ribbon)

EICHNER Norman Arthur Ens. Letter of Commendation (Ribbon)

ELLIOTT Jr. Herbert T. Major Bronze Star Medal

ELLIS Leon Stanley MM1 Letter of Commendation (Ribbon)

ELLIS Thomas Ollie S2 Letter of Commendation (Ribbon)

ELLIS William S. Lt. Navy Cross

ELSEY Gordon John EM1 Letter of Commendation (Ribbon)

ENSIGN Allen Garfield Mach. Letter of Commendation (Ribbon)

FELLOWS Jr. Clyde H. Lt. Bronze Star Medal

FINKENSTEDT Charles L. SSML3 Bronze Star Medal

FINNEY Jr. Charles Fenton S1 Letter of Commendation (Ribbon)

FITZGERALD Donald J. Lt. Letter of Commendation (Ribbon)

FOWLER Alvin L. Ch.PayClerk Bronze Star Medal

FOWLER William J. AOM1 Bronze Star Medal

FOX Elmer L. Lt. Bronze Star Medal

FOX George William LCDR.(MC) Navy Cross (Post)

FRANCIS Edward (n) StM2 Letter of Commendation (Ribbon)

FRANDLE Gerald Truman F2 Letter of Commendation (Ribbon)

FRANK Robert H. Lt. Bronze Star Medal

FREEK Jr. George Marshall F2 Letter of Commendation (Ribbon)

FREGGENS Robert Alfred F1 Letter of Commendation (Ribbon)

FRIEDMAN Herman S. SF2 Bronze Star Medal

FRIEND Alon Louis S2 Letter of Commendation (Ribbon)

FRISBEE Marion Boatswain Silver Star Medal

FUELLING James J. LCDR. Navy Cross

FULLER Billie (n) BM1 Letter of Commendation (Ribbon)

FURROW John Harry F2 Letter of Commendation (Ribbon)

GARY Donald A. Lt.(jg) Medal of Honor

GASSMAN Robert Francis F1 Letter of Commendation (Ribbon)

GATALUS Joseph William GM2 Letter of Commendation (Ribbon)

GATLIN Grimes W. Lt. Silver Star Medal

GEHELNIK Dave George S2 Letter of Commendation (Ribbon)

GEHRES Leslie E. Capt. Navy Cross

GEIR Jr. Philip O. Lt. Bronze Star Medal

GIBSON Howard (n) StM2 Letter of Commendation (Ribbon)

GILES Raymond Gerald WT3 Letter of Commendation (Ribbon)

GLASBERG Irving (n) S1 Letter of Commendation (Ribbon)

GLOSSOM Sylvester (n) StM1 Letter of Commendation (Ribbon)

GOBRIGALL Calvin Frank MM3 Letter of Commendation (Ribbon)

GORDON Arnold E. CK2 Letter of Commendation (Ribbon)

GOWEN Michael (n) GM2 Bronze Star Medal

GRAHAM Stanley S. Lt.(jg) Silver Star Medal

GRANT Eugene Newton StM2 Letter of Commendation (Ribbon)

GRAVES Earl Eugene AMM2 Letter of Commendation (Ribbon)

GREEN William E. Mach. Silver Star Medal

GREENE Thomas J. LCDR. Navy Cross

GREGORY William Tency StM1 Letter of Commendation (Ribbon)

GRESHKO Stephen (n) S1 Letter of Commendation (Ribbon)

GRIER Edward A. StM2 Letter of Commendation (Ribbon)

GUBA Jr. Henry Arthur S1 Letter of Commendation (Ribbon)

GUDBRANDSEN James H. MM1 Silver Star Medal

GUGLIELMO William (n) S1 Bronze Star Medal

HALE Henry H. CDR. Navy Cross

HALE Roy G. Gunner Bronze Star Medal

HALL Fred M. Ens. Navy Cross

HALL Leonard Melford WT2 Letter of Commendation (Ribbon)

HALL Stanley David WT1 Letter of Commendation (Ribbon)

HAMEL William H. EM3 Silver Star Medal

HAMILTON George A. Ens. Bronze Star Medal

HAMM Robert Lee WT3 Letter of Commendation (Ribbon)

HAMPTON John Emmitt AOM2 Letter of Commendation (Ribbon)

HAND John Willard AMM3 Letter of Commendation (Ribbon)

HANDROP Jack Corbet S1 Letter of Commendation (Ribbon)

HANNA Isom (n) S2 Letter of Commendation (Ribbon)

HARRIS Fred Lt. Navy Cross

HARRIS James Houston F2 Letter of Commendation (Ribbon)

HARRIS James Samuel F2 Letter of Commendation (Ribbon)

HART Stephen C. SM3 Bronze Star Medal

HASSIG Gordon L. Lt.(jg) Gold Star in lieu of Second Bronze Star Medal

HATCHER Walter S. Ch.Gunner Bronze Star Medal

HAYLOR William Birch Ens. Letter of Commendation (Ribbon)

HEAD Albert Louis Mach. Letter of Commendation (Ribbon)

HEDDELL John Vincent Lt. Letter of Commendation (Ribbon)

HELZEL William K. Lt.(jg) Bronze Star Medal

HOFFNER Arthur H. Ch.Electrician Letter of Commendation (Ribbon)

HOGGE Wilton G. F1(WT) Bronze Star Medal

HOLSTROM Edward (n) MM2 Bronze Star Medal

HOPKINS Joseph P. S1 Bronze Star Medal

HOPKINS Leo Francis RM3 Letter of Commendation (Ribbon)

HOTTINGER Eugene J. S1 Bronze Star Medal

HUNTINGTON Theodore T. Lt. Bronze Star Medal

HUTTON Stanley Richard F2 Letter of Commendation (Ribbon)

HZER DeVon M. LCDR. Bronze Star Medal

JACKSON Dan (n) CK1 Letter of Commendation (Ribbon)

JACOBS Charles W. S1 Bronze Star Medal

JACOBS Harold Wilbury S1 Letter of Commendation (Ribbon)

JONES James Leonard EM3 Letter of Commendation (Ribbon)

JORTBERG Richard E. Ens. Bronze Star Medal

JURIKA Stephen CDR. Navy Cross

KALVIN John M. Ch.Torpedoman Bronze Star Medal

KASSOVER Martin Lewis SM3 Letter of Commendation (Ribbon)

KIDWELL Irving L. Y2 Bronze Star Medal

KIELISZAK Raymond John F1 Letter of Commendation (Ribbon)

KILPATRICK Mac G. LCDR. Navy Cross

KINCAIDE Robert Doane Mus2 Letter of Commendation (Ribbon)

KISSELL Lynn M. AOM2 Bronze Star Medal

KLEIBER Bernard (n) WT2 Bronze Star Medal

KLIMKIEWICZ Wallace L. Pvt. Bronze Star Medal

KNOELLER William Warren WT3 Letter of Commendation (Ribbon)

KRAUSE Leonard Robert F2 Letter of Commendation (Ribbon)

KREAMER Walter H. LCDR. Navy Cross

KUSY John Michael Prtr3 Letter of Commendation (Ribbon)

LA BLANCO Joseph (n) S2 Bronze Star Medal

LA ROLE Arthur Dorsey F1 Letter of Commendation (Ribbon)

LAKE James (n) GM3 Letter of Commendation (Ribbon)

LANGLEY John Steward S2 Letter of Commendation (Ribbon)

LARSEN Stephen Lorang S2 Letter of Commendation (Ribbon)

LAWSON David Vernon S1 Letter of Commendation (Ribbon)

LAZERSKI Richard Joseph S1 Letter of Commendation (Ribbon)

LEBLANC Harold Acting Pay Clerk Bronze Star Medal

LECUS Edward (n) MM1 Letter of Commendation (Ribbon)

LEFF Marvin Lt.(jg) Bronze Star Medal

LEIPEL Clayton Buford WT3 Letter of Commendation (Ribbon)

LEITCH George Kennedy Lt.(jg) Letter of Commendation (Ribbon)

LEPORE Frank Peter MM3 Letter of Commendation (Ribbon)

LIGHTFOOT Frederick S. Ens. Bronze Star Medal

LINDBERG John H. EM2 Bronze Star Medal

LITTLE Major (n) StM1 Letter of Commendation (Ribbon)

LITTLEFIELD Dewey Carl S2 Letter of Commendation (Ribbon)

LOCKE Jr. Robert (n) SF1 Bronze Star Medal

LONG Henry Arthur MM3 Letter of Commendation (Ribbon)

LONG James Moore WT3 Letter of Commendation (Ribbon)

LUDLOW Myron Edward S1 Letter of Commendation (Ribbon)

LUPTAK Louis William F1 Letter of Commendation (Ribbon)

MACALLISTER William H. EM1 Bronze Star Medal

MACOMBER Walter E. Mach. Silver Star Medal

MAGEE Paul Leland MM1 Letter of Commendation (Ribbon)

MAGNUSON Herbert A. LCDR. Bronze Star Medal

MANTONE Antonio S1 Letter of Commendation (Ribbon)

MARKS Leon (n) StM2 Letter of Commendation (Ribbon)

MARQUESS Lawrence Calvert S1 Letter of Commendation (Ribbon)

MARSHALL Guy S. Ens. Bronze Star Medal

MARTIN Voley Arval S2 Letter of Commendation (Ribbon)

MASON Peter T. Lt.(HC) Letter of Commendation (Ribbon)

MASSEY Clyde 'T.' Ens. Letter of Commendation (Ribbon)

MATSON Ernest (n) SM2 Letter of Commendation (Ribbon)

MATTHEWS William R. StM2c Letter of Commendation (Ribbon)

MAYER Norman C. S1 Silver Star Medal

MCCAFFREY John W. WT1 Bronze Star Medal

MCCLELLAN William A. Ens. Bronze Star Medal

MCCRARY Robert D. Ens. Silver Star Medal

MCGOUGH William Joseph Y3 Letter of Commendation (Ribbon)

MCGUIRE William Lt. Letter of Commendation (Ribbon)

MCKINNEY William R. LCDR. Navy Cross

MCMEEL Joseph F. Lt. Letter of Commendation (Ribbon)

MCRAE Donald Elliott WT2 Letter of Commendation (Ribbon)

MEGGINS Charles Curtis MM1 Letter of Commendation (Ribbon)

MIHAL Victor Michael RM3 Letter of Commendation (Ribbon)

MILLER Charles E. SF1 Silver Star Medal

MILLER George Edward S1 Letter of Commendation (Ribbon)

MITCHELL Harrison D. Ens. Letter of Commendation (Ribbon)

MOLLETT Samuel Wesley S1 Letter of Commendation (Ribbon)

MONKUS Frank (n) SF1 Bronze Star Medal

MONSOUR Edward Lt. Bronze Star Medal

MORGAN Lindsey E. Lt.(jg) Navy Cross

MOSES Benjamin (n) WT2 Letter of Commendation (Ribbon)

MOZDIAK Henry J. S2 Bronze Star Medal

MUNZING Harry Ernest S1 Letter of Commendation (Ribbon)

MURPHY Rex Gluck B3 Letter of Commendation (Ribbon)

NARDELLI Walter Lt.(jg) Bronze Star Medal

NEWLAND Walter M. 1stLt. Silver Star Medal

NICHELSON Jack Alexander WT1 Letter of Commendation (Ribbon)

NOBLE Charles M. BM1 Bronze Star Medal

NOTT William J. MM2 Bronze Star Medal

NYCUM Edward C. RT1 Bronze Star Medal

O'CALLAHAN Joseph Timothy LCDR. Medal of Honor

O'CONNELL Richard Daniel S1 Letter of Commendation (Ribbon)

ODOM James P. MM1 Bronze Star Medal

O'DONNEL John B. Lt.(jg) Bronze Star Medal

O'DONOVAN John Richard QM2 Letter of Commendation (Ribbon)

OLIVER Audrey L. S1 Bronze Star Medal

O'NEILL Ernest Frank F1 Letter of Commendation (Ribbon)

ORENDORFF Carl S. ACOM Bronze Star Medal

OXFORD John Marvin F2 Letter of Commendation (Ribbon)

OXLEY Robert W. GM3 Bronze Star Medal

OXLEY Robert William GM3 Letter of Commendation (Ribbon)

PEARSON Ernest (n) StM2 Letter of Commendation (Ribbon)

PEDERSON Harry LeRoy S1 Letter of Commendation (Ribbon)

PERSONEN Veikko William WT3 Letter of Commendation (Ribbon)

PETERMAN John Allen FC2 Letter of Commendation (Ribbon)

PETRILL Frank Gilbert S2 Letter of Commendation (Ribbon)

PETRUNYAK Emery Louis F1 Letter of Commendation (Ribbon)

PHILLIPS Elmer C. Ch.Elect Gold Star in lieu of Second Bronze Star Medal

POFF Calvin Robert S2 Letter of Commendation (Ribbon)

PRATHER Donald Eugene AMM1 Letter of Commendation (Ribbon)

PRIVETT William Allen MM1 Letter of Commendation (Ribbon)

PROBST C. Ens. Bronze Star Medal

RAFUSE John Oscar GM3 Letter of Commendation (Ribbon)

RAMEY Glenn Thomas MMR2 Letter of Commendation (Ribbon)

RAUSCH Harold Edwin S2 Letter of Commendation (Ribbon)

RAY Gerald Abniwake F2 Letter of Commendation (Ribbon)

REID Clarence B. Ch.Mach. Silver Star Medal

REYNOLDS William W. AerM3 Bronze Star Medal

RHODES Robert Tiennie StM2 Letter of Commendation (Ribbon)

RICCHETTI Paul Anthony MM2 Letter of Commendation (Ribbon)

RICHARDSON Harold W. Lt.(jg) Letter of Commendation (Ribbon)

RICHARDSON Haron James CEM Letter of Commendation (Ribbon)

RICKS Benjamin M. S1 Bronze Star Medal

RITCHIE Edward Augusta S1 Letter of Commendation (Ribbon)

RITZ George B. Lt.(jg) Bronze Star Medal

RIZZI Vito (n) SK1 Letter of Commendation (Ribbon)

ROACH John Marvin F2 Letter of Commendation (Ribbon)

ROBERTSON Jr. Frederick S. Lt. Bronze Star Medal

ROBINSON John Wallace S2 Letter of Commendation (Ribbon)

ROCKHILL Kenneth Paul Lt.(jg) Letter of Commendation (Ribbon)

RODGERS Ernest B. Lt. Silver Star Medal

ROOT Gordon Henry F2 Letter of Commendation (Ribbon)

ROY Henry Napoleon F2 Letter of Commendation (Ribbon)

RUSSELL Allen Clarence S1 Letter of Commendation (Ribbon)

RUSSELL Donald H. Air.Tech. Silver Star Medal

RYAN Virgil R. QM2 Bronze Star Medal

RYDER John P. Lt.(jg) Bronze Star Medal

SCHMALZ Rudolph Ernest Ens. Letter of Commendation (Ribbon)

SCHWENKNER Edwin A. Ch.Machinist Letter of Commendation (Ribbon)

SEVERSON Royal Roscoe SK1 Letter of Commendation (Ribbon)

SHAW Dudley Emanuel StM2 Letter of Commendation (Ribbon)

SHEPARD Jr. John W. Ch.PayClerk Bronze Star Medal

SHERMAN Sam LCDR.(MC) Navy Cross

SHERWOOD John (n) S1 Letter of Commendation (Ribbon)

SIEBOLD Donald Alfred WT3 Letter of Commendation (Ribbon)

SKEAN William (n) MM2 Letter of Commendation (Ribbon)

SKORICH John 1stLt. Bronze Star Medal

SLATTERY Bart Lt. Bronze Star Medal

SLIFIES Robert Ulysses MM2 Letter of Commendation (Ribbon)

SMITH Francis K. CDR. Navy Cross

SMITH John F. F1 Bronze Star Medal

SNYDER Harold Thomas S2 Letter of Commendation (Ribbon)

SOLTVELDT John Phillip MM1 Letter of Commendation (Ribbon)

SPRIGGS Robert Lee EM2 Letter of Commendation (Ribbon)

ST. PETERS Robert Edward EM3 Letter of Commendation (Ribbon)

STACK John Major Bronze Star Medal

STEINBRON Harold Ray FCO3 Letter of Commendation (Ribbon)

STEWART Robert Charles CB Letter of Commendation (Ribbon)

STITES John Tabert GMM Letter of Commendation (Ribbon)

STONE George LCDR. Navy Cross

STONE Harold S. RT1 Silver Star Medal

STOOPS Thomas M. Gunner Navy Cross

STORK Glenn Dean F1 Letter of Commendation (Ribbon)

STRATTON John Ross F1 Letter of Commendation (Ribbon)

STREICH Hans A. WT3 Bronze Star Medal

SUTHERLAND Hiram David EM3 Letter of Commendation (Ribbon)

SWANN Bert (n) BM2 Letter of Commendation (Ribbon)

SWANSON Ernest A. Lt.(jg) Silver Star Medal

SWANSON Robert Walter WT2 Letter of Commendation (Ribbon)

TAMMEAID Niloai BM2 Bronze Star Medal

TAPPEN Melvin M. Lt. Gold Star in lieu of Second Bronze Star Medal

TARR Jr. Bernard (n) S2 Letter of Commendation (Ribbon)

TAYLOR Everett J. Lt.(jg) Bronze Star Medal

TAYLOR Joseph CDR. Navy Cross

THAYER Robert M. Lt.(jg) Gold Star in lieu of Second Bronze Star Medal

THOMAS Harold Leslie F1 Letter of Commendation (Ribbon)

THOMAS Jr. Earl Roy RdM1 Letter of Commendation (Ribbon)

TIARA Joseph B. Lt.(jg) Silver Star Medal

TUCKER Charles V. S1 Bronze Star Medal

TUCKER Jr. John Reilly Ens Letter of Commendation (Ribbon)

TUREK Charles B. Lt. Bronze Star Medal

TURNER James W. WT1 Bronze Star Medal

VALLONI Thomas J. CEM Bronze Star Medal

VARILEN William (n) QM1 Letter of Commendation (Ribbon)

VAUGHN William Thomas AMM2 Letter of Commendation (Ribbon)

VAUGHN Jr. James A. Lt. Bronze Star Medal

WALES Ross E. Lt. Letter of Commendation (Ribbon)

WALSH Eugene Thomas QM3 Letter of Commendation (Ribbon)

WASSMAN Edward H.R. Lt.(jg) Silver Star Medal

WATKINS George R. Lt. Bronze Star Medal

WATSON James Kenneth Mus2 Letter of Commendation (Ribbon)

WAYMAN Ronan Edward MM1 Letter of Commendation (Ribbon)

WEBSTER Hubert Cread F2 Letter of Commendation (Ribbon)

WEINLEY Harold DeWayne F1 Letter of Commendation (Ribbon)

WELLMAN Frederick E. MM2 Bronze Star Medal

WEST Jr. James W. LCDR. Bronze Star Medal

WHITAKER John D. LCDR. Bronze Star Medal

WHITE Bill J. Lt.(jg) Silver Star Medal

WHITE John Montague WT2 Letter of Commendation (Ribbon)

WILLARD Henry Kellogg S2 Letter of Commendation (Ribbon)

WILLIAMS Mack Henry StM1 Letter of Commendation (Ribbon)

WILLIAMS Wilfred 'J.' Y3 Bronze Star Medal

WILLS Scott William Cox Letter of Commendation (Ribbon)

WILSON Dorris W. S1 Bronze Star Medal

WINEMAN Robert J. Lt.(jg) Bronze Star Medal

WISE Charles Paul S2 Letter of Commendation (Ribbon)

WOLFE Joseph Jacobs Ch. Electrician Letter of Commendation (Ribbon)
WOLLETT Clair 'C.' WT3 Letter of Commendation (Ribbon)
WOOK Chester Roy S1 Letter of Commendation (Ribbon)
WOOKBURN Melvern C. Lt. Letter of Commendation (Ribbon)
YEARICK Robert Day F1 Letter of Commendation (Ribbon)
ZELLER Heinz (n) S2 Letter of Commendation (Ribbon)


*From the appendix (pp. 139-153) of: "I was Chaplain on the Franklin" by Father Joseph T. O'Callahan, S.J., Published 1956 The Macmillan Company, New York. NOTE: Air Group 13, Air Group 5, VMF-214 and VMF-452 were not included in Father O'Callahan's list. The list does not include Purple Heart recipients.*

UNITED STATES SHIP ____ FRANKLIN (CV13) _____ Monday  19  March  1945
                                                                 (Day)  (Date)  (Month)

**00-04** Operating off Southern Coast of Japan as part of Task Group 58.2 in company with Task Force 58. Zigzagging plan 6, USF 10A on course 345 (t and g), 350 (psc), speed 22 knots (166 rpm). All boilers in use. Formation is in disposition 5-VN, USF 10A on axis 030 (t and g) as followes: FRANKLIN (O.T.C., C.T.G. and Guide) in 2280, SAN JACINTO 2000, HANCOCK 2080, BATAAN 2180, other heavy ships plus destroyers in a circular screen on circle 5. Ship is darkened in condition of readiness III and material condition YOKE. 0008 ceased zigzagging, changed course to 045 (t and g), 021 (psc). 0041 went to torpedo defense, unidentified aircraft in vicinity. 0043 changed course to 345 (t and g), 350 (psc). 0044 set material condition ZEBRA below third deck. 0047 changed speed to 21 knots (158 rpm). 0054 changed course to 270 (t and g). 0100 changed speed to 15 knots (113 rpm). 0103 changed course to 345 (t and g), 350 (psc). Changed speed to 21 knots (158 rpm). 0107 commenced zigzagging plan 6, USF 10A. 0128 set condition of readiness III. Set material condition YOKE. 0135 went to torpedo defense , unidentified aircraft in the vicinity. 0139 set material condition ZEBRA below third deck. 0141 set condition of readiness 1-Easy in all batteries. 0149 set condition of readiness III and material condition YOKE. 0215 ceased zigzagging and steadied on course 005 (t and g), 001 (psc). 0221 changed speed to 23 knots. 0256 resumed zigzagging on base course 345 (t and g). 0301 changed speed to 21 knots. 0320 ceased zigzagging, resumed base cours 0326 went to torpedo defense, unidentified aircraft in vicinity. 0330 changed course to 32 and g). 0336 went to general quarters. 0339 set material condition ZEBRA. 0340 commenced zigzagging plan 6, USF 10A.

E. L. FOX,
Lieutenant, U. S. Navy.

**04-16** Steaming as before. 0501 changed course to 270 (t and g). 0517 changed course to 330 (t a g). 0529 changed course to 045 (t and g) and headed ship into wind for flight operations. 0535 commenced launching airplanes. 0554 completed launching airplanes. 0557 changed cour to 250 (t and g), changed speed to 17 knots (128 rpm). 0601 assumed cruising disposition 5 0611 set condition III except in batteries and fire control stations. 0630 changed speed t knots (136 rpm). Commenced zigzagging plan 6, USF 10A. 0649 changed course to 060 (t and changed speed to 24 knots (182 rpm) and headed ship into wind to launch airplanes. 0650 Be N. J., 623 14 12, AMM2c, was buried at sea. 0657 commenced launching aircraft of strike 2E 0708 ship under attack by enemy aircraft. Took two bomb hits, first bomb hit flight deck 1 68, exploded hangar deck frame 82; second bomb hit flight deck frame 133, exploded frame 14 0709 general quarters. 0712 set condition ZEBRA. At the time of the attack 36 VF and 9 VF air borne. 0725 (about) ship steadied on 355 (t). 0800 Rear Admiral R. Davison and staff transferred to U.S.S. MILLER (DD535). 0815 assumed starboard list 3 degrees. Fires and ex plosions occuring throught the ship. 0840 starboard list increased to 6 degrees. 0931 SA1 FE approached and lay to about 100 feet off starboard bow to remove wounded. 0945 lost st ing control and all communications except to steering aft from bridge. Set all engines ahe 8 knots and abandoned engine rooms due to smoke and heat. 0952 after 5"/38 magazines explo 1000 starboard list steadied at 13 degrees. Ship dead in water. 1015 SANTA FE backed off ping all lines. 1050 SANTA FE alongside for second time. All wounded and unnecessary pers were removed. 1225 SANTA FE cleared ship. 1254 Japanese JUDY made glide bombing attack, 1 missing starboard side of ship. 1404 FRANKLIN taken under tow by U.S.S. PITTSBURG on south course at 2 knots. Ships present include 3 screening destroyers, PITTSBURG, and SANTA FE. FRANKLIN headed 180 (t) at 6 knots under tow.

M. M. TAPPEN,
Lieutenant, U. S. Naval Reserve.

**16-20** Under tow as before. 1500 damage control parties commenced fighting fires, frame 170. 16 U.S.S. MILLER (DD535) came along port quarter to fight fires, frame 200 gallery deck. 1813 ship darkened except for small glow from fire, frame 200.

J. B. BARR,
Lieutenant, U. S. Naval Reserve.

**20-24** Under tow as before. The following named officers and men were killed or missing in actic this date: 2100 (about) first party entered No. 3 fireroom. Commenced counter flooding m ures to reduce list. 2230 lighted fires under boiler No. 5. 2200 (about) U.S.S. MILLER c along port quarter in an effort to extinguish fire in the after part of the ship.

C. G. DERN
Lieutenant, U. S. Naval Reserve.

APPROVED:

L. E. GEHRES, Captain, U.S.N. COMMANDING.

EXAMINED:

STEPHEN JURIKA, Commander, U.S.N. NAVIGATOR

A CALL TO DUTY

## E. Robert Wassman
### 15 Campbell Lane
### Larchmont, NY 10538

June 24, 2006

Dr. William J. Stewart
10031 Franklin Drive
Englewood, Fl. 34224

Dear Bill,

I think it is fine and generous of you to take the time to write a biography of Captain Leslie Gehres and I am most thankful to Rene Gauthier for suggesting my involvement.

I served on the bridge of the Carrier U.S.S. Franklin. (CV 13) as Watch Officer and Ass't. Navigator under the first Commanding Officer Captain Schoemacher and was aboard to welcom Capt. Gehries when he relieved Capt. Schoemacher and assumed the Command. He was a most affable senior officer and walked with a proud, upright swagger.

During our many hours of watch together underway the captain would remain involved with all the daily operations.

I was not present on the Bridge at 7:04 AM on the day of our tragic bombing but arrived there within a few hours after coming up from below deck and fighting fires on the flight deck forward and then trying to gain my battle station in Secondary Control which is aft in the island. Unable to remain there because of the fire, smoke and explosions I joined Captain Gehries ,the Navigator, Cdr. Steven Jurika, the Executive Officer with whom I would normally serve with during General Quarters in the Sec Con and the men of my "N" Division who were on the Bridge at the time.
We were all totally in shock from the terrible explosions that rocked the ship and the sight of themany men fleeing from the fire and smoke. Captain Gehres was most notable for his calm courage and acted in the finest traditions of the Navy when he responded to the Admiral who was transferring his Flag to another ship so he could ,"get on with the war" and he advised the Captain to leave the ship from the starboard side and Gehres replied, "Admiral, I don't intend to abandon my ship - good luck to you". AND HE DIDN'T ! .

When you think of what faced us, the rescue of shipmates trapped below and eventually getting the ship underway and the caring for the crew the Captains leadership was exemplary. And he remained calm, collected and friendly all the time.

What prompted his action to initiate investigation of those who didn't remain aboard and suggesting court marshall proceedings I'll never know. i for one testified against the idea on behalf of the crew. It was inmy opinion a bad mistake and none of the Senior Officers deserved their awards if they counseled him in this regard for many guided the men off the ship for their safety including Father O'Callahan. Some men have resented this for too long and discredit the glory and memory of our ship, the USS Franklin , the ship that wouldn't die!

Good luck Bill with the book and thank you'

Sincerely yours,
E. Robert Wassman, Lcdr. USNR
Assistant Navigator & "N" Division Officer

Robert L. Bartlett
3725 Caimbrook Ct.
Columbia, SC USA ~~29220~~
(803)-750-4930
bobbartlett37@hotmail.com

September 26, 2006
Mr. Bill Stewart
6610 Gasparilla Pines Blvd.
Englewood, FL 34224
Dear Mr. Stewart,

I was referred to you by Mr. Kevin Whitaker, principal of Newark (NY) High School as the person who is writing a biography of Leslie Gehres, commanding officer of the USS FRANKLIN. I am the cousin of Lt(jg) Stanley S. Graham, a survivor of 19MAR45. I vividly remember him taking me on board in Brooklyn Navy Yard in August of 1945. I have been collecting items on CV-13 for years and have found some criticism about both Capt. Shoemaker and Capt. Gehres, but nothing like what I have recently encountered.

Clark G. Reynolds has been an outstanding author and aircraft carrier expert for years. He has written CARRIER ADMIRAL(With Joko Clark 1967),THE FAST CARRIERS(1968),THE SAGA OF SMOKEY STOVER(1978),FAMOUS AMERICAN ADMIRALS(1978),ADMIRAL JOHN H. TOWERS(1991),and ON THE WARPATH IN THE PACIFIC(2005). The latter is a full biography of Admiral Joko Clark written after his death. Mr. Reynolds was the nephew of Frank Robert Reynolds who was Admiral Clark's flag lieutenant. Unfortunately, Clark Reynolds passed away in December, 2005.

In his last book, Mr. Reynolds has chosen to make what I consider to be some very disparaging remarks about Capt. Gehres without giving any source for these remarks. On page 407, he says "The carrier's (USS Franklin) martinet of a captain, Leslie H. Gehres, (A mustang and social friend of Joko's a decade earlier) had failed to initiate precautionary damage-control measures early enough and then tried to put the blame on the crew.....".

In my oppion, not only are these remarks disparaging, they are outright insulting and slanderous. Have you ever heard of such events from anyone on the FRANKLIN or from anywhere else? At the beginning of that book is a note on citations saying that most quotes are taken from recorded interviews by the Naval Photographic Center, Columbia University Oral History Program, or personal interviews by Reynolds. With Mr. Reynolds untimely death, I don't know how to determined where he obtained his information. Do you have any suggestion on how this might be done?

Cmdr. Stephen Jurika (Now deceased), was standing on the bridge with Capt. Gehres at the time of the attack. I am in contact with Jurika's two daughters and nephew. I will query them as what they may know about this. I have also asked the son of my cousin, Stanley Graham, Jr. what he knows from his farther (Now deceased) of Capt. Gehres.

Also, on page 320, he quotes an Enlisted man transferred to the FRANKLIN as saying she (The Franklin) was" not even 30 percent the quality of the YORKTOWN, that was due to a terrible and pompous skipper (Lesie H. Gehres)". At least this time Mr. Reynolds gives us his source. There is a comment on page 492 of FAST CARRIERS fr⋯ a letter to Admiral Nimitz from Admiral John Towers referring to Shoemaker as a poor commander. Gehres relieved him only seven days after the 30OCT44 attack (Strange?) Are you aware of these items?

What concerns me, is that in the future, authors will quote these remarks and perpetuate a myth that is entirely unfounded. As an example of such repeated errors, many authors quote the early Dictionary of American Fighting Ships" as the casualties on the FRANKLIN was 724. The correct figure from the USS FRANKLIN MUSEUM ASSOCIATION is 836. What do you thinks of all this? Please respond to these items by e-mail ,if possible.

Sincerely,

Bob Bartlett
PS: Enclosed is a copy of my FRANKLIN bibliography.

*Copy of a letter written to the author and his wife, dated January*
*6, 2005 from Rene N. Gauthier F1c, a crewmember aboard the USS Franklin on March*
*19, 1945*

January 06, 2005

Mr. and Mrs. Bill Stewart
10031 Franklin Drive
Englewood, FL 34224

Thank you for keeping in touch with me. I am so glad that you were able to get a plaque for the museum in Newark. It is only fitting that the Admiral Gehres Memorial Museum should have all the names of the crew members on the plaque. It certainly shows that all members of the crew were heroes.

I believe that your museum will show the true history of the USS FRANKLIN-CV13 and its crew during World War II. Combined with your book about Admiral Gehres and the UJSS Franklin-CV-13 will take its place in American history.

My experience while aboard the USS Franklin-13 on March 19, 1945, when we were fifty miles off the eastern shore of Japan was that the ship was dead in the water. All of Franklin's wounded and many able-bodied crewmembers were taken aboard the light cruiser Santa Fe. Other overboard Franklin crewmembers were picked up by ships in Task Force 52. Two hundred ninety-six members of the original crew were left clean up and bury the dead. We were very tired after fighting the fires. Our dungarees soaked with salt water and when dried, they were stiff as a board Our shoes rotted from the salt water, our feet were very cold and broken out with fungus. My feet were swollen up to my knees and thighs chaffed and bleeding.

When Capt. Gehres heard of our situation, he immediately sent part of the 296 men crew to locate stores for some dry clothes. I don't remember how long it took because we were under attack by Japanese aircraft. The search party did come up with some clothes. We had new dry -dungarees, rubber boots and heavy woolen socks. What a relief! We were still not able to take a shower and continued to be attacked all the time.

One of Captain Gehres' first orders was to the Engineering Department to ascertain how much damage there was to the boilers and turbines, and estimate how soon we could get the Franklin underway (we were still under attack). The engine room crew felt that fire room #3 was our best bet- we were able to successfully
fire up the first boiler which provided power for the electric generators that allowed the water evaporators to operate, providing fresh water. Shortly thereafter, there was enough power to operate several turbines that moved the screws and got the Franklin under way.

Once we had our crew back on their watch, the Capt. started the work details, cleaning the ship. We picked up bodies that had drowned in the lower compartments and where they had suffocated and boiled to death. The only way they could bury them was to pick them up with a shovel and put their body parts in trash cans.

The chaplains blessed them and buried them at sea. From the day we were dead in the water, we only had one meal a day, same thing every night (beef on the shingle) and a pack of cigarettes. All through the above activities we were under attack by the enemy.

When we arrived at the island of Ulithi, the ship and its crew of 296 officers and enlisted men were exhausted. While the Franklin remained at Ulithi for a few days for repairs and refueling, Capt. Gehres instructed his officers to pick 408 former officers and enlisted crewmembers from the remaining pool of Franklin crewmembers who were still aboard the rescue ships that had been moved earlier from the battle zone to Ulithi. The men presently in charge of the 704 Club are from the 408 crewmembers that were reinstated at Ulithi, and these men were not there at the time of real peril.

I am certain that the 408 crewmembers that were reinstated had their moments of survival, but never knew of Capt. Gehres leadership, seamanship or passion for his crew.

Sincerely,
Rena Gauthier F1c
3 Harmhill Drive
Plainville CT 06062-1014

12 April 1945

Captain L. E. Gehres, USN
USS Franklin - CV 13
c/o Fleet Post Office
San Francisco, California

Dear Captain:

I flew in to see you but you had just left. I am sorry I missed you. I talked to Father Sheehy and heard of the splended work of the Chaplains. During the evening I was at the hospital visiting the men, several of whom I knew very very well. Their many examples and stories of courage and heroism made me extremly proud, especially of my dear friend Dr. Fox. I know there were many others. One of the men by the name of Walter Kniss, of the V-1 Division, said after telling his story: "Boy, the old Captain can be proud of bringing her back." I too say the same and I am glad because after thirteen months aboard my heart is with her. She's a good old ship in best traditions of the United States Navy.

Upon leaving the ward I said to the nurse, "Take good care of the Franklin men because they're important people."

Kindly give my regards and highest tribute to those who remain with you, and may the Lord bless our dead.

With all good wishes and sincere tribute to you Captain, I remain,

Very respectfully yours,

EDWARD J. HARKIN
Chaplain - USNR

EJK/rgr

DEPARTMENT OF THE NAVY – NAVAL HISTORICAL CENTER
805 KIDDER BREESE SE – WASHINGTON NAVY YARD
WASHINGTON DC 20374-5060

# Oral Histories - Attacks on Japan, 1945

**Recollections of LCDR Samuel Robert Sherman, MC, USNR, Flight Surgeon on USS *Franklin* (CV-13) when it was heavily damaged by a Japanese bomber near the Japanese mainland on 19 March 1945**

**Adapted from:** "Flight Surgeon on the Spot: Aboard USS *Franklin*, 19 March 1945," Navy Medicine 84, no. 4 (July-August 1993): 4-9.

I joined the Navy the day after Pearl Harbor. Actually, I had been turned down twice before because I had never been in a ROTC [Reserve Officer Training Corps - located at many colleges to train students for officer commissions] reserve unit. Since I had to work my way through college and medical school, I wasn't able to go to summer camp or the monthly week end drills. Instead, I needed to work in order to earn the money to pay my tuition. Therefore, I could never join a ROTC unit.

When most of my classmates were called up prior to Pearl Harbor, I felt quite guilty, and I went to see if I could get into the Army unit. They flunked me. Then I went to the Navy recruiting office and they flunked me for two minor reasons. One was because I had my nose broken a half dozen times while I was boxing. The inside of my nose was so obstructed and the septum was so crooked that the Navy didn't think I could breathe well enough. I also had a partial denture because I had lost some front teeth also while boxing.

But the day after Pearl Harbor, I went back to the Navy and they welcomed me with open arms. They told me I had 10 days to close my office and get commissioned. At that time, I went to Treasure Island, CA [naval station in San Francisco Bay], for indoctrination. After that, I was sent to Alameda Naval Air Station [east of San Francisco, near Oakland CA] where I was put in charge of surgery and clinical services. One day the Team Medical Officer burst into the operating room and said, "When are you going to get through with this operation?" I answered, "In about a half hour." He said, "Well, you better hurry up because I just got orders for you to go to Pensacola to get flight surgeon's training."

Nothing could have been better because airplanes were the love of my life. In fact, both my wife and I were private pilots and I had my own little airfield and two planes. Since I wasn't allowed to be near the planes at Alameda, I had been after the senior medical officer day and night to get me transferred to flight surgeon's training.

I went to [Naval Air Station] Pensacola [Florida] in April 1943 for my flight surgeon training and finished up in August. Initially, I was told that I was going to be shipped out from the East Coast. But the Navy changed its mind and sent me back to the West Coast in late 1943 to wait for Air Group 5 at Alameda Naval Air Station.

# A CALL TO DUTY

## Air Group 5

Air Group 5 soon arrived, but it took about a year or so of training to get up to snuff. Most of the people in it were veterans from other carriers that went down. Three squadrons formed the nucleus of this air group--a fighter, a bomber, and a torpedo bomber squadron. Later, we were given two Marine squadrons; the remnants of Pappy Boyington's group.

Since the Marine pilots had been land-based, the toughest part of the training was to get them carrier certified. We used the old [USS] *Ranger* (CV-4) for take-off and landing training. We took the *Ranger* up and down the coast from San Francisco to San Diego and tried like hell to get these Marines to learn how to make a landing. They had no problem taking off, but they had problems with landings. Luckily, we were close enough to airports so that if they couldn't get on the ship they'd have a place to land. That way, they wouldn't have to go in the drink. Anyhow, we eventually got them all certified. Some of our other pilots trained at Fallon Air Station in Nevada and other West Coast bases. By the time the [USS] *Franklin* [CV-13] came in, we had a very well-trained group of people.

I had two Marine squadrons and three Navy squadrons to take care of. The Marines claimed I was a Marine. The Navy guys claimed I was a Navy man. I used to wear two uniforms. When I would go to the Marine ready rooms [a ready room is a room where air crew squadrons were briefed on upcoming missions and then stood by "ready" to go to their aircraft. Each squadron had a ready room.], I'd put on a Marine uniform and then I'd change quickly and put on my Navy uniform and go to the other one. We had a lot of fun with that. As their physician, I was everything. I had to be a general practitioner with them, but I also was their father, their mother, their spiritual guide, their social director, their psychiatrist, the whole thing. Of course, I was well trained in surgery so I could take care of the various surgical problems. Every once in a while I had to do an appendectomy. I also removed some pilonidal cysts and fixed a few strangulated hernias. Of course, they occasionally got fractures during their training exercises. I took care of everything for them and they considered me their personal physician, every one of them. I was called Dr. Sam and Dr. Sam was their private doctor. No matter what was wrong, I took care of it.

Eventually, the *Franklin* arrived in early 1945. It had been in Bremerton [Washington] being repaired after it was damaged by a Kamikaze off Leyte [in the Philippine Islands] in October 1944. In mid-February 1945 we left the West Coast and went to [Naval Base] Pearl [Harbor, Hawaii] first and then to Ulithi [in the Caroline Islands, west Pacific Ocean. It was captured by the US in Sept. 1944 and developed into a major advance fleet base.]. By the first week in March. the fleet was ready to sail. It took us about 5 or 6 days to reach the coast of Japan where we began launching aerial attacks on the airbases, ports, and other such targets.

## The Attack

Just before dawn on 19 March. 38 of our bombers took off, escorted by about 9 of our fighter planes. The crew of the *Franklin* was getting ready for another strike, so more planes were on the flight deck. All of a sudden, out of nowhere, a Japanese plane slipped through the fighter screen and popped up just in front of the ship. My battle station was right in the middle of the flight deck because I was the flight surgeon and was supposed to take care of anything that might happen during flight operations. I saw the Japanese plane coming in, but there was nothing I could do but stay there and take it. The plane just flew right in and dropped two bombs on our flight deck.

I was blown about 15 feet into the air and tossed against the steel bulkhead of the island. I got up groggily and saw an enormous fire. All those planes that were lined up to take off were fully armed and fueled. The dive bombers were equipped with this new "Tiny Tim" heavy rocket and they immediately began to explode. Some of the rockets' motors ignited and took off across the flight deck on their own. A lot of us were just ducking those things. It was pandemonium and chaos for hours and hours. We had 126 separate explosions on that ship; and each explosion would pick the ship up and rock it and then turn it around a little bit. Of course, the ship suffered horrendous casualties from the first moment. I lost my glasses and my shoes. I was wearing a kind of moccasin shoes. I didn't have time that morning to put on my flight deck shoes and they just went right off immediately. Regardless, there were hundreds and hundreds of crewmen who needed my attention.

## Medical Equipment

Fortunately, I was well prepared from a medical equipment standpoint. From the time we left San Francisco and then stopped at Pearl and then to Ulithi and so forth, I had done what we call disaster planning. Because I had worked in emergency hospital service and trauma centers, I knew what was needed. Therefore, I had a number of big metal containers, approximately the size of garbage cans, bolted down on the flight deck and the hangar deck. These were full of everything that I needed--splints, burn dressings, sterile dressings of all sorts, sterile surgical instruments, medications, plasma, and intravenous solutions other than plasma. The most important supplies were those used for the treatment of burns and fractures, lacerations, and bleeding. In those days the Navy had a special burn dressing which was very effective. It was a gauze impregnated with Vaseline and some chemicals that were almost like local anesthetics. In addition to treating burns, I also had to deal with numerous casualties suffering from severe bleeding; I even performed some amputations.

Furthermore, I had a specially equipped coat that was similar to those used by duck hunters, with all the little pouches. In addition to the coat, I had a couple of extra-sized money belts which could hold things. In these I carried my morphine syrettes and other small medical items. Due to careful planning I had no problem whatsoever with supplies.

I immediately looked around to see if I had any corpsmen [Hospital Corpsman is an enlisted rating for medical orderlies] left. Most of them were already wounded, dead, or had been blown overboard. Some, I was later told, got panicky and jumped overboard. Therefore, I couldn't find any corpsmen, but fortunately I found some of the members of the musical band whom I had trained in first aid. I had also given first-aid training to my air group pilots and some of the crew. The first guy I latched onto was LCDR MacGregor Kilpatrick, the skipper of the fighter squadron. He was an Annapolis graduate and a veteran of the[USS] *Lexington* (CV-2) and the [USS] *Yorktown* (CV-5) with three Navy Crosses. He stayed with me, helping me take care of the wounded.

I couldn't find any doctors. There were three ship's doctors assigned to the *Franklin*, CDR Francis (Kurt) Smith, LCDR James Fuelling, and LCDR George Fox. I found out later that LCDR Fox was killed in the sick bay by the fires and suffocating smoke. CDR Smith and LCDR Fuelling were trapped below in the warrant officer's wardroom, and it took 12 or 13 hours to get them out. That's where LT Donald Gary got his Medal of Honor for finding an escape route for them and 300 men trapped below. Mean while, I had very little medical help.

Finally, a couple of corpsmen who were down below in the hangar deck came up once they recovered from their concussions and shock. Little by little a few of them came up. Originally, the band was my medical help and what pilots I had around.

## Evacuation Efforts

I had hundreds and hundreds of patients, obviously more than I could possibly treat. Therefore, the most important thing for me to do was triage. In other words, separate the serious wounded from the not so serious wounded. We'd arranged for evacuation of the serious ones to the cruiser [USS] *Santa Fe* (CL-60) which had a very well-equipped sick bay and was standing by alongside.

LCDR Kilpatrick was instrumental in the evacuations. He helped me organize all of this and we got people to carry the really badly wounded. Some of them had their hips blown off and arms blown off and other sorts of tremendous damage. All together, I think we evacuated some 800 people to the *Santa Fe*. Most of them were wounded and the rest were the air group personnel who were on board.

The orders came that all air group personnel had to go on the *Santa Fe* because they were considered nonexpendable. They had to live to fight again in their airplanes. The ship's company air officer of the *Franklin* came up to LCDR Kilpatrick and myself as we were supervising the evacuation between fighting fires, taking care of the wounded, and so forth.

# A CALL TO DUTY

He said, "You two people get your asses over to the *Santa Fe* as fast as you can." LCDR Kilpatrick, being an [US Naval Academy at] Annapolis [Maryland] graduate, knew he had to obey the order, but he argued and argued and argued. But this guy wouldn't take his arguments.

He said, "Get over there. You know better." Then he said to me, "You get over there too."

I said, "Who's going to take care of these people?"

He replied, "We'll manage."

I said, "Nope. All my life I've been trained never to abandon a sick or wounded person. I can't find any doctors and I don't know where they are and I only have a few corpsmen and I can't leave these people."

He said, "You better go because a military order is a military order."

I said, "Well what could happen to me if I don't go?"

He answered, "I could shoot you or I could bring court-martial charges against you."

I said, "Well, take your choice." And I went back to work.

As MacGregor Kilpatrick left he told me, "Sam, you're crazy!"

## Getting *Franklin* Under Way

After the Air Group evacuated, I looked at the ship, I looked at the fires, and I felt the explosions. I thought, well, I better say good-bye right now to my family because I never believed that the ship was going to survive. We were just 50 miles off the coast of Japan (about 15 minutes flying time) and dead in the water. The cruiser [USS] *Pittsburgh* (CA-72) was trying to get a tow line to us, but it was a difficult job and took hours to accomplish.

Meanwhile, our engineering officers were trying to get the boilers lit off in the engine room. The smoke was so bad that we had to get the *Santa Fe* to give us a whole batch of gas masks. But the masks didn't cover the engineers' eyes. Their eyes became so inflamed from the smoke that they couldn't see to do their work. So, the XO [Executive Officer, the ship's second-in-command] came down and said to me, "Do you know where there are any anesthetic eye drops to put in their eyes so they can tolerate the smoke?"

I said, "Yes, I know where they are." I knew there was a whole stash of them down in the sick bay because I used to have to take foreign bodies out of the eyes of my pilots and some of the crew.

He asked, "Could you go down there (that's about four or five decks below), get it and give it to the engineering officer?"

I replied, "Sure, give me a flash light and a guide because I may not be able to see my way down there although I used to go down three or four times a day."

I went down and got a whole batch of them. They were in eyedropper bottles and we gave them to these guys. They put them in their eyes and immediately they could tolerate the smoke. That enabled them to get the boilers going.

## Aftermath

It was almost 12 or 13 hours before the doctors who were trapped below were rescued. By that time, I had the majority of the wounded taken care of. However, there still were trapped and injured people in various parts of the ship, like the hangar deck, that hadn't been discovered. We spent the next 7 days trying to find them all.

I also helped the chaplains take care of the dead. The burial of the dead was terrible. They were all over the ship. The ships' medical officers put the burial functions on my shoulders. I had to declare them dead, take off their identification, remove, along with the chaplains' help, whatever possessions that hadn't been destroyed on them, and then slide them overboard because we had no way of keeping them. A lot of them were my own Air Group people, pilots and aircrew, and I recognized them even tough the bodies were busted up and charred. I think we buried about 832 people in the next 7 days. That was terrible, really terrible to bury that many people.

## Going Home

It took us 6 days to reach Ulithi. Actually, by the time we got to Ulithi, we were making 14 knots and had cast off the tow line from the *Pittsburgh*. We had five destroyers assigned to us that kept circling us all the time from the time we left the coast of Japan until we got to Ulithi because we were under constant attack by Japanese bombers. We also had support from two of the new battlecruisers.

At Ulithi, I got word that a lot of my people in the Air Group who were taken off or picked up in the water, were on a hospital ship that was also in Ulithi. I visited them there and was told that many of the dead in the Air Group were killed in their ready rooms, waiting to take off when the bombs exploded. The Marine squadrons were particularly hard hit. having few survivors. I have a list of dead Marines which makes your heart sink.

The survivors of the Air Group then regrouped on Guam. They requested that I be sent back to them. I also wanted to go with them, so I pleaded my case with the chaplain, the XO, and the skipper [ship's commanding officer]. Although the skipper felt I had earned the right to be part of the ship's company, he was willing to send me where I wanted to go. Luckily. I rejoined my Air Group just in time to keep the poor derelicts from getting assigned to another carrier.

The Air Group Commander wanted to make captain so bad, that he volunteered these boys for another carrier. Most of them were veterans of the [USS] *Yorktown* and [USS] *Lexington* and had seen quite a lot of action. A fair number of them had been blown into the water and many were suffering from the shock of the devastating ordeal. The skipper of the bombing squadron did not think his men were psychologically or physically qualified to go back into combat at that particular time. A hearing was held to determine their combat availability and a flight surgeon was needed to check them over. I assembled the pilots and checked them out and I agreed with the bombing squadron skipper. These men were just not ready to fight yet. Some of them even looked like death warmed over.

The hearing was conducted by [Fleet] ADM [Chester W.] Nimitz [Commander-in-Chief, Pacific Fleet and Pacific Ocean Areas]. He remembered me from Alameda because I pulled him out of the wreckage of his plane when it crashed during a landing approach in 1942. He simply said, "Unless I hear a medical opinion to the contrary to CDR Sherman's. I have to agree with CDR Sherman." He decided that the Air Group should be sent back to the States and rehabilitated as much as possible.

In late April 1945, the Air Group went to Pearl where we briefly reunited with the *Franklin*. They had to make repairs to the ship so it could make the journey to Brooklyn. After a short stay, we continued on to the Alameda. Then the Navy decided to break up the Air Group, so everyone was sent on their individual way. I was given what I wanted--senior medical officer of a carrier--the [USS] *Rendova* (CVE-114), which was still outfitting in Portland. OR. But the war ended shortly after we had completed outfitting.

I stayed in the Navy until about Christmas time [1945]. I was mustered out in San Francisco at the same place I was commissioned. As far as the Air Group Officer, who said he would either shoot me or court-martial me, well, he didn't shoot me. He talked about the court-martial a lot but everybody in higher rank on the ship thought it was a really bad idea and made him sound like a damned fool. He stopped making the threats.

# A CALL TO DUTY

Oral History: As I Saw It, Lt. (jg), George K. Leitch,USNR, USS Franklin

The following is a transcript of some notes a few days after the scrap - - excuse the personal angle.

Early March 13, 1945, Tuesday, we steamed into Ulithi Harbor and saw a sight we had seen only a few times before. The entire fleet was there - practically every major warship afloat and hundreds of others. We learned that the night before one of our carriers, a brand new one, had been crash-dived, and another "Betty", a twin-engine bomber had crashed on the island. It was not a safe place to be! For that reason, we had an all-out loading program and set out again at 0700 the next morning. With us went the fast carrier task groups.

We steamed 000, due north, for a couple of days, then north-west. Our destination was still speculation, but we knew "pretty well".

The first strike was to be Sunday the 18th. All day Saturday we expected to be intercepted, but no planes appeared. However, "Tokyo Rose" did include in her broadcast this warning, "To the fleet steaming northward, turn back. We have 1000 suicide planes waiting for you."

Night came and most of us, over-confident as always, really expected us to reach our launching point without interception. Both Friday and Saturday nights we had sunset General Quarters and then late supper. So it was about 9 o'clock when we turned in.

About 10 o'clock, the shrill spine-chilling call to Torpedo Defense woke us. At a time like that you leap out and right into your socks, and then wonder if you heard correctly. We secured at 0100 even though all of the enemy planes had not been accounted for. I went to "Combat", our radar detection center, which is always an intriguing place to be and watched them work, until our night fighter had "splashed" a twin-engine bomber. Another was still in the area but he was eluding the fighters successfully.

At 0245 we were again routed out by Torpedo Defense. This time we had the pleasure of seeing fairly close by the second enemy plane mentioned above shot down. A plane shot down at night is a sight to remember. Tracers light up the sky, all converging on one point. Then a small light shows on the plane and soon a huge mass of flames plunges into the ocean and the fire flattens and goes out. That was not the only plane. We tracked many by radar that morning. Through the whole night, the screen was never clear. The Japanese planes orbited constantly north and south of us, apparently keeping their headquarters advised of our position.

Everyone feared that hour of pre-dawn. Our air group

got up and in the darkness prepared their planes and bomb loads.
We knew that the Japs knew our position.  The four task groups
were strungalong on an East/West axis, steaming due North, into
the wind, less than 100 miles from the Japanese main islands.
Single planes came out constantly - then suddenly we got the word -
"large group of planes 70 miles away, closing".  And we could see
other groups being silhoutted by flares.  That was the attack
we had feared.  The first of our planes were ready to go and they
were launched.  They joined our night fighters and together they
intercepted the large group at about 35 or 40 miles, breaking
it up.

     Day came, but we stayed at our battle stations.  (Mine
was as Ass't Control Officer of #1 Mark 37 Director - from where
we could position and fire any or all of the 5" guns on the ship.)
Our planes swarmed on and off the ship all day.  Several failed
to return, but the damage to the enemy mounted with each strike.
The big news was that our fliers discovered major units of the
Jap fleet across the island on the Inland Sea.  We would have to
stay close to the mainland in order for our planes to go over
there and have enough gas to make it clear back to the ship.
It was planned for our planes to strike the next day with new
and powerful rockets recently developed and which the Franklin
was to experiment with.  Photographers were aboard to photograph
the results.

     During that day and two nights I saw within our horizon
at least 15 planes shot down either by ship's guns or by combat
planes.  We stayed at General Quarters until about 0630 the
following morning, March 19.  We were still within about 70 miles
of the Japanese mainland and enemy planes were constantly
appearing onthe screen.  However, the Admiral of the fleet on
board with us considered it wise to relax for awhile and give
the boys a rest, so Condition III was set, during which only
half of our guns were manned.  Breakfast was begun and the sailors
formed their chow lines which originate on the Hanger deck and
extend down two decks to the mess hall.  I intended going to
"Combat" again but I was too tired and so I had breakfast in the
wardroom - 3 pancakes and juice.  On my way out I saw Lt.Comdr.
Magnuson, the dental officer.  I had an appointment to see him
between 7 & 8, but asked him to call it off.  He had been up a
good deal and gladly agreed.  I state these facts to show an odd
sequence of events. "Combat" and "Sick Bay" later yielded about
50 bodies between them.  Let me add another coincidence.  In
Bremerton, I was transferred out of Gunnery and became Aide to
the Executive Officer and Personnel Officer.  The day before we
started back out a Lt. Hathaway came aboard to be Aide to the
newly appointed Exec. and I went back to  Gunnery.  He was
killed at his desk - previously my desk.

     Well, after breakfast I went to my room and "hit the sack".
I was dead to the world in nothing flat.  I remained fully dressed
including shoes and a heavy sweater my sister had knit for me.
The first bomb - at 0707 - woke me and I knew instantly we had
been hit.  It sounded right over me, but it proved to be a little

aft of there. However, the force of that original explosion
wrecked the forward elevator which is forward of where I sleep.
That huge elevator is about 45' square, but was lifted about
8' and let to fall sideways. It is situated at least 150' from
where the bomb hit!

I put on a fowl weather jacket and dashed out, first aft
and then forward to the forecastle and then up to the flight
deck to see if I could get to my battle station, the forward
director, almost the highest spot on the Island. Smoke was so
thick that I couldn't see anything aft of the forward elevator,
so I stopped and helped with a foam hose line until our foam
was exhausted. I returned to the forecastle intending to go to
the burning hanger deck but then rockets and bombs seemed to all
break loose at once, although there had been continuous heavy
explosions before that too. We all flattened on the deck and
the shipshuddered again and again. Rockets and pieces of wreckage
could be seen flying by.

Then we turned to getting more hoses to the hanger deck,
for if fire was allowed to burn forward we could not stay aboard.
The wounded were being brought forward - the only part of the
ship that was not damaged. We lost track of time, but I think
that about 1000 we were dead in the water with a starboard list
of about 15 degrees. The heavy cruiser Santa Fe came along side
to take off the wounded and some unnecessary personnel like the
air group. The admiral had also taken his staff to another ship.
To do its job, the Santa Fe had to just bang its way in close.
All of our starboard walkways and guns were badly damaged as
well as the portside of the Cruiser. Many lines were thrown
across and a disorderly exodus took place. There seemed to be no
direction from the bridge and there was great confusion as to
who was to leave. All in all, about 1700 left the ship in one
way or another - and lived. Half of these were picked up out
of the water by other ships. I heard that one destroyer rescued
440 men.

Early afternoon, the heavy cruiser Pittsburgh was directed
to move forward of us and take us in tow, a very difficult task
because we had no power and the towline was a 3" steel cable.
The job was completed about 1500 and we were towed at about 3 or 4
knots until the next morning. At this rate for about 18 hours
didn't give us a very secure feeling!

Dusk came and we were given our first food - a half sandwich with spam or sausage filling, nothing to drink. Up to then
my efforts had been divided supplying hoses and equipment to the
hanger deck where the fire was kept from spreading to officers
country, helping to get wounded to the flight deck to be transferred to the Santa Fe, helping to rig the towline and other
miscelaneous work. It is useless to describe the extent of the
fire and explosions, but at times it appeared that the ship was

blowing apart. Those from other ships reported that from the moment of the first hit, our hanger deck for its full length of about 750' was one mass of flames. They said explosions blasted 1500' into the air. Planes reported we looked like a huge funnel of black smoke and the ship could not be seen, but every once in a while a great roll of flame and smoke would billow up as another explosion took place. The cruiser reported distinguishing 37 very large blasts. Hundreds of feet of film on ships and planes recorded it all. Our own cameras were constantly in operation, too.

Fires continued to break out that night, and from dusk until after 2100 I had a group of 6 or 8 men at the after end of the flight deck with hoses soaking suspicious places. A fairly bright moon helped, but the next day when we saw the deck we wondered how we kept a sure footing. Before dark, we had laid a hose along the only path you could follow from mid-ship to the aft-end of the ship without danger of falling through! All night fire parties followed that hose.

Often during the night, large parties were called out to fight fires. Once we had an eerie feeling when the ship tipped from 8 degrees to starboard to 8 degrees port in a matter of a few minutes. One of our damage control officers, Lt(jg) Graham, had tried to correct the list by counter-flooding, but because of all the free-surface water and the total lack of controls, the ship slipped over to the opposite side. We still expected another major attack during the night. We learned that a 50-plane raid had come to the exact spot where we should have been had we not been towed, but our combat air patrol from other ships of course had intercepted them and downed every plane. That alone saved us because we could not have survived a torpedo attack. If we slept, we slept fully clothed with our life jackets on.

Next day we had another meat sandwich and a glass of water. Some found canned juice in rooms, but that didn't go far. The engineers had performed miracles. They went into extremely hot areas, lit off boilers and developed about 15 knots. We cast off the towline. Some sections up forward were given light. Some sections were again being ventilated and fresh water was being made in sufficient quantity. It wasn't long before we could get up to 20 knots and phone connections were being established. That day certain guns were put back in operation and a make-shift P.A. system was in order.

It was lucky some guns were manned, for during the morning we were attacked again. This time a Judy dove out of the sun. Our only 40mm quad mount couldn't see the plane, but they saw where the cruiser was sending their 5" shells and they opened up at the exact spot. The plane faltered, leveled off a bit, then dove again. That change ruined her dive and her bomb splashed only a few yards astern. At the time, I was back aft digging up charred bodies. In the afternoon we were attacked again. This time I was on the second deck below the hanger deck helping to remove heavy bodies from a Marine compartment which was not burned. There were 60 in all.

That brings me to the most hideous detail of all.  It was imperative that bodies be removed as soon as possible.  Several parties set out, but the Skipper had directed since we were still in dangerous waters, we officers could not force any man to go back aft against their wishes.  So, the safe forecastle remained crowded!  We tried to make identification where possible, but many were not wearing their dogtags and there was nothing left to distinguish.  These weren't too obnoxious, but others died of suffication or concussion (as in that Marine compartment) and had already begun to deteriorate. Description is impossible.  Only a few could continue working with these for any length of time. Dr. Smith, Dr. Feulling and an ex-ministerial student, Steinbron FCO3cl, were ones who really worked.  We had very little help below decks; lots of help up where the air was clear.  When we knocked off for the day, I threw my gloves down - I couldn't stand the thought or the smell of them and I went over near the low side of the deck, sat down and stared out over the smooth water toward the setting sun.  It was cool and fresh, and I found myself shaking like a leaf and wondering if I was going to lose the Spam sandwich I had for lunch which I had long since digested.  Those few hours had been far harder to take than a bit of fire and explosions.

For some reason it was two days before the Admiral on the Guam took us farther than 300 miles from major Jap positions, but gradually we worked South and then after 3 days in Ulithi harbor, we headed East.  Like planting enough beans for the bugs to get their fill, and still have some for you, someone had to take a share of the Jap bombs that we knew the Fleet had to take, but if added up against the toll the Fleet had exacted against the enemy, we didn't lose.  But just looking at the history of one Carrier, the cost was heavy.  We were last knocked out of action on October 30, 1944 by a suicide plane near Leyte.  We returned to Bremerton for repairs.  On March 3,1945, we left Pearl Harbor and arrived in Ulithi on March 13th.  We left Ulithi the next day heading North.  Twenty-five hours after our planes left for their first strike we were out of action again with perhaps a $50 million loss - for another year or more.

We were struck with 1 or probably 2 bombs.  Having our planes ready on both decks, we were especially vulnerable.  It is estimated that at least 30 tons of our own bombs exploded on the ship, plus hundreds of rockets, ready-service ammunition for our guns; at least 400 5" shells and even more 5" powder cans, plus pyrotechnic magazines and well over 15000 gallons of gasoline in our planes alone.  Half of our gasolene system was open and poured fire over the side.  At least 52 planes burned or were blown apart. Everything from the forward elevator aft, and from the second deck below the hanger deck up was demolished, and the Island except for the forward edge which houses the bridge, the Flag bridge and the #1 Director.  Even our mast had been clipped by a large rocket.

At present writing, it appears that almost 1000 are dead; over 200 are wounded; 1700 went over to the Santa Fe or were picked up out of the water by other ships; and 704 remained aboard and brought her back to Brooklyn.

There weren't too many heroes. Most of us did far less than we might have done. The Catholic Chaplain, Father O'Callahan, brand new on the ship, was everyplace getting men to fight fires in the face of explosions. He went everywhere to speak to dying men. He was recommended for the Medal of Honor. Lt(jg) Don Gary, also new on the ship, found himself in the messhall with 300 men, trapped and getting panicky. Smoke was terrific. He remembered a possible escape route through an uptake he had discovered a few days before. He started with 10 men, and enforcing discipline, he led all 300 to safety. The men had been there for 3 hours before rescue. He was also recommended for the Congressional Medal. Another man, a 1st class carpenter's mate, led about 100 men to safety, then on his last trip found his way blocked. He finally found another escape and came topside where he was blown off the ship. He was picked up. Lt(jg) White heard a dramatic choking appeal over the Engineering P.A. system for help. He put on a rescue breather and successfully released several men trapped and suffocating in the engine rooms.

We lost 17 ship's officers, some were my closest friends. Of the two divisions I've been associated with on board, over half the men were lost - more than the ship's average. As stated before, the officer that replaced me as Aide to the Executive Officer in San Francisco was killed at his desk and also four of our yoemen.

This we believe was the greatest naval tragedy of the war to that time - perhaps of any war. It was likely the most photographed. We were CV 13. Our air group was #13. "Lucky 13" That name might well be renamed "Frightened Lady".

We returned to Pearl one month to the day after leaving Pearl to go West. There it was decided that the job was too big for the West Coast, so we went through the Canal to Brooklyn. First they had to strip the sides of our deck-edge elevator and the 5" gun sponsons on the port side, for without them we still had only 8" clearance in the Canal!

We had several "firsts". We broke all records in getting from keel laying to the fighting area. We were the first carrier to return through the Canal. We took the first Kamikazi crash. The first to take a Marine squadron, the first to use the smaller 5" rockets, the first to use the new 12" Tiny Tim rockets. Our Air Groups only in the action a short time chalked up more tonnage sunk than any other. And, of course, the first to sustain <u>most</u> serious damage and return to port.

A CALL TO DUTY

REAR ADMIRAL LESLIE EDWARD GEHRES
UNITED STATES NAVY, RETIRED

Rear Admiral Gehres was born in Newark, New York, September 23, 1898 attended Western High School in Rochester, and Union High School in Newark before enlisting in 1914 in the Naval Militia, New York State, Sixth Division, Third Battalion. Mobilized with that unit on April 6, 1917, he was appointed Ensign, USNRF,on May 24, 1918. In September of that year was transferred to the regular Navy in the rank of Ensign, having completed the course in the Fourth Reserve Officers Class at the Naval Academy, Annapolis, Maryland. He subsequently progressed in grade until his promotion to Captain, June 17 1942. He was appointed Commodore for temporary service, July 5, 1943 to continue while serving as Commander, Fleet Air Wing 4, and upon detachment from that assignment on August 28, 1944 reverted to his permanent rank of Captain. He was transferred to the Retired List of the Navy on May 1, 1949 in the rank of Rear Admiral by reason of combat citations.

Mobilized in April, 1917 as an enlisted man in the Naval Reserve Rear Admiral Gehres served in the USS SALEM, USS INDIANA, and USS MASSACHUSETTS, until discharged in May, 1918. Following his transfer to the regular Navy in the rank of Ensign, he served from September until June, 1919 in the USS NORTH DAKOTA, which operated on escort duty during the World War, and during the subsequent five years had duty in the destroyers TINGEY, GILLIS, AULICK, JACOB JONES, and FARENHOLT.

From June, 1924 until November, 1926 Rear Admiral Gehres had duty at the Navy Yard, Pearl Harbor, Hawaii, and returning to San Diego in January, 1927 he was ordered to report for flight training at Naval Air Station, Pensacola, Florida. Designated Naval Aviator August 30, 1927, he has served continuously with naval aviation since that time. In November, 1927 he joined Aircraft Squadrons, Battle Fleet, and was assigned to Fighting Squadron One, based on the air craft carrier LANGLEY, and later on the carrier SARATOGA. During his service with that Squadron, which extended to December, 1929, he trained and led "The Nine High Hats", a nine-plane acrobatic formation which performed in the National Air Races at Cleveland, Ohio, in 1929.

Rear Admiral Gehres was on duty at the Naval Air Station, San Diego, California, from December, 1929 until June, 1932. During that assignment he headed the naval aerial expedition to Honey Lake, California, in April 1930, to photograph the moon's shadow on the earth during the total eclipse. For the next two years, he served with Fighting Squadron 5, based on the aircraft carrier LEXINGTON. After fifteen months with the Naval Examining Board, Navy Department, Washington, D. C., on duty involving flying, he returned to the Pensacola Naval Air Station in September, 1935, where he commanded a training squadron, and for one year before his detachment in 1937 was Officer in Charge of Corry Field there. In 1935-36 he led the stunt team at the All-American Air Maneuvers, Miami, Florida, which won the trophy for the best team in acrobatics.

Rear Admiral Gehres was operations officer on the staff of Commander Carrier Division 2, USS YORKTOWN, flagship, from July, 1937 until June, 1938. He then joined the USS RANGER, and from May to

185

Rear Admiral Leslie E. Gehres, USN Ret.                    Page 2

December, 1939 served as air officer of that carrier. He next had
duty as executive officer of the Naval Air Station, Pearl Harbor,
Hawaii, from January, 1940 until October 31, 1941 when assigned
duty as Commander, Patrol Wing 4. He was later designated Commander
Aircraft, Northwestern Sea Frontier and Commander, Fleet Air Wing
Four, with the accompanying rank of Commodore.

Under command of Rear Admiral Gehres, planes of Patrol Wing 4,
and later Air Wing 4, took part in the Aleutians campaigns, flying
in an area where weather conditions are the worst in the world for
aerial operations. In June, 1942 his planes (Catalina flying boats)
defended Dutch Harbor from attack by the Japanese, and for two weeks
maintained daily patrols over thousands of square miles of ocean.
During June and July, working in conjunction with submarines, they
prevented enemy reenforcements from landing on Kiska and Attu. They
participated in the occupation of Adak in August, 1942 and of
Amchatka in January, 1943; in the attack on, and occupation of, Attu
in May, 1943, meanwhile continuing almost daily raids on Kiska until
that town was occupied in August, 1943. The Aleutians campaign
ended successfully with the occupation of Kiska, and planes of Air
Wing 4 were enabled to continue bombing and photographing Paramushiro in the Kuriles.

For his services in the Aleutians and succeeding operations
against the Kuriles, Captain Gehres received the Distinguished
Flying Cross from the Army, and was awarded the Legion of Merit,
and Gold Star in lieu of a second Legion of Merit, with citations
as follows:

LEGION OF MERIT
"For exceptionally meritorious conduct in the performance
of outstanding services to the Government of the United
States as Commander of a Patrol Wing and later as Commander
of a Fleet Air Wing in action against enemy Japanese forces
in the Aleutian Islands. Despite extremely unfavorable
weather conditions and limited communication facilities,
Commodore Gehres directed the operations of his planes with
such excellent tactical skill and sound judgment as to enable them to locate, attack and destroy hostile ships and
installations, and to provide our forces with vital weather
data and detailed information of enemy activities. The
expert professional ability and valiant devotion to duty
of Commodore Gehres greatly contributed to the success of
his command in frustrating Japanese plans for invasion of
the eastern Aleutians."

GOLD STAR in lieu of second Legion of Merit
"For exceptionally meritorious service to the Government of the United States as Commander Fleet Air Wing FOUR
and Commander Task Group NINETY POINT TWO between September
1943 and August 1944. Operating with aircraft unsuited for
the tasks performed, Commodore Gehres initiated and successfully continued sustained air operations from the Aleutian
Island bases against Japanese installations in the Northern
Kuriles with patrol planes and medium landplant bombers.
His professional skill, devotion to duty and perseverance

Rear Admiral Leslie E. Gehres, USN Ret.                          Page 3

Gold Star, cont'd
— were in keeping with the highest traditions of the
United States Naval Service."

Following detachment from command of Fleet Air Wing 4, on August
28, 1944, Rear Admiral Gehres joined the Air Force of the Pacific
Fleet and assumed command of the USS FRANKLIN in November of that
year.   That carrier was so severely damaged on March 19, 1945, while
in combat operations with remnants of the Japanese fleet in the
Inland Sea, that her return to the Navy Yard, New York, New York
for repair, under her own power was an outstanding triumph in itself
For his services in command of the FRANKLIN, Rear Admiral Gehres was
presented the Navy Cross and following citation:

NAVY CROSS
   "For extraordinary heroism as Commanding Officer of the
USS FRANKLIN, in action against enemy Japanese forces off
the Southern Coast of Honshu, Japan, on March 19, 1945.
When his ship was struck by enemy bombs which caused tremendous fires and explosions among the fully armed and
fueled planes on the flight deck and in the hangar; Captain
Gehres displayed outstanding resourcefulness in directing
measures which, in spite of severe damage to the ship's
fire-fighting equipment and communications, eventually
brought the fires under control and restored the power
to his ship, enabling the vessel to withdraw from the
hostile coast.  His gallant conduct and devotion to duty
were in keeping with the highest traditions of the United
States Naval Service."

When relieved of command of the FRANKLIN, Rear Admiral Gehres
reported, in July, 1945, for duty as Commander, Naval Air Station.
San Diego, California, and in September, 1948, he assumed the duty
as Director, Naval Officer Procurement, at Los Angeles, and was
serving when relieved of active duty pending his retirement on May
1949.

In addition to the Navy Cross, the Legion of Merit with Gold
Star, Distinguished Flying Cross from the Army, and the Purple Hear
Medal, Rear Admiral Gehres has the Victory Medal, Escort Clasp, and
is entitled to the American Defense Service Medal, Fleet Clasp,
Asiatic-Pacific Campaign Medal, and World War II Victory Medal.  He
also has the Philippine Liberation Ribbon awarded by the Government
of the Philippines.

His wife is the former Miss Rhoda E. Cooley of LaMesa, Califor
nia.  Then have one daughter, and reside in Coronado, California.

— — — —

12 July 1949

```
              SECRETARY OF THE NAVY
           OFFICE OF PUBLIC RELATIONS
              WASHINGTON, 25, D.C.
```

MEMORANDUM TO THE COMMANDING OFFICER:

1. THE ATTACHED COPY OF A PRESS RELEASE ISSUED BY THE PRESS SECTION, OFFICE OF PUBLIC RELATIONS, IS SENT TO YOU TO SHOW THE USE MADE OF MATERIAL RECEIVED THROUGH THE PUBLIC RELATIONS OFFECER, CINCPAC, MENTIONING YOUR VESSEL BY NAME.

2. FORWARDING OF THIS MATERIAL DOES NOT MEAN THAT OTHER MATERIAL CONCERNING YOUR VESSEL HAS NOT BEEN USED. A GREAT VOLUMN OF THE MATERIAL NOW BEING PREPARED IN THE FLEETS IS BEING FORWARDED TO THE FLEET HOME TOWN DISTRIBUTION CENTER DIRECT FROM THE FLEETS, OR IS BEING FORWARDED BY THIS OFFICE TO THE DISTRICT PUBLIC RELATIONS OFFICERS FOR RELEASE WITHIN THEIR DISTRICTS AND COPIES OF SUCH RELEASES ARE NOT AVAILABLE HERE.

---

### USS HICKOX RESCUED SURVIVORS OF USS FRANKLIN

WHILE THE USS FRANKLIN LAY DEAD IN THE WATER, BURNING FIERCELY AFTER THE ATTACK BY A JAPANESE BOMBER MARCH 19, A DARING DESTROYER CAME ALONGSIDE THE STRICKEN CARRIER TO RESCUE 21 SURVIVORS CUT OFF FROM RESCUE ABOARD BY THE FIR

THE BOLD RESCUE OCCURRED LITERALLY UNDER THE CARRIER'S BLAZING FLIGHT DECK AND LESS THAN 100 MILES FROM THE JAPANESE HOME ISLAND OF KYUSHU. SIMULTANEOUSLY, ON THE HORIZON FROM THE DESTROYER AND CARRIER, THEIR TASK GROUP WAS UNDERGOING AIR ATTACK BY ENEMY PLANES WHICH MIGHT HAVE AT ANY MOMENT DIVERTED THEIR ATTENTION TO THE TWO SHIPS DEAD IN THE WATER.

THE OPERATION WAS SIMILAR TO THE ONE WHICH COST THE USS BIRMINGHAM 649 CASUALTIES, MORE THAN ONE-THIRD OF THEM INSTANTLY KILLED, WHEN THAT VESSEL SOUGHT TO AID THE STRICKEN USS PRINCETON WHICH EXPLODED DURING THE MANEUVER.

THE DESTROYER WAS THE USS HICKOX, COMMADED BY COMMANDER JOSEPH J. WESSON, U.S.N., WHOSE USUAL ADDRESS IS 470 West 24th STREET, NEW YORK, NEW YORK, AND WHOSE WIFE, MRS. ANN WESSON, LIVES AT 698 EAST CALIFORNIA STREET, PASADENA, CALIFORNIA. IN THIS AND OTHER PHASES OF THE DESTROYER'S RESCUE OPERATIONS, 91 OFFICERS AND MEN OF THE FRANKLIN WERE RESCUED.

MAJOR ROLE IN THE HEROIC DRAMA WAS PLAYED BY THE DESTROYER'S MOTOR WHALEBOAT WHICH MADE FIVE TRIPS IN A CHOPPY SEA FROM THE HICKOX TO THE FLAMING CARRIER. THE DESTROYER SUBSEQUENTLY WENT IN ALONGSIDE THE LARGER VESSEL TO TAKE ABOARD THE 21 STRAINED SURVIVORS.

AS THE HICKOX CAME ALONGSIDE THE FRANKLIN, RESCUE PARTIES WERE FORMED ON THE DESTROYER'S FORECASTLE. THE PARTY MEMBERS BEING EXPOSED UNDER THE FLATTOP'S BLAZING FLIGHT DECK. DIRECTING THE RESCUE PARTIES WAS LIEUTENANT WILLIAM W. POTTS, U.S.N.R., OF 2647 EAST FOURTEENTH PLACE, TULSA, OKLAHOMA.

WHILE LIEUTENANT POTT'S RESCUE PARTIES WERE OCCUPIED WITH SURVIVORS FIRE-FIGHTING TEAMS SUPERVISED BY LIEUTENANT (JUNIOR GRADE) FORREST D. HECKMAN, US.N.R., OF 625 WEST BRIDGE AVENUE, BLACKWELL, OKLAHOMA, AND C.H. BRENNAN, SHIPFITTER, FIRST CLASS, U.S.N.R. OF 946 NORTH NINTH STREET, ST. JOSEPH, MISSOURI, WERE DIRECTING STREAMS OF WATER AT THE CARRIERS STERN.

**Oral History – Rear Admiral Leslie R. Gehres – By Pete Wilson, former California governor**

Some years after the death of Rear Admiral Leslie E. Gehres, a friend gave me a necktie as a present for my efforts to arrange for permanent berthing of the Missouri at Hunter's Point in San Francisco. That tie is special to me. On it is inscribed the proud battle cry of the U.S. Navy, "Don't give up the ship." It is because it brings to mind memories of the remarkable World War II naval hero, Les Gehres, commander of the aircraft carrier, U.S.S. Franklin, who refused an order to abandon ship when to do so you would have cost the lives of some two hundred men trapped below. The distinguished naval historian Samuel Eliot Morison described the Franklin as the most heavily damaged warship in naval history to survive attacks that should have sunk her.

The extraordinary performance and heroism of Captain Gehres and his crew won for the Franklin not only survival but the distinction of having the most decorated crew in naval history. Two Congressional Medals of Honor were awarded, and there should have been a third – Les Gehres, but he declined to accept it, declaring that he had only performed his duty to his ship and crew. But he had performed it with such inspiring leadership and tenacity in the face of incredible danger and loss of life that the Navy insisted he accept the Navy Cross, second only to the Medal of Honor as recognition of conspicuous gallantry under fire. He managed to save his ship a charred hulk after exploding ordinance and gasoline fires had rendered it a floating inferno and killed over nine hundred of his crew – and with a skeleton crew of volunteers sailed it back some 13,000 miles to New York harbor.

Some twenty years later, the hero of the Franklin had retired from the Navy and was a successful businessman living in San Diego and by then was in his twelfth year as the chairman of the county Republican committee. I was a young lawyer working for him as the executive director and legal counsel of the committee. I was privileged to work closely with him, and to develop a fast friendship with an extraordinary leader and an extraordinary and generous friend. He was a strong personality who expressed firmly held opinions that were the result of strong convictions. He was exceptionally thoughtful in both senses of the word, and was truly eloquent both on paper and as an extemporaneous speaker.

Paul Peterson, a very bright and articulate young lawyer, was then the chairman of the Democratic county committee. Paul was a very good debater, but he laughs and shakes his head recalling the times that he had to face Les in a debate setting. "It was not a fair fight," he chuckles. "Les was unfailingly gracious to me. There was non animus, there were no cheap shots. He was confident, pleasant and good humored – and a gifted natural orator. When it was over, he would congratulate me on my performance, but we both knew it was Les who had held the audience hanging on his every word." The Freedoms Foundation at Valley Forge evidently held the same high opinion of Les as a writer of great persuasive powers: They repeatedly recognized speeches and columns he had penned with their highest awards.

And I know why. I know his secret. He was articulate to be sure, but he had something much more important – something of far greater value:

When I wear that tie, I think of Les not just because of his Navy Cross-winning performance in saving his ship and the lives of hundreds of his crew, but because of the moral as well as physical courage that sustained him to hold on to principled positions with the same integrity and tenacity as when he refused to abandon ship. I've known many people in public life who were easily bright enough to know the right thing to do, but who lacked the courage to do it. I have known too many who backed away from confrontation and principle and chose the much easier path of ducking or choosing not to become involved. But not Les Gehres. Never. He was loyal to what he believed in and to people he believed in. He did not abandon either under pressure. And he did not wait to be asked for help. When it was needed, he acted to do what was needed.

I was walking behind him as we left the Cow Palace at the end of a session of the Republican National Convention in 1964. About two steps ahead of him, a teenage girl was enthusiastically marching along carrying a campaign placard. Suddenly a scruffy unshaven man in his mid 30's stood scowling in her path, knocked the placard from her hands and thrust his face into hers, shouting an obscenity at her. Les was then in his late 60's, wearing glasses and a stylish straw fedora. But he was a big man, burly and powerfully built. In two lightning fast strides he was suddenly between the young girl and the shouting man, had pinned the man's arms against his sides, lifted him and slammed him down on the hood of the nearest parked car.

"I ought to break your rotten neck, you gutless thug! – picking on a little girl!" The gutless thug was not only gutless, but speechless and plainly scared witless, as he started up at Les, unable to move. Neither he nor I were in any doubt that the strong, very angry man holding him pinned to the car hood could in fact break his neck if he decided to. His eyes grew round with fear the next instant when Les picked him up, grabbed him by the scruff of his neck and the seat of his pants and yelled at him, "Now get the hell out of here before I change my mind and do it!" With that, Les gave the thug a mighty shove that sent him flying. He just managed to keep his feet. When he was about fifteen feet away, he turned, red-faced and scowling and yelled, "You old bastard!" Les took a quick step in his direction and the coward turned and ran like a rabbit.

A small crowd had gathered by this time. Les said in a loud, clear voice, "How dare he call me old!" and then bellowed with laughter, as did the crowd who broke into enthusiastic applause and cheers. Les turned to the teenage girl who looked up adoringly at her rescuer. He removed his hat and softly asked, "Are you alright, Miss? Did that bum hurt you?" She shook her head and gave him a dazzling smile. He bent down, picked up her placard, and handed it to her. "Oh, thank you!" she said, and kissed Les on the cheek. "Well, thank you, Honey!" he laughed as she ran off.

I'm sure she never learned that her knight in glasses and the straw fedora was the Hero of the Franklin. A small incident but a revealing one. It was not the last time I would see that same instinct in Les, the proper action in almost instant response to a threat to a person or cause he cared about, or simply to prevent injury or injustice to innocents as with the teenager and the bullying thug.

Les was naturally chivalrous, decent and generous of spirit. It doubtless gave him satisfaction and pleasure to be on the side of right after the victory. But what truly set him apart was his readiness to take action to defend those in need without counting the possible cost. He did not wait to weigh threats to his own safety in war or his own interest in peace. He was decisive because he had already decided which side he was on and why, without being asked and before the need for his action had arisen. The men he led in war sensed that in the standards he set and met himself, with a style of leadership that demanded of them and of himself energy, discipline, courage and focus on victory arising from clear values and purpose.

I sensed it, working for him in a time of peace, to achieve the kind of country he had fought for with such selflessness and distinction. It was a priceless learning experience and one that taught me to anticipate worst case scenarios and options available to meet and deal with them in my chosen career of public service. It also taught an even more valuable lesson: How to set up a goal and pursue a course to make that goal happen, to put in place step by step the prerequisites for success. But basic to that success is having what Les had, the fundamental foundation of value upon which to rely and build, the premises which give purpose and direction to the course you chose.

Les loved his country, his family, and his friends. He understood that freedom is precious because it is essential for the creation of opportunity, and for progress that

191

advances learning and quality of life. He also knew that freedom is not free, that it cannot be taken for granted by those of us fortunate to be born to it, but must be defended against tyrants foreign and domestic. He knew that America's military strength must be maintained and defended over the objections of those among us too naive to understand that strength in arms and the resolve to use it if necessary are far more effective and far less costly deterrents to aggression and war than weakness that invites attack.

Les knew that American weakness and isolationism have required the bloodshed and lives of young Americans to repurchase our freedom in every generation. He knew that because he had himself suffered as the skipper of the Franklin the terrible heart-rendering pain of losing more than 700 young lives under his command. Strong and tough as he was, the Captain of "The Ship That Wouldn't Die" (as NBC-TV entitled its hour-long special on the Franklin on April 6, 1969) felt that pain excruciatingly as he described in a poignant interview (American Heritage, April 1969, Volume XX, Number 3, at page 83) the nightmare of the wholesale burials at sea "[T]he ship was full of death and...it was terrible."

I visited Les for the last time as he lay dying of cancer in a hospital bed in Balboa Naval Hospital. His daughter had just emerged from his room as I was about to enter. She was in tears, but pulled herself together after a moment and said, "Pete, don't stay long. He loves you but he is in unbearable pain that they can't help. He'll try to be strong as long as you are there, but don't stay long, please." I put my arms around her and managed to mumble, "OK."

I didn't stay long. He was obviously suffering terrible pain and had grown terribly weak, but true to her prediction, was trying to be strong and upbeat for my sake. I told him that I loved him, that I admired him, and owed him more than I could ever repay or even express for all that he has done to help me, and to teach me about courage and honesty by example. Then I told him he was truly a great man. I managed to get that out and then I couldn't speak. I squeezed his hand and he squeezed back. Then he managed a faint smile, closed his eyes and let go of my hand. I turned and left so he would not see or hear me as I had begun to weep and could not stop.

I got out of the room and just stood there for a time, feeling terrible loss and grief. Then I became aware that the young doctor who had been treating Les was at my side trying to comfort me. He had his hand on my shoulder. He said, "Mr. Mayor, I am terribly sorry. I know how much you cared for Admiral Gehres. And he told me how much he cares for you, and... how proud he is of you. He is quite a remarkable man, from all accounts a real hero. Won the Navy Cross." I nodded, thanked him for his kindness and could say no more. I wanted to get away before the tears started flowing again. I went down to the parking lot and sat in my car and let the grief wash over me. Finally the tears stopped. I knew they would come again, but I knew he would chide me, gently, and say, "OK, Pete, come on now. You've got work to do and a city to run. Lots of people depending on you. Move on, Marine, do your duty."

The first duty I felt was to help see that Les got the kind of memorial that all of us who loved him knew he deserved, with the Naval Training Center on hand there to play the Navy Hymn invoking the protection of the "Eternal Father...For those at peril on the sea." In the long proud history of naval warfare, few have been more at peril on the sea than Admiral Les Gehres, and very few have responded with such conspicuous gallantry, such coolness under fire and enormous pressure, such daring leadership. The crew of the Franklin deserves the enormous credit they have received as the most decorated of any ship in the history of the U.S. Navy. But with all respect to those who earned those decorations, they would not have done so had not their gutsy skipper refused to abandon ship and led and inspired them to make the Herculean efforts that saved the Franklin and the hundreds of lives of those sailors trapped below decks.

In his obituary, I said that "Les Gehres would have been a giant in any age and in my company. He had the moral courage and stamina that made him an imposing patriot and spokesman for freedom, American strength and peace through strength." More than three decades later, I feel even more strongly today that Les deserves that tribute and more. He was an inspirational leader and fighter for freedom in peace and war who could and did summon others to greatness. He declined the Medal of Honor as unwarranted by the simple performance of his duty as captain of his ship to save it and his crew.

I don't dispute his definition of his duty. But the performance of that duty which provided such inspirational leadership to his crew, the courageous decision to save a ship that by all rights should not have survived, and the sheer tenacity of the effort he sustained and inspired in others to succeed in actually saving the Franklin are uniquely deserving of a special and enduring recognition: To preserve his unique and inspiring leadership for future generations, a future warship of the United States Navy should be christened the U.S.S. Leslie E. Gehres. A great fighting ship launched and equipped to preserve peace and enduring freedom deserves the name and proud heritage of a great fighting patriot.

# Courier-Gazette
## DIGITAL EDITION

# Newark's hero - Rear Admiral Gehres ceremony Saturday

The school district, village and town will honor the late Rear Admiral Leslie Gehres on September 28 at Newark High School.

The public is invited to attend this historic ceremony at 1:30 p.m.. outside the main entrance of the school.

Rear Admiral Gehres is a World War II hero who rescued more than 300 sailors trapped below deck in a burning aircraft carrier. the *USS Franklin*. on March 19, 1945. They were 60 miles off the coast of Japan. under attack by Japanese aircraft. More than 1000 crew members. from a crew of 3000, were killed and injured.

Leslie Gehres was born in Newark on September 23, 1898. He and his sisters attended Newark.

The village recognized Captain Gehres at its Rose Festival in 1945. but his outstanding accomplishments are worthy of being remembered with a memorial. The Sept. 28 ceremony will move into the gym and conclude in the school's foyer with the unveiling of an exhibit.

**The Village of Newark and Town of Arcadia have both proclaimed September 28, 'Leslie E. Gehres Day.'**

September 2, 2002

# Memorial Tribute To
# Rear Admiral Leslie E. Gehres
# Brings Countless Expressions
# Of Praise And Gratitude

Congressman James T. Walsh was just about to share his thoughtful reflections on the extraordinary accomplishments of Rear Admiral Leslie E. Gehres in the Newark High School gymnasium September 28, when he quickly shifted gears.

Hoping to surprise Gehres family members and even organizers, William J. Stewart and wife, Eleanor, it was not known exactly when the mystery call would come in.

Governor George Pataki was on the line, calling from an event he was attending in Elmira. Walsh, who represents the 25th district, graciously put his remarks on hold and introduced him.

Applause swept through the expansive room after the Governor greeted the more than 400 people attending the event sponsored by the school district and the village. But it quickly stilled as everyone listened to Pataki's warm and encouraging remarks that were followed by voluminous applause.

The call from the Governor further charged the atmosphere in which emotions had already swelled to a heightened, patriotic pitch after a monument in the Rear Admiral's memory had been dedicated in a somber service outside in the crisp fall air.

Led by former Newark Mayor, Lt. Col. Fred Pirelli and featuring remarks from leaders of local veteran's organizations and Gold Star Mother Dolores Wagemaker, the dedication was punctuated with heartfelt, hometown pomp and pageantry befitting this man's distinguished Naval career.

### An Extraordinary American And Newark Native

Rear Admiral Gehres' accomplishments are many, but certainly his greatest - the one that captured the attention of the world and the national media in 1945 - was when he served as captain of the U.S. aircraft carrier, the U.S.S. Franklin. On March 19, 1945, when the ship was 60 miles off the eastern coast of Japan, it was attacked by Japanese aircraft. More than 1,000 members of the crew of 3,000 were immediately killed or injured and with the ship extensively damaged and in danger of sinking or capsizing, Captain Gehres refused to abandon it and rescued more than 300 sailors trapped below deck and safely removed the injured to other ships. The direct bomb hit caused the ship to burn for 15 hours and with the number of casualties, it was one of the worst U.S. Naval disasters at sea.

Amazingly, Captain Gehres was also able to save the damaged ship and bring it back over 12,000 miles through enemy waters to the Brooklyn Navy Yard with a skeleton crew of 704. This remarkable story was the subject of a NBC television-sponsored documentary entitled "The Ship That Wouldn't Die," narrated by actor Gene Kelly and a book entitled, "I Was Chaplain On The Franklin" by Father Joseph T. O'Callahan, S.J.

Rear Admiral Gehres was also responsible for driving the Japanese out of the Aleutian Islands in World War II. He was promoted to the rank of Commodore for his leadership skill in this campaign - a rank that had not been given to any Navy officer since the War of 1812 when

*This is the scene looking down from the bleachers in the gymnasium during the ceremony.*

Commodore Oliver Perry chased the British out of Lake Erie.

Following his retirement in 1948 from the Navy, he ultimately became the general manager of the National Marine Terminal Company in California. He also served as chairman of the San Diego Republican Central Committee, organizing support for former Gov. Ronald Reagan, former Senator George Murphy and former Presidents Dwight D. Eisenhower and Richard M. Nixon. Rear Admiral Gehres ran for Congress in 1950 but was unsuccessful.

Newark School Superintendent Robert Christmann promised at the beginning of the formal, indoor program, that those who might not know much about Rear Admiral Gehres would come to be as proud of him as the organizers of the event.

"He was described as an imposing patriot and a spokesman for freedom, strength and peace," Christmann said of Rear Admiral Gehres. "The life that began in Newark in 1898, was given to every American in defense of liberties during the second World War. We will do our very best to hold sacred his ideals and communicate what he represented to future generations."

The tribute then moved into a lockstep military cadence with a formal procession into the gymnasium by an honor color guard from the Rochester Navy & Marine Center, and contingent of midshipmen from the NROTC program at the University of Rochester. A stirring rendition of the National Anthem, by Lynne Mooney, was accompanied by the NHS band under the direction of David Schwind.

### A Tribute Befitting A Hero

The program that ensued was lengthy. But every word of tribute and appreciation expressed by the varied list of speakers - and in letters from those unable to attend - continually drove home the point that Rear Admiral Gehres' exceptional life and selfless acts serve as an incredible lesson to us all.

"Admiral Gehres is a symbol of what's been called "the Greatest Generation," a title given to those who valiantly rose to meet the challenges presented by World War II, both at home and abroad," said Congress-

*Lynne Mooney sings the National Anthem at the indoor ceremony and is accompanied by the Newark High School Band under the direction of David Schwind*

*Members of the Rochester Navy Honor Color Guard, back left, and Midshipmen from the University of Rochester NROTC program stand at attention throughout the ceremony,*

man Walsh. "They were protectors of liberty and defenders of freedom throughout the world, and their work and sacrifice ensures that today the United States remains the world's beacon of democracy. It will be difficult for any subsequent generation to ever match their selfless sacrifice and valor."

### One Of The State And Nation's Greatest Heroes

State Senator Mike Nozzolio, who represents the 53rd district, spoke of the countless "national heroes" whose birthplace was New York like Presidents Franklin Delano Roosevelt, Teddy Roosevelt, Martin VanBuren and Millard Fillmore; Sojurner Truth, Emma Willard, Lou Gehrig and Norman Rockwell, Elizabeth Cady Stanton, Susan B. Anthony, Harriet Tubman, William Seward and Elizabeth Blackwell.

"And, of course, Rear Admiral Leslie Gehres," he said, noting what then Captain Gehres did aboard the U.S.S. Franklin was remarkably similar to the heroes of 9/11 - "the worst disaster ever to take place on American soil, followed by Pearl Harbor.

"Admiral Gehres did what thousands of heroes did on September 11. . . . the firefighters and police officers who rushed into the burning towers to help the victims and refused to leave, ultimately sacrificing their lives. It is estimated that the selfless actions of these New York heroes saved 25,000 lives."

Continuing, the Senator said the dedication of the monument in Gehres' memory and the opening of the memorial exhibit in the school, is an honor that is "long overdue and a fitting tribute to this national hero from Newark, a member of the "Greatest Generation."

"... It reminds us all, and especially our children, who REAL heroes are," he continued. "Not athletes, rock stars or celebrities, but people like our firefighters, police officers and emergency medical workers. People like our veterans and the men and women of the military currently serving to defend and protect our freedom. People like Rear Admiral Leslie E. Gehres.

Citations in honor of Gehres were read,

196

including one from Pataki; from 27th district Congressman Tom Reynolds; and 128th district Assemblyman Bob Oaks. Proclamations announcing September 28, as Leslie E. Gehres Day in Wayne County and Newark were also read or acknowledged.

### Gehres Family Members Introduced

Leslie Van Huben, nephew of Rear Admiral Gehres, introduced the 10 members of Gehres' extended family who had come from as far away as California to attend the event.

"This family has always been proud of his (Gehres') accomplishments," Van Huben said. "His patriotism. His loyalty and dedication to duty. His concern and compassion for the men he led and his heroism in discharging his duties.

"He was a great military man, a great airman, a great seaman and a great family man," he continued. "We also wish to thank Dr. William Stewart and his wife, Eleanor, for conceiving, organizing and ramrodding this project. We thank the (school district) personnel who helped so artistically with arranging the exhibit. And we are especially grateful to Superintendent Robert Christmann and Mayor Blandino and to the people of Newark for the recognition and honor you are bestowing this day on our grandfather, our uncle, but more importantly your native son - Rear Admiral Leslie Edward Gehres United States Navy hero."

### Newark Mayor Blandino Shares His Thoughts

After Van Huben's introduction of family members, Mayor Blandino said he wished the tribute had "been done on this scale when the Rear Admiral was alive and could have been here with us.

"But even now, we can tell his family how proud our community is of this man whose relentless courage refused to let him take the easy road and abandon his horribly damaged ship, the USS Franklin - when he was given an order to do so," the mayor said. "Only God knows the difference that single decision made in the history of the lives of those that otherwise would have been lost like Rene Gauthier, who has traveled here today from Plainville, CT, to tell us a bit of his story," the mayor said.

Newark resident Maurice Boutelegier, who later changed his name to Boutell, was aboard the U.S.S. Franklin and was one of the seaman who survived. Another Newark resident,

*Members of the Gehres family are seen here after they were introduced by Rear Admiral Gehres' nephew, Leslie Van Huben, who was at the podium.*

Harvey Blann, was lost in the tragedy. Blann's name is among those inscribed on the WWII plaque on the monument in Central Park.

"How many children, grandchildren, and great grandchildren of those brave men aboard the Franklin - many who were in their late teens on March 19, 1945 - are alive today because of Captain Leslie Gehres' stubborn refusal to give up when everything around him looked so hopeless?" Blandino asked.

"What lessons can we learn from this man? Many. We will learn some of them today as we reflect on all that is being said by so many distinguished guests," the mayor said.

Board of Education President John Strait said Newark students will learn much from studying Gehres' life.

"As students look into the display cases containing the Rear Admiral's uniform, his many medals, and the pictures, newspaper and magazine articles tracing his extraordinary career, they will be reminded that those who grow up in small communities like ours are capable of achieving greatness," he said. "I will never forget the rapt attention afforded Dr. William Stewart by Participation in Government students when he shared some of the riveting details of Rear Admiral Gehres' life at a Board of Education meeting. The looks on their faces registered great amazement."

Strait said having the memorial exhibit in the High School will instill a great deal of pride in students when they see students and staff from other schools in the region - and hopefully, as word gets out, tourists from all over - who will come to Newark, NY to learn more about this great man.

Representing the Town of Arcadia, and the Wayne County Board of Supervisors, Joseph De Santo said that had Gehres lived and been able to attend the ceremony, he probably would not have thought what he did aboard the Franklin was heroic.

"He had a job to do and he did it," De Santo said. "And I bet every man aboard that ship said 'Don't worry about anything, the old man will take care of it.' And I bet you that's exactly what he did. He had a job to do and he did it. And I am so proud that he's from Newark, New York."

NHS Student Council president Caitlin Sloane said she was honored to represent the NHS student body and participate in the memorial tribute. She also said when she learned about his accomplishments, she was "amazed."

197

"He obviously was thinking more about his country than his own life," she said. "His integrity, courage and leadership should inspire us all to think more of others than ourselves. Rear Admiral Leslie E. Gehres, and all other veterans who served our country, paved the way for all of us today to live in such a wonderful nation where freedom reigns."

### Honorary Diploma Presented

Because young Leslie Gehres left high school at 16 to enlist in 1914, his grandsons received a Newark High School diploma in his honor. Before making the presentation, NHS Principal Tom Miller noted that like during World War II, many thousands of brave individuals also selflessly left hearth and home to serve their country during World War I and were not able to finish high school. He said most of them died without hope of ever receiving their high school diploma.

"And so today, just five days after what would have been Rear Admiral Gehres' 104th birthday had he lived, it is thrilling and a great privilege to posthumously award a Newark High School degree in his honor to his grandsons Leslie John Girard and Peter Gehres Girard, who have come from California to participate in this ceremony." Miller said. "We all owe their grandfather a tremendous debt of gratitude."

*With U.S.S. Franklin survivor to his immediate right, Lt. Col. Fred Pirelli, at the podium, presents colors to Rear Admiral Leslie E. Gehres' grandsons - Peter Gehres Girard and Leslie John Girard, both of San Diego.*

Miller also thanked the people of Newark for helping to provide such a great high school in which to house the Gehres museum.

Another memorable moment during the program involving the Rear Admiral's grandsons, was the presentation to them of colors by Pirelli. Flanked by Rene Gauthier, Navy representatives Capt. Gavin Lowder and Capt. Roosevelt "Rick" Wright, Pirelli and the others saluted as the members of the audience stood to honor the deceased hometown hero.

### Navy Men Remember One Of Their Own

It would be difficult to say that any part of the program was better than another, but speeches by Capt. Lowder, Gauthier, and Capt. Wright were certainly highpoints. "Heroes begin as ordinary people are faced with extraordinary circumstances," asserted Capt. Lowder , who is commander of Naval Reserve Officers Training Corps Unit, University of Rochester, recalling some of the Rear Admiral's life, Lowder noted he was born on September 23, 1898, and began his naval career at the tender age of 16, enlisting in the Navy in the first year of the First World War.

"He rose through the ranks as a naval aviator, devoting 32 years of service distinguished by leadership, commitment and dedication to his sailors and his country," Lowder continued. "Rear Admiral Gehres was one of the first aviators to fly off our first aircraft carrier, the USS Langley, and in the interwar years he was a founding member of the "High Hats", direct ancestors of today's Blue Angels. At the outset of the Second World War he played a large role in the defense of the Aleutian Islands. But it was as Captain of the USS Franklin that he faced his ultimate challenge. Much has been written about this event and many of you know the story. But allow me to revisit this harrowing tale with you.

### The Ship That Wouldn't Die

"The Franklin's keel was laid on December 7, 1942, one year to the day after the Japanese attack on Pearl Harbor. For ten months naval engineers and ship builders worked furiously to construct a mighty carrier. She would have an 872-foot long flight deck rising 60 feet above the sea and become home to over 3,000 men. She would carry a compliment of 100 planes; hold thousands of gallons of aviation fuel, fuel oil; and tons of bombs, rockets and anti-aircraft ammunition.

"The Franklin was launched on October 14, 1943, and formally commissioned at the Norfolk Navy yard on January 31, 1944. This magnificent vessel would ultimately fight through five major Pacific campaigns. But it was on March 19, 1945, that she found her place in naval history.

"On the morning of March 19, the "Big Ben" was operating 60 miles off the shores of Kyushu, Japan, a unit of Task Force 58 of the American Fifth Fleet — a task force that covered a fifty square mile area of ocean. This was the greatest armada of ships the world had ever seen. Big Ben's new commanding officer was Captain Leslie Gehres. Captain Gehres was considered a strict officer - a mustang, an officer who had risen through the enlisted ranks. The Franklin was flagship for Admiral Davison - Commander, Carrier Division Two.

"As the Task Force approached the Japanese homeland, the enemy threw everything they had into the fight. For two days and nights, kamikazes and torpedo bombers attacked the task group. The Franklin's crew was at a constant state of alert, running to and from battle stations at all hours of the

198

day and night. As dawn broke on March 19th, general quarters were secured, flight quarters were called away, and the first hot meal in days was prepared for the tired and hungry men." "Just past 7 a.m., while flight quarters were in progress, a small speck appeared out of the overcast. Rapidly closing on the ship, the Japanese dive-bomber flew straight down the flight deck, finding its mark with two five hundred pound bombs that penetrated the flight deck and exploded in the hangar deck below. Three quarters of the ship was engulfed in smoke and fire. The Franklin, fully loaded with ammo and armed planes was a 30,000-ton bomb. The open aviation lines ignited and planes on her flight deck fueled the raging inferno. Bombs and rockets exploded while the blast of 40,000 gallons of aviation fuel billowed across the hangar deck like a flaming Niagara. Those on the hangar deck were vaporized.

"The damage was incredible. Ready service magazines exploded and the 32-ton forward deck elevator lifted into the air and crashed back through. The explosions literally lifted the carrier out of the sea and shook it from side to side. No one thought the Franklin would survive, as a mushroom cloud of black smoke rose hundreds of feet into the air.

"Captain Gehres reacted swiftly and decisively. He swung the ship's wheel to starboard, allowing firefighters to work fore and aft. As her boilers shut down the Franklin lost power, and she began to drift towards the Japanese shore. Rear Admiral Davison and his aide came to the bridge and told Captain Gehres that he would have to transfer his flag. The Admiral's Chief of Staff suggested to Gehres that he issue the order to abandon ship. Captain Gehres said years later, "That was none of his d. . . business. I had no intention of abandoning the ship."

"The Captain had in mind the lessons learned at the Battle of Midway. He had heard that when the U.S.S. Yorktown was severely damaged our own destroyers had to deliver the torpedoes that sank her, and she had gone down with men still trapped below. Truth or rumor, Capt. Gehres would not send his own sailors to a similar fate.

"The fleet closed around Franklin, cruisers, destroyers and battle cruisers formed in a tight screen to protect her. A group of steward's mates, mess attendants, latched onto the messenger line from the cruiser Pittsburgh and heaved the 540 foot steel cable towline by hand.

"The ship had lost all electrical power and the four for-

*Congressman James Walsh, left, and Newark Superintendent applaud just before U.S.S. Franklin survivor Rene Gauthier began to speak at the podium.*

ward boilers were damaged beyond repair. The ship's electricians routed steam pressure from the after boilers to her forward engines, and by the morning of the second day Captain Gehres was able to write on his bulletin board for the crew – "We are under our own power and will be making fifteen knots by noon."

"Out of 3,400 men on board the Franklin, 724 died in the fires. One third were wounded and a small but courageous crew of 704 sailed the Franklin home. Six weeks later the Franklin passed by the Statue of Liberty with all hands lining the rails in salute. The 12,000 mile journey had ended for the most damaged warship in the history of the US Navy ever to make it back to port under her own power."

"The crew of the U.S.S Franklin became the most decorated crew in US Navy history, recognized by two Congressional Medals of Honor, 19 Navy Crosses, 22 Silver Stars, and numerous Bronze Stars and Citations. Mindful of the incredible heroism of so many of his crew that day, Captain Gehres was humble about his own accomplishments. Called before the Board of Decorations in Washington and asked if he should receive the Medal of Honor, he replied, "No. It is the commanding officer's primary duty to save his ship and I had done nothing beyond the call of duty."

"What he had done, in truth, was something no other man could have done. On that ship on that day he shouldered ultimate responsibility for countless life and death decisions made on a moment's notice. He directed the fight that saved his ship. He inspired his crew by personal example. He refused to surrender. He proved that "a ship that won't be sunk can't be sunk.

"Such is the nature of heroism ... an ordinary person called to extraordinary deeds," Lowder concluded.

### Survivor Speaks

Some of the most poignant moments of the program came as Gauthier came to the podium. Given a standing ovation by the crowd, the U.S.S. Franklin survivor, understandably struggled at times and fought back tears in his attempt to recall the events leading up to and the day of the unforgettable attack of the ship in 1945. A short and powerful video narrated by actor Charles Derning was then shown, bringing the audience an even greater understanding of the horrors faced by the ship's crew after the attack.

With emotions so heavy at this point, Capt. Roosevelt Wright Jr., a media consultant for the Assistant Secretary of the Navy and professor at S. I. Newhouse School of Public Communications at Syracuse University, quickly changed the mood with upbeat remarks including his reading the famous Edgar Guest poem entitled "Navy Epic" about the U.S.S. Franklin.

Wright, who is also a board member of the National Naval Officers Association, said he was thrilled to be speaking at the program because of several connections he has to the U.S.S. Franklin.

Growing up in Elizabeth City, NC, he recalled his father, Roosevelt Wright Sr., was a civilian electrician who worked at the Norfolk Naval ship yard where the U.S.S. Franklin was built. His father's cousin was a member of the Franklin crew.

"My hometown is a Navy town. The U.S.S. Franklin. What a story. I've been hearing the story all of my life," he said excitedly. "God Bless each and every one of you. What a wonderful high school this is. Thank God I finally got to Newark, NY."

### Grandsons Speak

Both Leslie John Girard and Peter Gehres Girard briefly shared some of their recollections of their grandfather and each expressed gratitude to the school district and village, on behalf of the entire Gehres family for dedicating a monument to and opening a memorial exhibit in memory of their grandfather.

"I want to thank you all very, very much," said Leslie Girard. "This has been a wonderful experience and you can rest assured I will bring my family back to Newark so they can see the memorial and this wonderful town.

Peter Girard, also thanked everyone.

"Our mother regrets that she could not attend, but I know she is deeply moved. It means so much to her that you should consider awarding the diploma that my grandfather never achieved. And that you should recognize him here today in these wonderful surroundings," he said. "We will take this diploma and flag back to our mother. For our grandfather. For our mother. I thank you all."

### Organizers Speak

Lastly, but certainly not least, Dr. William Stewart and wife, Eleanor, spoke and by their applause, the audience seemed to be saying thanks for not giving up their exhausting quest of seeing a lasting memorial to Rear Admiral Gehres in his hometown.

A retired University of Cincinnati College of Education professor emeritus, Stewart, who lives in Florida with his wife and who is writing a biography about Rear Admiral Gehres doggedly determined some time ago that this native hero would not be forgotten and that he would have the prominent place in local history he deserves.

Gehres and his sisters attended Newark schools with Stewart's mother here before he enlisted in 1914.

"I knew his family as I am sure many people in Newark did," Stewart said. One of Stewart's favorite pastimes as a youngster was walking from his South Main Street home to visit Newark's old air strip called "Bailey's Lot" on the south side of the village - to watch then Lieutenant Gehres fly his plane.

"I used to go there with some of my buddies to see his plane," Stewart recalled.

Stewart shared many such recollections and spoke at length about the Rear Admiral's many accomplishments, awards and recognitions.

"By honest efforts, he worked his way up the ladder on his own and his career indicates a high level of performance consistently above and beyond the call of duty," he said.

Before closing the formal program and proceeding with the unveiling of the exhibit in the high school foyer, Christmann pledged, "From this day forward, this village of Newark, NY and this Newark Central School District will never forget the integrity, the courage and the leadership of our native son, Rear Admiral Leslie E. Gehres."

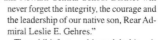

The exhibit features his medals, his uniform, numerous books and magazine articles, U.S.S. Franklin artifacts including a portion of the ship's deck; numerous citations and more. It can be seen from 9 a.m. to 4 p.m. Monday through Friday at Newark High School off Peirson Avenue.

"Do return to the museum again and again," Eleanor Stewart urged at the program's end. "Bring family and friends. Tell others around the nation. Bill and I will be forever in deep gratitude to all the participants of this "Leslie E. Gehres Day" event."

*Eleanor and Dr. William J. Stewart, who spearheaded and organized the event, spoke last at the program at Newark High School, September 28.*

Stewart said his book will be published sometime next summer. Profits, if realized, will be given to Newark High School to help institute an ROTC program there. ■

# A CALL TO DUTY

Prepared speech for Captain Gavin D. Lowder
Rear Admiral Leslie E. Gehres Memorial Dedication Ceremony
Newark
28 September 2002

It has been said that any formal act of remembrance, whether in ritual or
recollection, certifies our humanity.   Let us take today as an opportunity to appreciate
the mystery of human heroism.  Heroes begin as ordinary people put in extraordinary
circumstances.  Today we honor a hero who saw himself as someone who was simply doing his
job.  We honor courage, bravery, dedication and commitment.  We honor lives lost and
lives saved.

Rear Admiral Leslie Gehres was a native of your village.  Born on September 23,
1898, he began as an enlisted man in our Navy and rose through the ranks as a naval
aviator, giving 32 years of illustrative service through his leadership, commitment and
dedication to his sailors and his country.

His career included many heroic endeavors.  Rear Admiral Gehres was one of the
first aviators to fly off the USS Langley and was responsible for driving the Japanese
out of the Aleutian Islands.  But it was his role as Captain of the USS Franklin that
created his ultimate challenge of leadership, courage and commitment.

Much has been written about this event and many of you know the story.  But
allow me to revisit this harrowing tale with you, sharing with you the recounting the
story shared from the USS Franklin homepage and other sources.

One year after the Japanese attack on Pearl Harbor, the Franklin's story began
on December 7, 1942. Her keel was laid at the Newport News Shipbuilding Company in
Virginia.  For ten months naval engineers and ship builders worked furiously to
construct a mighty carrier. She would have an 872-foot long flight deck rising 60 feet
above the sea and become home to over 3000 men.  She would carry a compliment of 100
planes, hold thousands of gallons of aviation fuel, fuel oil, tons of bombs rockets and
anti aircraft ammunition.

The Franklin was launched on October 14, 1943 and formally commissioned at the
Norfolk Navy yard on January 31, 1944.  This magnificent vessel would ultimately
fight through 102,000 combat miles participating in 5 major Pacific campaigns.

But on March 19, 1945, she would become a part of naval history.

On the morning of March 19, the Franklin, nicknamed "Big Ben" was about 60 miles
from the shores of Kyushu, Japan.  She was part of Task Force 58 of the American
Fifth Fleet -- a task force that covered a fifty square mile area of ocean.  This was
the greatest armada of ships the world had ever seen and Big Ben's new
commanding officer was Captain Leslie Gehres.  Captain Gehres was considered a strict
officer, a mustang, who had risen through the ranks from an enlisted man - a mustang.
The Franklin was the Flagship for Admiral Davison and had a new air group on board - Air
Group 5, the famed (or infamous) Black Sheep squadron of Gregory Pappy Boyington.

For two days and nights, the Japanese attacked this task group.  The crew of the
Franklin were at a constant state of alert, running to and from battle stations every
time the alarms sounded. Finally at 6:10 am on March 19th, the battle stations
were secured - and the first hot meal in days was being prepared for hungry and
tired men.

Suddenly two five hundred pound bombs were dropped on the Franklin by a Japanese
Judy dive-bomber.  Three quarters of the ship was inundated by smoke and fire.
The Franklin, fully loaded with gasses and armed planes was a 30,000-ton bomb.  The
open aviation lines ignited and planes warming on her flight deck turned into raging
infernos, with bombs and rockets aboard exploding while 40,000 gallons of aviation fuel
poured out on the hangar deck like a flaming Niagara.  Those on the hanger deck were
vaporized.

The damage was incredible. Ready service magazines exploded and the 32-ton forward deck elevator lifted into the air and crashed back through. The explosions literally lifted the carrier out of the sea and shook it form side to side. No one thought the Franklin would survive as a mushroom cloud of black smoke rose hundreds of feet into the air.

Captain Leslie Gehres reacted decisively. He swung the ship's wheel to starboard, permitting firefighters to work fore and aft. The Franklin began drifting once her boilers shut down and came within 50 miles off the Japanese shore. Rear Admiral Davison and his aide came to the bridge and told Captain Gehres that he would have to transfer his flag. The Admirals aide suggested to Gehres that he issue the order to abandon ship. Captain Gehres said years later " That was none of his damn business. I had no intention of abandoning the ship."

Captain Gehres kept in mind the lessons learned at the Battle of Midway. He remembered that when the U.S.S. Yorktown, CV 5 was sunk, that our destroyers had to deliver the torpedoes that sank her and had heard the rumor that there were men trapped below when the Yorktown went down. Capt Gehres said he would not send hundreds of his own sailors to a similar fate. Captain Gehres set his mind to saving his ship and his crew.

The fleet closed around Franklin, cruisers, destroyers and battle cruisers placed a tight screen to protect her. And a group of steward's mates, mess attendants, latched onto the messenger line from the cruiser Pittsburgh and heaved the 540 foot steel towline by hand while singing gospel spirituals. Think of it. By hand, they pulled a 540 foot steel cable through the sea to enable Franklin to be towed.

The ship had lost all electric all power and the four forward boilers were damaged beyond repair. The ship's electricians routed steam pressure from the after boilers to her forward engines - something never tried before. On March 20th, Captain Gehres wrote on his bulletin board for the crew - "We are under our own power and will be making fifteen knots by noon."

That same morning, two of the crew met on the flight deck near the island. They looked at the wreckage of the command structure and saw the radio mast bent over haphazardly. The gun mounts were riddled with shrapnel holes and fire damage. The flag mast was hanging tenuously to the island by a single role - the ship's flag was wrapped around it at half-mast. "Who put the flag at half mast," a sailor asked. The answer - "No one. She slid down there by herself," his shipmate answered.

The stars and stripes were torn by rocket and shrapnel holes, the white stripes turned gray by smoke; the red stripes a darker shade of crimson. And yet, the stars and blue field were unscathed.

This is America's secret - our nation holds together. Our field of stars on blue remains vibrant under any and all challenge and adversity. And when America is hurt, we fight back, we stick together and we win.

Out of 3500 men on board the Franklin, 836 died in the fires. One third were wounded and a small but courageous crew of 704 sailed the Franklin home. Amazingly, on April 30,1945 the Franklin passed by the Statue of Liberty with all hands standing on deck at salute. The 12,000 mile journey had ended for the most damaged warship in the history of the US Navy to ever make it back to port under her own power.

The crew of the USS Franklin was the most decorated crew in US Navy history. Captain Gehres later stood before the Board of Decorations in Washington and when asked if he should get the Medal of Honor, he replied, "No. It is the commanding officer's primary duty to save his ship and I had done nothing beyond the call of duty. "

This is an American hero. An ordinary person responding to extraordinary

# A CALL TO DUTY

circumstances.

We all know where we were on September 11th, last year. Our nation once again lost family, friends, and fellow Americans. It has been said that America lost our sense of safety, security, even our innocence.

Today, we remember... and honor... those that were lost on the USS Franklin just as we honor the heroism of Rear Admiral Gehres. We are linked in time and memory to the recent observances held at Ground Zero in New York, where names of the dead and missing have been read; at the Pentagon, and in Shanksville, Pennsylvania, where the first battle in the war on terrorism was fought.

One September 11th, ordinary men and women also responded to extraordinary events. We remember those who were carrying out their daily activities on that day, working in their offices, flying to destinations never reached, responding to help others. Some never knew what happened. Others knew the dread and fear as they struggled to escape danger. Still others clearly knew their own lives were on the line, as they moved toward the danger, to save others.

Today, we honor the past, we honor the present and we prepare for the future. We must honor, too, every life saved -- The lives saved in March of 1945 aboard the USS Franklin and the lives saved on September 11th 2001.

As we dedicate this monument to Rear Admiral Leslie Gehres let us not forget to remember those who have deployed overseas to take the battle to the terrorists and those who have harbored them. Let us not forget to celebrate our response to the tragic events of September 11th in the spirit of the men of the USS Franklin.

We have much to celebrate. Every American in this country has exemplified the spirit and dedication of Rear Admiral Gehres and his crew. In moments of uncertainty... uncertainty for personal safety... our people have stayed at their posts, driven by their sense of service. The work of the first responders, the work of recovery and rebuilding, and the work of each of you contributes to our recovery, our future and our victory.

As Rear Admiral Gehres said, "I had no intention of abandoning my ship." We cannot abandon America. So, today is a day of honor and remembrance and it is a day of celebration and rededication. Let us honor all those who did not live to see America after March 18th 1945 or September 11th 2001. Let us honor those who did not live to see the new unity of America. Let us honor every life saved and their rescuers. Through your daily and continued devotion, dedication and commitment, each of you illuminates each lost life with honor.

It is the bright light of Liberty, and the reflection of freedom, which will blind our enemies and guide us into our future - a future of freedom, prosperity and equality for all.

God bless America, and God bless each of you.

"I just wanted to call and congratulate you as you honor the memory of Rear Admiral Leslie E. Gehres. . . . I'd like to congratulate the community, Mayor Blandino, Supervisor De Santo, Senator Nozzolio and Congressman Walsh on everything you are doing today to honor one of the great heroes of World War II. What he did, in particular in saving the U.S.S. Franklin, is something future generations have to remember to appreciate the courage, heroism and inspirational leadership he provided. I simply want to thank the Newark High School for hosting this memorial exhibit. It's critical that our young people and future generations never forget the courage that this Newark native - Rear Admiral Gehres - showed. That's one of the reasons we are the finest nation in the world and I think it is incredibly important and appropriate that Newark is honoring his memory and keeping it alive. I wish I could have been there in person.. .

Governor George Pataki
September 28, 2002

THE SECRETARY OF THE NAVY
WASHINGTON, D.C. 20350-1000

September 16, 2002

GREETINGS TO THE CITIZENS OF NEWARK, NEW YORK,
AND THE HEROIC VETERANS WHO SERVED ABOARD USS FRANKLIN

On behalf of the Department of the Navy, I am honored to send greetings as you dedicate the Rear Admiral Leslie E. Gehres Memorial. Hailing from Newark, New York, Admiral Gehres was a patriot, an exemplary officer and leader, and one of the United States Navy's greatest heroes.

To the volunteers who have worked so hard to make this memorial a success, please accept my deepest thanks. The valiant crew of the USS FRANKLIN will not be forgotten and will stand as an example of exemplary service and valor.

Admiral Gehres and the crew of the aircraft carrier USS FRANKLIN suffered an attack to their ship that cost the lives of 1000 of their shipmates and damage that would have sunk a lesser ship and a lesser crew. Instead, these Sailors, the most decorated crew in U.S. Navy history, and their leader, Admiral Gehres, overcame incredible odds and sailed the FRANKLIN more than 12,000 miles through enemy waters to the safety of the New York Harbor.

Their profound sacrifice, courage and commitment continue to serve as an inspiration for every generation of men and women in uniform who stand watch across our Country and around the globe.

As we reflect on the remarkable accomplishments of Admiral Gehres, we can take pride in the knowledge that there are many brave men and women who continue to follow in his footsteps, protecting freedom, liberty and our way of life. God bless our men and women in uniform, our veterans, the people of Newark, and God Bless America!

Gordon R. England

## United States Department of the Interior

NATIONAL PARK SERVICE
1849 C Street, N.W.
Washington, D.C. 20240

IN REPLY REFER TO:

October 9, 2002

Robert W. Christmann
Superintendent
Newark Central School District
Newark, New York

It was with great enthusiasm that I learned of your museum project to commemorate the ship and crew of U.S.S. Franklin, CV-13, that participated in the great Pacific War and launched air attacks against the Japanese homeland, in late Winter of 1944 – 45.

She was struck by a single Japanese kamikaze plane on the 19th day of March, 1945. And despite more than half of the crew being casualties (724 killed; 265 wounded), those remaining were able to arrest the fire that had turned the ship into a raging inferno. The ship and the remaining crew were saved.

U.S.S. Franklin, CV-13, and her gallant crew, perpetuated the memory of thousands of soldiers in the American Civil War, both the Grey and Blue, who were participants in the Battle of Franklin, Tennessee, which was fought November 30th, 1864. The linkage between the crew of the World War Two U.S.S. Franklin and the soldiers of 1864 is particularly relevant as the Confederate charge at Franklin underscores the type of people who stood tall in defense of what they believed. The obvious comparison serves also to suggest that like them, the officers and men on Franklin stood tall in defense of the principles in which they believed, despite horrific experiences.

U.S.S. Franklin, CV-13, also commemorates the four ships of the United States Navy that preceded her with the venerable and honored name of "Franklin."

Respectfully,

Edwin C. Bearss
Chief Historian Emeritus
National Park Service

Please note that the information indicated in paragraph 1 above is not entirely accruate. The USS Franklin (CV-13) was struck by two 500 pound bombs on March 19, 1945, with the casualty numbers considerably higher. The Japanese Kamikaze attack took place in an earlier battle in the South Pacific, when Captain W. R. Shoemaker was in command. Captain Leslie. E. Gehres was in command of the USS Franklin on March 19, 1945.

THE SECRETARY OF DEFENSE
WASHINGTON

September 13, 2002

Mr. Robert W. Christmann
Superintendent
Newark Central School District
100 East Miller Street
Newark, NY 14513

Dear Mr. Christmann:

Thank you for your kind invitation to take part in the exhibit opening at Newark High School in honor of Rear Admiral Leslie Gehres. I regret I will have to decline, as the schedule is very full these days.

Throughout our history, the United States has been blessed with inspirational leaders such as Admiral Gehres, who always seem to shine brightest when the country needs them the most.

I commend you for honoring him, and I wish you the very best for a successful event.

With best wishes,

Sincerely,

*[signature]*

# Index

# H

# I

# J

# K

# L

# M

# N

# Notes

Newark, N.Y. The Early Years

[1] Cecilia B. Jackson. *Annals of Arcadia*. Vanderbrook Press, 1978. 10-13.

[2] Ibid., 12.

[3] Robert L. Hoeltzel. *Hometown History*. Arcadia Historical Society, 2000. 90-103.

[4] Birth Certificate of Leslie Edward Gehres. September 28, 1898, by Arcadia Town Clerk, Diane Allerton, 2004.

*Prutzman, Thelma. Interview. Newark, New York: 2005.

[5] Information furnished by Leslie Gehres' daughter and other Gehres family members and friends.

[6] Information furnished by Gehres family members and friends.

[7] McNett, D.T. *Great Sodus Bay: A Beautiful Historical Sketch of The Famous Resort*. Sodus Bay Improvement Association, 1912-13, Reprinted by the Sodus Bay Historical Society in 1988.

[8] Information furnished by author's father, Joseph Stewart, and Gehres' family and friends.

[9] McNett, op. cit., 4-5.

[10] Ibid., 9. Common knowledge among Gehres' family and friends.

[11] Information furnished by author's family, friends, and local Gehres' family members.

[12] Masefield John. *Sea Fever: Salt Water Ballads*. McMillan Company, 1923.

[13] McNett, op. cit., 9-10.

[14] Ibid., 9.

[15] Information furnished by author's family, friends, and local Gehres' family members.

[16] McNett, , op. cit.

[17] Information furnished by author's family, friends, and local Gehres' family members.

Rochester; Early Service

[18] Information furnished by Gehres' relatives living in Rochester, New York.

[19] Stickler, Merrill. *Glenn H. Curtiss and The Evolution of Naval Aviation*. Glenn H. Curtiss Museum, 1986.

[20] Reynolds, Clark G. *Admiral John H. Towers: The Struggle for Naval Air Supremacy*. Annapolis: Naval Institute Press, 1991.

[21] Ibid.

[22] Information furnished by Gehres family and friends.

[23] Nilo, James R; St. Peters, Robert. USS *Franklin (CV-13): The Ship That Wouldn't Die*. Paducah, Ky. Turner Publishing Company, 1996.

[24] Ibid.

[25] Information furnished by Gehres family and friends.

[26] Ibid., Marriage certificate.

Barnstorming Days, Science and Technology

[27] Ewing, Steve. *Thach Weave: The Life of Jimmie Thach*. Annapolis: Naval Institute Press, 2004. 12-13.

[28] Ibid., viii.

[29] Nilo, op. cit.

[30] Ibid.

[31] United States Navy Information Services.

[32] Reynolds, Clark G. *Admiral John H. Towers: The Struggle for Naval Air Supremacy*. Annapolis: Naval Institute Press, 1991.

[33] Nilo, op. cit.

[34] Krepinevich, Andrew. *Transforming to Victory: The U.S. Navy, Carrier Aviation, and Preparing for War in the Pacific.* http://www.csbaonline.org/4Publications/PubLibrary/A.20000000. Transforming_to_Vi/A.20000000.Transforming_to_Vi.php. Center for Strategic and Budgetary Assessments. 2000.

[35] Lewis, Isabel M. "Observations of the Central Eclipse of the Sun of April 28 1930 at Honey Lake, California." *Popular Astronomy*, (28:8).

[36] Ibid.
Nilo, op. cit.

[37] "USS *Akron* (ZRS-4)." *Wikipedia*: Wikimedia Foundation. [insert date accessed 16 Mar. 2016]. < http://en.wikipedia.org/wiki/USS_Akron_%28ZRS-4%29>

[38] Interviews, Gehres family members.

[39] Ibid.

[40] Palmer, Robert. Personal interview. [insert date.]

[41] Boyne, Walter J. *Clash of Titans: World War II at Sea.* New York: Touchstone, 1995.

Rumors of War; The USS Franklin is Born

[42] "Army and Navy: Job with Japanese." *Time* Magazine. 27 July 1936.

[43] "John Semer Farnsworth." *Wikipedia*. Wikimedia Foundation. <http://en.wikipedia.org/wiki/John_Semer_Farnsworth>

[44] Layton, Edwin T.; Pineau, Roger; Costello, John. *And I Was There: Pearl Harbor and Midway—Breaking The Secrets* Annapolis: Naval Institute Press, 2006. 59.

[45] Reynolds, Clark G. *The Fast Carriers: The Forging of an Air Navy.* Annapolis: Naval Institute Press, 1968.

[46] Sheridan, John. *Essex Class Aircraft Carrier Data.* <http://www.steelnavy.com/essex_data.htm>

[47] Doehring, Thoralf. *Unofficial U.S. Navy Website* 1999– 2009. <http://www.navysite.de/cv/cv13.htm. >

[48] "USS Franklin." *Wikipedia*. Wikipedia Foundation. <http://en.wikipedia.org/wiki/USS_Franklin_%28CV-13%29>

[49] Wright, Roosevelt, Jr. *Interview*

[50] "Essex-Class Aircraft Carrier." *Wikipedia*. Wikimedia Foundation. <http://en.wikipedia.org/wiki/Essex_class_aircraft_carrier>

[51] Ibid.

[52] Bearss, Edward H. Personal interview.

[54] "Carnton Plantation and Battlefield." *Battle of Franklin Trust*. <http://www.carnton.org/history.htm>

[55] Crutchfield, James A. *The Harpeth River: A Biography.* Johnson City: Tenn.: Overmountain Press, 1994. 23-25.

Guarding the Gate: The Captain Assumes Command

[56] Nilo, op. cit., 80.

[57] Hoehling, A.A. *The* Franklin *Comes Home.* Annapolis: Naval Institute Press. 1974. 6.

[58] Freeman, Elmer. *Those Navy Guys and Their PBY'S: The Aleutian Solution.* Spokane: Kedging Publishing Company, 1999. 19-58.

[59] Young, Donald J. *Japanese Submarines Prowl the U.S. Pacific Coastline in 1941.* HistoryNet.com. <http://www.historynet.com/japanese-submarines-prowl-the-us-pacific-coastline-in-1941.htm/7.> Weider History Group, 2010.

[60] Cloe, John Haile. *The Aleutian Warriors: A History of the 12ᵗʰ Air Force and Fleet Air Wing 4*. Missoula: Anchorage Chapter–Air Force Association and Pictorial Histories Publishing Company, 1990. 38.

[61] Conn, Stetson; Engelman, Rose C.; Fairchild, Byron. *Guarding The United States and Its Outposts*. Washington, D.C., Center of Military History, United States Army, 2002. 223-52. *Building the Navy's Bases in World War II: History of the Bureau of Yards and Docks and the Civil Engineer Corps, 1940-1946*. Washington: United States Government Printing Office, 1947. 163.

[62] Wetterhahn, Ralph. *The Last Flight of Bomber 31: Harrowing Accounts of American and Japanese Pilots who fought in World War II's Arctic Air Campaign*. New York: Carroll & Graf, 2004. 22-23.

[63] Cloe, op. cit., 38.

[64] van der Vat, Dan. *The Pacific Campaign: The U.S. Japanese Naval War 1941-1945*. New York: Touchstone, 1991. 162-63.

[65] *Battle of the Coral Sea*. Naval History & Heritage Command. <http://www.history.navy.mil/photos/events/wwii-pac/coralsea/cs-1.htm>United States Navy, 2009.

[66] Morison, Samuel Eliot. *The Two-Ocean War: A Short History of the United States Navy in the Second World War*. Boston: Little, Brown and Company, 1963. 140-144.

[67] "Battle of the Coral Sea*." Wikipedia*. Wikimedia Foundation. <http://en.wikipedia.org/wiki/Battle_of_the_Coral_Sea>

[68] Costello, John. *The Pacific War*. New York: Rawson, Wade Publishers, Inc.,1981. 262-63.

[69] Reynolds, op. cit., 36-50.

[70] Boyne, Walter J. *Clash of Titans: World War II at Sea*. New York: Touchstone, 1995. 278-80.

[71] Morison, Samuel Eliot. *The Two-Ocean War: A Short History of the United States Navy in the Second World War*. Boston: Little, Brown and Company, 1963. 146-63.

[72] van der Vat, op. cit., 177-78.

[73] van der Vat, op. cit., 180-95.

[74] Davidson, David. "Captain of the Franklin." *American Heritage* Magazine, 20:3 (April 1969).

[75] Morison, op. cit., 146-63.

[76] Ibid., 21.

[77] Costello, op. cit., 283.

[78] van der Vat, op. cit., 196.

[79] Hanson, Shannon. "Attack on America: Dutch Harbor 60 years later: this may come as a surprise, but the nation was attacked twice during WWII. The second time was at the Pearl Harbor of the North in the Aleutian Islands. The National Park Service is making sure we all remember with a new visitor's center." *VFW Magazine*. 2002 via. *accessmylibrary*.). < http://www.accessmylibrary.com/coms2/summary_0286-25533720_ITM.> 8 May 2010.

[80]Goldstein, Donald M., Dillon, Katherine V. *The Williwaw War: The Arkansas National Guard in the Aleutians in World War II*. Little Rock: University of Arkansas Press, 1992. 187.

[81] "Lt. Bill Thies." Personal Web site. (2007) < http://www.angelfire.com/wa/wathies/billthies1.html.>

[82] Seattle Post-Intelligencer

[83]Rearden, Jim. *Koga's Zero: An Enemy Plane That Saved American Lives*. 13:2 (Fall, 1997) .

[84]Creed, Roscoe. *PBY: The Catalina Flying Boat*. Annapolis: Naval Institute Press, 1985. 129.

[85] Springer, Joseph A. *Inferno: The Epic Life and Death Struggle of the USS* Franklin *in World War II*. St. Paul, Minn.: Zenith Press, 2007. 171.

[86] Hanable, William S. "Theobald Revisited." *Alaska at War, 1941-1945: The Forgotten War Remembered*. Anchorage: University of Alaska Press, 2007. 75-80.

[87] Henderson, Bruce. *Down to the Sea*. New York: HarperCollins Publishers, 2007. 56-58.

[88] MacGarrigle, George L. *Aleutian Islands*. U.S. Army Center of Military History.
<http://www.history.army.mil/brochures/aleut/aleut.htm>
[89] Freeman, op. cit., 242.
[90] "Aerology and Naval Warfare: Fleet Air Wing Four Strikes." Chief of Naval Operations, Aerology Section, Washington, D.C., June, 1945.
[91] Ibid.
[92] Ibid.
[93] Dixon, 1st Lt. Jacob W. *Appreciation*.
[94] Hoehling, op. cit., 7.
[95] Wetterhahn, op. cit., 114-19.
[96] Freeman, op. cit., 252.
[97] Ibid., 242.
[98] Wetterhahn, op. cit., 138-141.
[99] Ibid., 119.
[100] Ibid., 124-129; 239-84.
[101] "The Aleutian Islands Campaign." *Wikipedia*. Wikimedia Foundation.
<http://en.wikipedia.org/wiki/Aleutian_Islands_Campaign>
[102] Cloe, op. cit., 321-22.
[103] Bell, Norman. "Paramushiro Hit on Schedule." The *Seattle Times*. Monday, 24 January 1944.
[104] Creed, Roscoe. *PBY: The Catalina Flying Boat*. Annapolis: Naval Institute Press, 1985. 142.
[105] Hoehling, op. cit., 6.
[106] "USS *Franklin*." *Wikipedia*. Wikimedia Foundation.
<http://en.wikipedia.org/wiki/USS_Franklin_%28CV-13%29>
[107] Ibid., 7.
[108] Tuohy, William. *America's Fighting Admirals: Winning the War at Sea in World War II*. St. Paul, Minn. Zenith Press, 2007. 221.
[109] Nilo, op. cit., 10.
[110] Ibid., 204-05.
[111] Reynolds, Clark G. *On The Warpath in the Pacific*. Annapolis: Naval Institute Press, 2005. 397.
[112] Hoehling, op. cit., 18.
[113] Springer, Joseph A. *Inferno: The Life and Death Struggle of the USS Franklin in World War II*. St. Paul, MN: Zenith Press, 2007. 193.
[114] "Deck Log – Remarks Sheet." USS *Franklin* for Monday, March 19, 1945.
[115] Hoehling, op. cit., 15.

The Battle for Survival

[116] Ibid., 29.
[117] O'Callahan, Father Joseph T. *I Was Chaplain on the Franklin*. New York: MacMillan 1956. 65-66.
[118] Toon, Jackson. Interview with the author.
[119] Baumann, Warren L. Letter to author, 2003.
[120] Frajman, John E. Letter to the author. 2003.
[121] Toon, op. cit.
[122] Springer, op. cit., 229-30.
[123] Baumann, op. cit.
[124] Payak, Julius F.
[125] O'Callahan, op. cit., 121.
[126] Davidson, David. *Captain of the* Franklin. American Heritage Magazine: April 1969; Volume 20, Issue 3

[127] Toon, op. cit.

[128] Jackson, Steve. *Lucky Lady: The World War II Heroics of the USS* Santa Fe *and* Franklin. New York: Carroll & Graf Publishers, 2003. 384-88.

[129] Hoehling, op. cit., 79.

[130] Nilo, op. cit., 21; Jackson, op. cit., 422.

[131] Frajman, op. cit.

[132] Ibid.

[133] Baumann, op cit.

[134] Caruso, John A. Letter to the author, 2003.

[135] Foster, Irvin. Interview with the author, 2003.

[136] Gauthier, Rene N. Interview. 2003.

[137] Davidson, David.

[138] Wisse, John. Interview with the author, 2003.

[139] Baumann, Warren. Personal interview, 2003.

[140] Fowler, Donald. Personal interview. 2003.

[141] Kraft, Casey. Personal interview. 2003.

[142] Gauthier, op. cit.

[143] Need attribution.

[144] Wassman, Robert L. Personal interview 2003.

[145] Callahan, op. cit., 98.

[146] Jackson, op. cit.

[147] Gauthier, op. cit.

[148] Gauthier. Ibid.

[149] Nilo, op. cit.

[150] Callahan, op. cit., 103.

[151] Ibid., 125.

[152] Wassman, op. cit.

[153] Nilo, James R; St. Peters

[154] Callahan. (pp t.k.)

[155] Springer, Joseph A.

[156] Nilo, James R; St. Peters

[157] Springer, Joseph A.

[158] Van Huben, interview, 2003.

[159] Callahan. (pp t.k.); Nilo, James R; St. Peters

[160] Gehres, Leslie R. letter, ---1945.

[161] *Rochester Democrat & Chronicle*

[162] Slotnick, Al, letter to author,

[163] Nilo, James R; St. Peters

A Civilian Career of Service

[164]"The Ship that Wouldn't Die: USS Ben Franklin." https://www.youtube.com/watch?v=Lk-39CgV1g4

YouTube: Periscope Film, "Saga of the USS Franklin 2093, and Aircraft Carrier CV13USS Franklin 'The Saga of the Franklin' produced by the U.S. Navy (attributed to circa 1945). No credits.

YouTube: Periscope Film. "Fire and Explosion Damage to Aircraft Carrier USS Franklin 32902, produced by the U.S. Navy (attributed to circa 1945). No credits.